JOHN REID
A CRICKETING LIFE

by Joseph Romanos

Hodder Moa Beckett

ISBN 1-86958-826-6

Front cover photo: Microdot
All photographs reproduced in the book are from John Reid Private Collection
unless otherwise credited.

Published in 2000 by Hodder Moa Beckett Publishers Limited,
[a member of the Hodder Headline Group]
4 Whetu Place, Mairangi Bay, Auckland, New Zealand

Produced and designed by Hodder Moa Beckett Publishers Ltd

Scanning and colour separations by Microdot, Auckland.
Printed by South China Printing Co., Hong Kong

ACKNOWLEDGEMENTS

Many people assisted me while I was writing this book. First, John Reid, a dream cricketer, has also been a dream co-author. I have never worked with anyone who made the writing of a book easier. He was not only methodical, organised and thorough – traits he brings to his duties as an I.C.C. match referee – but he handwrote page after page of notes for me. Displaying the fortitude he must have shown while leading New Zealand through some of its more barren years in the international arena, he never once blanched, despite my seemingly endless requests for "just one more" piece of writing. That this book covers such a wide range of topics, and addresses some in an unusual manner, is entirely due to John.

Before leaving the Reid family, I must also thank Norli, John's wife, for her contribution. Her proof-reading and timely suggestions added much to the final product and she was a fine hostess during my stays with the Reids in Taupo.

In these days of commercialisation, profit is often the bottom line. How inviting a proposition would it be for a publisher to produce a book on a cricketer, no matter how great, who departed the test scene in 1965? Two people, John Oakley and Sir Ron Brierley, acted as part-sponsors of this book and because of this generosity, enabled it to be published. Both have been extremely generous benefactors of cricket for many years now, and must surely be the target of many people seeking financial assistance with various worthy cricket projects. I was delighted that they were so willing to help with this book and took it as an indication of their love of cricket and a reflection of their friendship with John Reid and their admiration for the way he played his cricket.

The Lord Cowdrey of Tonbridge, known to cricketers around the world as Colin, and Sir Wilson Whineray, arguably New Zealand's greatest All Black captain, generously wrote forewords for the book.

A number of cricket identities helped me in my research. I would like to thank Gren Alabaster, Jack Alabaster, Brian Aldridge, Willie Basson, Don Clarke, Artie Dick, Ted Dexter, Martin Donnelly, Graham Dowling, Bill Fraser, Sam Guillen, Walter Hadlee, Tony MacGibbon, Noel McGregor, Roy McLean, Frank Mooney, Tim Murdoch, Bruce Murray, Don Neely, Alan (Ming) Nightingale, Geoff Rabone, John F. Reid, Richard Reid, Richie Romanos, David Shepherd, Barry Sinclair, Bert Sutcliffe, Eric Tindill and Merv Wallace. Most of these people assisted me with inquiries directly relating to this book.

Finally, to the publishers, Hodder Moa Beckett, a very big thank you. There were some false starts before this book finally got under way. I very much appreciated the way Hodder Moa Beckett took on this project, reworking cost structures and print schedules until it became feasible. I must mention two people in particular, Kevin Chapman, the company's New Zealand managing director/publisher, who supported the book when it would have been easier to turn it down, and Warren Adler, a long-time friend, who brought his usual high level of enthusiasm and expertise to the project.

Joseph Romanos
Wellington, December 1999

SIR RON BRIERLEY AND JOHN OAKLEY CBE

Sir Ron Brierley

John Oakley

I am sure these two gentlemen will not mind being bracketed together in the context of a sincere personal vote of thanks.

Both have made an exceptional contribution to New Zealand cricket, and continue to do so. The feeling of well-being between New Zealand and Australian cricket was strained owing to our cricket at test level being virtually ignored for nearly 30 years, but has been repaired in no small measure because of the many acts of generosity of these two men. Both have spent parts of their business lives in Australia and have developed many friendships among Australian cricket players and officials. It was appropriate that Alan Davidson, during his speech at his 70th birthday dinner, should make a point of mentioning John and Sir Ron and the contributions they have made. He said he counted both among his closest friends.

Only recently, the 1946 Australian team, with Bill Brown as captain, was invited to a reunion at the Basin Reserve to mark the 50-year anniversary of the first Australia-New Zealand test match. It was terrific to welcome back such identities as Keith Miller, Ernie Toshack, Ray Lindwall and Ian Johnson, along with special guests Bert Sutcliffe, Neil Harvey and Alan Davidson. Their 1946 New Zealand opponents, including Wal Hadlee, Merv Wallace and Eric Tindill, delighted in rekindling old friendships. The occasion, a big success, was made possible only by the generosity of Sir Ron Brierley and John Oakley.

In 1999, a 50th reunion of the Forty-Niners was held at the Basin Reserve. This was a major undertaking, with wives and special guests invited. The occasion, marvellously nostalgic, would not have been feasible without the backing of Sir Ron and John.

The generosity of these two men has been amazing. Who knows how many clubs and schools around the country have benefited from their kindness? Then there is the New Zealand Cricket Foundation and, situated under the old stand at the Basin Reserve, the National Cricket Museum, a particular favourite of John Oakley.

John was once my solicitor, cricket team-mate and opponent. He was a foundation director of John Reid's Squash Centre. Ours has been a long and happy friendship. Sir Ron, who in his youth manned the scoreboard at the Basin when I was playing for Wellington, was a foundation member of the squash centre. Our association, too, is one of long standing.

I can never repay their generosity in kind, but I wish to recognise and salute these two friends of mine and of the game of cricket.

—John Reid
December, 1999.

CONTENTS

FOREWORD

BY THE LORD COWDREY OF TONBRIDGE

John Reid was a great all-round cricketer. Had he played today, he would have lived comfortably with the best men of recent times, be it Ian Botham, Imran Khan, Richard Hadlee, Kapil Dev, Malcolm Marshall and, on his 1999 form in England, Chris Cairns. He would have matured and improved so much faster with the increased cricket played today.

John could do everything on a cricket field – bat correctly and defensively or attack belligerently, bowl with a new ball or some slower off-cutters, field anywhere and keep wicket. As well, he was able to balance being a tough competitor on the field, but always the supreme sportsman, with a ready smile. He studied the game of cricket and was a good captain as well.

I am delighted that he has asked me to write a foreword for what I know will be a fascinating biography. One of the charms of international cricket for me has been the opportunity to meet with all the outstanding players from the various cricketing countries and to make lifelong friendships through the game. I have come to know John Reid and his delightful wife, Norli, so well that they have stayed with me in England.

Happily, it was on my suggestion that John be considered as a possible match referee in test cricket. He has enjoyed that role and has become one of the best, working meticulously always to defend the traditional aspects of the game which need to be preserved.

It was in 1949 when I first became aware of John. It was an important year for me as I made my first appearances for the Kent second eleven, to make my debut in first class cricket in 1950. John, at 20, was the youngest member of the fine team Walter Hadlee led to England that year. Even in a lineup that included such fine batsmen as Martin Donnelly, Bert Sutcliffe, Mervyn Wallace and Hadlee himself, John was an important player, a hard-hitting batsman, useful reserve wicketkeeper, outstanding fieldsman anywhere and handy back-up pace bowler. His attitude and ability suggested that a long and successful career might be in store, and for the next 16 years, he more than fulfilled that promise.

Over the years John and I did battle often. I played against him in New Zealand in 1954, 1959 and 1963 and in England when he led touring teams in 1958 and 1965. John was always a formidable opponent. Leading New Zealand teams which often struggled for depth, he was a dominant figure. Often John and Bert Sutcliffe were the only two New Zealand batsmen of true international calibre, which must have made life difficult for them. John was generally a strong and punishing batsman with scoring strokes all around the wicket. However, he could defend when the occasion demanded. I recall his tremendous fighting innings against England at Christchurch in 1963, when he scored 74 and 100 (out of 150 off the bat), both outstanding solo innings against a lively and eager England attack.

John's international career wound down in 1965 when he was chosen to captain a Rest of the World XI against England. His team included famous players such as Sir Garfield Sobers, Rohan Kanhai, Wes Hall, the Nawab of Pataudi, Eddie Barlow, Hanif Mohammad, Lance Gibbs and Wally Grout. It was a significant honour and one that was well-deserved, for when John retired, world cricket lost a giant figure.

Generally, this book about John, tracing a career in cricket that stretches back to the end of the Second World War, is one of celebration – rejoicing in the great games, the great players, the friendships and the memories. John's involvement in cricket stretches from Sir Leonard Hutton to Alec Stewart, Sir Everton Weekes to Brian Lara.

His observations on cricketers and on the changing face of the game are interesting and informative and I am pleased to commend this book to any lover of cricket.

Colin Cowdrey
December 1999

FOREWORD

BY SIR WILSON WHINERAY

John Reid was one of the greatest sporting figures of my era. He captained the New Zealand cricket team from 1956 to 1965 and I led the All Blacks from 1958 to 1965. It was an era which preceded television, but still produced some truly legendary and unforgettable sports personalities. Colin Meads and Don Clarke, Peter Snell and Murray Halberg, Bert Sutcliffe and John Reid were all giants of the time and had world stature in their chosen sports.

In John's case, rugby's loss was cricket's gain. I'm told that he was an outstanding schoolboy rugby player, the first five-eighth and goal-kicker in the champion Hutt Valley High School team just after the Second World War. But for an illness he suffered in his last years at college, he might well have gone on to be an All Black, as did several of his college team-mates. Instead he devoted himself to his cricket.

It is not easy to explain to today's cricket followers just what a dynamic player John Reid was. He was a great, in the real meaning of the word, and would have excelled in any team in the world during his career. It was fitting that he was chosen to lead a World XI in his final season. John enlivened many a day I spent watching the cricket at Eden Park with his blazing batting, his bowling – either spin or pace – and his brilliant fielding. He was even chosen as New Zealand's reserve wicketkeeper on his first overseas tour. He was a genuine all-rounder. Strength, power and aggression were some of his key attributes. The cricket always became more exciting when he was involved because he invariably played positively, trying to make things happen.

He led New Zealand to their first test win, in 1956, and continued captaining New Zealand, in good times and bad, for another decade. It can't have been easy. When I led the All Blacks out for a test, we expected to win. We knew if we played up to our ability, we would be very hard to beat. It wasn't like that with the cricketers, where our amateurs were often matched against talented fulltime players from overseas. But John remained an optimistic and positive leader and showed New Zealanders that winning test matches was not beyond reach. He had confidence in his own ability, and showed time and time again that such confidence was not misplaced. That must have helped his team-mates immeasurably.

John had many great days, but one that must stand very high was his world record of 15 6s during his innings of 296 at the Basin Reserve in 1963. It was a Plunket Shield match, Wellington against Northern Districts, and one of the bowlers who made up the N.D. attack was Don Clarke, a fine pace bowler of near international class when he wasn't performing memorable deeds as one of the most famous All Black fullbacks. Not long after that famous match at the Basin, Don was taking part in a pre-season charity rugby match and naturally we began ribbing him about the assault John Reid had made on the N.D. attack.

We asked him quietly how the game had gone and he replied, equally quietly, that his team had lost. We pressed him a little more, inquiring how Reid had batted. "Okay," Don offered. We wouldn't let it go at that and asked him how he'd bowled. "Not too bad," he felt. "But Don, your figures didn't look too good."

Finally Don opened up, and the story, as I recall, went something like this: "I'll tell you," he said. "It got to the stage where no one wanted to bowl. John was hammering everyone. I was pushed into having another over. My first ball was quite full and he drove it through the covers for four. Then I bowled a dot ball. My third ball was on his sticks and he hit it through mid-wicket for another four. Then I bowled another couple of dot balls. I thought I'd drop the last one a bit short and he hooked it over the fence so far that we never did get it back. You couldn't bowl to him that day – he was superb."

It would be wrong to regard John as simply a thrasher of the ball. Like the other great New Zealand player of his time, Bert Sutcliffe, he had lovely timing and all the strokes. He was a batsman of style and elegance who could bowl well and was a lethal fieldsman. What a one-day player he would have been!

I used to meet John from time to time at various sporting functions, and got to know him better when he opened his squash centre in Kelburn, near the centre of Wellington. It was always nice to call in there for a game of squash and a chat.

For more than 20 years John and I have been trustees for the Halberg Trust. He has been our central North Island representative, turning out when asked to at various golf days and other fund-raising events.

He has continued to offer his time to help others and it is good to see that he has remained involved in cricket, using his experience to become one of the world's leading test match referees.

I am delighted that John has asked me to contribute this foreword. Such a book, spanning as it does more than half a century of cricket, will provide happy reading for those of us who remember his days as a player and may help the younger generation realise just why John is still regarded as a must selection in any all-time New Zealand team.

Wilson Whineray
December 1999

INTRODUCTION

The best way to judge a player, in any sport, is to ask his peers about him. If you want to know how good Laver was, talk to Rosewall, Newcombe and Roche. If you want to know about Michael Lynagh, ask Grant Fox and Rob Andrew. For a judgement on Steve Ovett, the best people to go to would be Seb Coe and Steve Cram. So it is with cricket. No one knows better than those in the middle who performs well in a crisis, and who doesn't.

It is revealing seeking opinions on Reid from his contemporaries. Of course, in terms of the New Zealand record book, he was supreme. When he retired in 1965, he held the New Zealand test record for runs, wickets, appearances and catches. He'd been a test wicketkeeper and had captained New Zealand to all three of their test wins. That's fairly conclusive.

But what was he really like as a player? Barry Sinclair, who during the mid-1960s took over from Reid as New Zealand's leading batsman, describes Reid as the biggest cricket drawcard ever produced by this country. When he was a youngster, Sinclair tried to watch Reid every time he batted. "When you knew Bogo [Reid] was batting, you'd hop on a tram at Miramar and head for the Basin. And you were dirty if he got out. There was no one else who could match John for excitement."

Walter Hadlee led New Zealand through England in 1949, when the youngest member of his side was Reid. He later became a national cricket administrator. In the late 1950s, he decided to take two of his boys, Martin and Dayle, for a trip north to the Bay of Islands over the Christmas holiday break. "We had decided to have a day of fishing, but when I asked the boys what they wanted to do the next day, they said they would really prefer to go to Eden Park to watch John Reid bat. We slept in the car that night, got up at about 5am for a couple of hours' fishing, grabbed something to eat at a dairy and set off for Auckland. That was the impact John had. He was a compelling figure as a cricketer. At the wicket he had a commanding presence. He was an imperious, dominating character and thrilling to watch."

Bert Sutcliffe's test career almost exactly paralleled Reid's and for all that time, he was New Zealand's one other true world-class batsman. He wrote in his autobiography, *Between Overs*, "What a debt New Zealand cricket owes John. I defy anyone to name a player today who can set a ground alight as Reid does when he comes out to bat...with due respect to those who have a claim to consideration, I do not know of any player to whom the term all-rounder more properly belongs than to Reid."

The tributes from overseas have been just as fulsome. John Woodcock, for so long the much-respected cricket writer for *The Times* of London and then the editor of *Wisden*, recently caused much discussion by naming his top 100 cricketers of all time. He had W.G. Grace and Don Bradman heading a list which included just two New Zealanders, Richard Hadlee at No 29, and Reid, at No 100. "There can have been very few sides at any time that would not have been stronger and better balanced for having John Reid as a member," Woodcock wrote. "His lot, in fact, was to spend most of his career trying to make New Zealand sides competitive, often with little support of much substance." Woodcock described Reid as an "immensely strong, completely natural, extraordinarily versatile cricketer".

Even 35 years after he departed big-time cricket, the memory of Reid's cricket remains vivid among those who saw him. He'd stride out to bat, a couple of shirt buttons undone. Merv Wallace described him as all hair and teeth and he was remarkably hirsute. Once when he was walking off a ground in Scotland in 1949, a woman in the stands turned to her companion and asked why Reid was wearing a dark singlet.

At the crease he was exciting. He took a big backlift and was always looking to attack. But he was not a slogger, or a hitter. He was a beautiful stylist with strokes all around the wicket. The feeling of power was always there, though. Even forward defensive shots travelled at a brisk pace to mid-off or cover. He wasn't a player who sought to keep the score ticking over with judicious pushes and prods. He liked to get on top of an attack and belt boundaries. He had such power he could smash 6s on any ground.

Watching Reid, there was always an impression of strength. He had "intent", as Dick Brittenden once so memorably described it. Reid was not particularly tall – perhaps 5ft 10in – but had very broad shoulders that could generate the power to hit 6s, or bowl a mean bouncer off a run-up of just a few paces. He had a rolling walk to the wicket and always looked slightly bow-legged, which was perhaps accentuated by the knee problems he suffered.

At the wicket he looked every inch the cricketer. No one ever played harder, or more fairly. It is noticeable, watching footage of the New Zealanders playing in South Africa in 1961-62, that when Reid, the bowler, is hit for a boundary, he claps the batsman. He was the most tenacious, determined of opponents, but he understood the concepts of fair play, sportsmanship and etiquette, which is probably why he has become one of the world's senior test referees.

On the field, he had mannerisms that New Zealand cricket followers got to know so well. He would brush his hand over his hair before settling down to face the first ball. He would whip off his right glove after starting out for a single, or what looked like it might be a three. He liked to be free of it when he was the non-stroker, because he did not want perspiration on his gloves to make his grip slippery. He seldom batted in a cap because he found he was forever knocking it off playing his shots. When bowling his off-cutters, he would amble in off a few paces and then make a sudden jink to alter the line of his delivery.

Reid could generate impressive pace off virtually no run-up. He would whip his arm over violently – cricket watchers got used to the sight of Reid rolling up his right sleeve as he walked back to bowl – and during a spell of gentle off-cutters was capable of bowling a mean bouncer. There is a standing joke in Wellington cricket circles about the effect Reid's bowling had on Trevor McMahon, who kept wickets to him for many years for Wellington and New Zealand. These days McMahon has a shock of totally white hair. It's said his hair changed colour prematurely through repeatedly having Reid's surprise bouncer kick up at him.

Though there can be little argument that Reid remains the finest all-rounder produced by New Zealand – what other opening bowler/spinner also kept wickets in test cricket, quite apart from being his team's best batsman and captaining the side? – for me his most admirable quality was his optimism. How depressing it must have been leading New Zealand over the years and going into battle knowing that his team was wielding pop guns and their opponents machine guns.

John Arlott, in *John Arlott's 100 Greatest Batsmen*, wrote of him: "Even when the going was toughest, he had a splendid and generous smile which completely lit up his face."

There were times when he needed that smile. During a period when only Reid and Sutcliffe were world class batsmen, the opposition included May-Cowdrey-Dexter-Graveney, or Boycott-Barrington-Dexter-Cowdrey or Barlow-Graeme Pollock-Bland-Waite or McGlew-Barlow-Waite-McLean-Bland or Flavell-Simpson-Harvey-Craig-Burge-O'Neill.

He had reasonable pace bowlers like Cave, MacGibbon, Motz and Cameron at his disposal. But they were hardly Trueman-Tyson-Statham, or Adcock-Heine. And while Alabaster was a good leg-spinner, he didn't offer the firepower of Lock-Laker, or Venkataraghavan-Chandraeskhar-Nadkarni, or Benaud or Tayfield.

"I told a lot of lies," Reid confides. "We'd gather as a team, and naturally I'd try to be as positive as possible. You never know what will happen in a cricket match. But it was difficult going into a match when we had unproven young players and the opposition had seven or eight world stars. I'd try to encourage our fellows, to explain that everyone was human, that they all got nervous, had failures. But in the back of your mind there was this knowledge that all things being equal, we were in for a tough time."

It was this ability to remain positive, to try to be inventive, that most appealed to Eric Tindill, one of the special figures in New Zealand sport. Tindill is the only New Zealander to have played test rugby and test cricket, and in addition he umpired or refereed both sports at test level. Tindill was near the end of his first class career when Reid arrived in the Wellington team, fresh from Hutt Valley High. But he was to see a lot of Reid over the years, as an umpire and a selector.

"In all the years I have known John, his outlook has never changed. He's always retained a boyish enthusiasm for anything he's attempted. When he was fielding he was brilliant anywhere, and had a fast, accurate throw. You had to be on your toes when you were keeping, because his returns came in very swiftly. He loved to attack, and was always trying to make something happen. When he was batting, he'd be walking around waiting for the bowler to get back to his mark, wanting to get on with it. He was ebullient, always on the go. What an example he was to his team."

While Reid was in every sense of the word an all-rounder, there should be no mistake: he was a batsman first. As Ted Dexter says, "John was a handy bowler, who would have been ideal today, when teams are looking for a fifth bowler to plug one end for 10 overs. But the main danger he presented to his opposition was his batting. He was a fine player who hit as hard as anyone could."

Arlott described Reid as "a kind of Atlas-type figure of New Zealand cricket" and said he was "a basically correct right-hander constantly prepared, when his side was in trouble, to hit his way out of it".

It's natural, in a sport dominated by statistics, to ask why Reid's batting average wasn't better. Compared to other recent New Zealand batsmen such as Martin Crowe, John Wright and Andrew Jones, Reid's test figures are not outstanding. Reid scored 3428 test runs at 33.28. Crowe averaged more than 45, Wright 37 and Jones 44.

How would Reid measure against today's best players? His contemporaries swear by him. Colin Cowdrey, in his foreword to this book, ranks Reid alongside Kapil Dev, Ian Botham, Hadlee and Imran Khan among recent world class all-rounders. Reid ponders the question. "It would have been lovely to have batted in the sides of the 1980s, when almost the whole team had scored test hundreds. Having that sort of solidity takes some of the pressure off the individual. I suppose I could have increased my average by half again under today's circumstances."

It's only fair to mention that Wright and Jones didn't bowl at all in test cricket, and Crowe only occasionally. Jones never captained New Zealand. Wright and Crowe had short stints. By comparison Reid did a huge amount of bowling. When he retired, he'd bowled 2698 overs for New Zealand. Only Harry Cave (2034) of the others had bowled even 2000 at that point.

Merv Wallace says it is not fair to judge Reid the batsman purely by his average. "There were causes for that. It's true he was not as sound a batsman as some of the top overseas players, though he certainly matched anyone for range of strokes and had more power than anyone. John was inclined to try to take over when at the crease, as if he was trying to let his team-mates see that the bowling was not as tough as it looked. He would take more risks than he should have.

"But I loved his attitude towards the game. That's what made him one of the best players around. He was always seeking to attack, so when you play that way, there is more likelihood of a dismissal. A plodder will play up and down the line for hours, but someone who is really going after the bowling offers more opportunities.

"I would say that without question, if John Reid was in the New Zealand team now, he would be the best player in the team. He would be a superb one-day player and would not have to change his natural game one iota. But he would also be the first player chosen in our test side."

These days our test players are basically professionals. In Reid's time, however, our test cricketers were amateurs: Wally Hadlee was an accountant, Wallace ran a sports shop. Reid was the closest to a professional. He played English league cricket for a couple of seasons and his all-round ability made him a huge attraction. Later he was a cricket coach in Wellington. But then he worked as a travelling rep for BP and in 1963 he opened his own business – John Reid's Squash Centre in Kelburn, Wellington.

If Reid played today, with the fierce commitment he had, he would be every schoolboy's hero. And, as such, the commercial opportunities would be vast. But, he says, he never thinks of it as money lost. "I suppose I'm old-fashioned. I always felt tremendously proud to be able to represent New Zealand. Things like having the gates at the Basin Reserve named in my honour and being voted into the Sports Hall of Fame mean a great deal to me. Maybe I didn't make as much straight-out money as the top players do today, but the reputation I got as a cricketer certainly helped me in business. It enabled me to start the squash centre and helped me when I went to live in South Africa, so there have been spin-offs."

Two New Zealand players often discussed in comparison to Reid are Richard Hadlee and Martin Crowe, Hadlee for his all-round ability and Crowe because of his dominance for a time in the test side. Don Neely, who played with Reid and was a selector during the Hadlee and Crowe careers, has interesting views on both: "Reid and Hadlee were both genuinely great all-round cricketers, but their approach to the game was vastly different. Hadlee was a clever, scheming bowler who weighed the odds and played the percentages. He knew he needed slip fieldsmen to take the catches and relied on his team-mates. Reid, on the other hand, was more like a Mississippi gambler, a larger-than-life character who was often willing to take on the opposition on his own. Lance Cairns occasionally hit the ball as hard as Reid, but Reid was a world class batsman who had soft hands and could manipulate the field with the placing of his shots.

Roy Ullyett's cartoon illustrates Reid's standing in New Zealand cricket in 1965.

"It's true that Crowe and Reid exerted a good deal of influence over the New Zealand team while they captained them. But whereas Crowe was a complicated character, Reid was relatively straightforward. He knew what he wanted, and often bluntly said so. There was never any feeling that he was running an agenda. He did what he thought was best for the team."

John Reid fills a unique role in New Zealand, even world, cricket. He played first class cricket with pre-war heroes such as Stewie Dempster, Les Ames and Bill Brown. He played with and against the best cricketers in the world from the end of the war until 1965. After that he remained involved in cricket as a selector, broadcaster, coach and manager. Since 1993, he has been an I.C.C. test match referee and has been able to see all the current world greats in action.

He is also an interesting mix as an individual. He was a spontaneous, intuitive cricketer, but one who thought deeply about technique. He is a stern disciplinarian, but cares passionately about the traditions of cricket. He gives the impression of being a man of action, with little time for detail, but in fact is meticulously organised and attacks projects with methodical diligence.

His span and his involvement with cricket enable him to comment with insight on virtually every leading cricketer who has emerged since the Second World War. And because he is Reid, and has never been one to shy away from expressing an opinion, his views carry authority.

1 | PRECOCIOUS TALENT

Most talented cricketers who go on to reach test level excelled at school. Ken Rutherford, Gary Bartlett, Bruce Edgar, Graham Vivian, Richard Hadlee and many others were tagged as future stars while still at college.

Occasionally a youngster is absolutely outstanding. Martin Crowe and Chris Cairns played with such maturity at college that it was really like men playing against boys. But it's doubtful if any New Zealand schoolboy since the war has dominated at sport like John Reid. From the time he began attending Hutt Valley High School in 1943, it was only a matter of time before he became a New Zealand cricket rep and an All Black.

Reid had one great advantage. By the time he was 13, he was much bigger and stronger than his contemporaries. He wasn't necessarily taller, but he had the body of a man, with powerful shoulders and arms. He went straight into his college First XI and First XV in the third form, which is virtually unprecedented at such a big school. "It was unusual to get into the First XI as a third-former, but I suppose it was even rarer to make the First XV that young. I always played at first-five, and I was big enough not to let the sixth-formers give me a hard time. At Hutt High, third-formers would get shoved down the rubbish chute by the sixth-formers, but they never did that to me!"

In addition, Reid became a swimming champion at college and represented Hutt Valley High School in the inter-collegiate athletics competition, the McEvedy Shield, as a sprinter and in the shot put and discus. He was into any sport that was going and happened to be at the college at a time of great sports riches. Among his schoolmates were future All Blacks Ron Jarden and Jim Fitzgerald, future sprint stars Don Jowett and Lionel Smith, and future New Zealand cricket rep Trevor Meale. Even in such august company, Reid stood out.

He was a school hero in every sense of the word. By his last year, 1946, he was also the head prefect, which pointed not only to his ability at sport, but to his level-headed, mature nature.

When we recall Reid now, we think of a rather gregarious, outspoken personality with a keen sense of humour and a wide grin. Because of his deeds on the cricket field, he tended to dominate most situations, and he became a forceful and forthright captain, as one would expect of such a dynamic, aggressive player.

In 1949, he toured England as the youngster in Walter Hadlee's fine team. Team-mates tell of his boyish sense of humour. They paint a picture of a young man who loved to have fun and really had no idea of his own strength. "It was mayhem in the dressing room sometimes," says Geoff Rabone. "He'd punch you playfully on the arm and the muscle would be temporarily paralysed. Or he'd shake your hand and your fingers would be tingling in pain. There was never anything malicious. He was just having fun, but he was incredibly strong, much stronger than he realised." Martin Donnelly used to joke that his body never really recovered from the wrestling match Reid "invited" him into during the train journey through Germany at the end of the tour.

Strange then that by all accounts, Reid was a quiet, shy schoolboy. He was born in Auckland on June 3, 1928, the son of Norman and Iris. His family moved to Wellington when he was just four. After a short time living at Worser Bay, his father, a mechanic, took the family to Lower Hutt. Though a first class mechanic, Norman Reid found the going hard during the Depression and turned to other means of employment. He became involved in the tourist industry, driving buses and cars for tourists. Then during the Second World War he became a test driver of tanks for the Ford Motor Company.

In the Hutt Valley, John Reid attended Waiwhetu Primary School, where Claude Browning was the headmaster and a strong supporter of children playing sport. "It was our headmaster," says Reid, "who first suggested I needed to control my visits to the toilet – 'morning and night' he used to say, as there was to be no leaving the field for a toilet break when we were out there in the middle batting or fielding. It was advice that was to benefit me throughout my life."

Even at primary school, Reid shone at sport, making various Hutt Valley age rep sides. "When I first got in the Hutt Valley primary school reps our fast bowler was Jackie Rata, who also went to Waiwhetu school. He was the gun fast bowler in those days!"

At primary school, the boys used to play pick-up games of cricket called "Missing on the Off". "There were no stumps and the rule would be that you were out if you missed a ball on the off side. If you were not out at the end of the day, you kept the bat and took it home for the next day."

Reid's father had once been a good wrestler and he showed his son the rudiments of self-defence. Though he never did don the leotard and hop into the ring as a wrestler, Reid did have one bout as a boxer at college. "I wasn't particularly scientific, but I did break the other fellow's nose. Despite this, or maybe because of it, I decided I didn't like the sport and never boxed again." Potential opponents would not have been unhappy about that.

"Mum and dad were very supportive of me, and, being an only child,

I received a lot of their time. Mum was a pianist and a music teacher and had her own band. My Uncle Les played the banjo very well and he was in the band, too. That sparked dad's interest, so he learned to play the banjo and accompanied them in the band. When they used to be playing, they'd take me along and I would sleep in the back of the car. I had several attempts at becoming a pianist, but the lure of the outdoors was too strong and I was soon hopping out the window to play cricket."

Reid's grandfather, Henry Edward Sherwood, was also an important early influence in his sport. He had been a good club cricketer in Dunedin and a champion diver and was then foreman in the foundry at the Woburn railway workshops. "My grandfather had a lot to do with me when I was a youngster. Even though he was getting on a bit when I played cricket, he'd take me into the paddock next door and bowl to me. The paddock had a slope. I had to hit the ball up the slope so it would roll back to him, or else grandad would get tired of retrieving it and would go inside. He also used to take me fishing. He'd have a fit when I jagged a trout. You had to have a licence to catch trout, so there was always a·bit of a fuss when I pulled one out. He taught me a love of fishing which has stayed with me to this day. I still love to get out on Lake Taupo and have a few hours' fishing."

While it was his grandfather who encouraged his cricket, Reid's father was keener on football. He had been a well-known Auckland rugby league fullback, and a particularly accurate goal-kicker. Come winter, he would take his son to the same paddock next door and practise the various rugby skills. Branches would be lashed together to form goal posts and there would be hours of goal-kicking. Tackling was another skill that was not neglected and the couch in the lounge took a hammering while that skill was practised.

Reid had a group of good friends nearby. Often Reid, Bill Fraser, Laurie Judd, Ming Nightingale and others would play cricket in the Nightingales' concrete driveway. "As kids do," says Nightingale, "we'd pretend to be famous cricketers. The only rule was that John was always Bradman. We could be Hammond or Herbert Sutcliffe or anyone else, but Bradman was reserved for him. John was always good fun, but when it came to sport, he was single-minded and purposeful. That competitiveness and determination was there back then."

Away from sport, Reid fitted in well. "We had a great life in the middle of the war," says Nightingale. "We'd go fishing off 'the groin' in the Hutt River. It was the ideal place for fishing because it was right by the sausage factory and all the offal from the factory would pour out the pipe into the river where we were. It really smelt, but it certainly attracted the fish. One day we caught three trout and about 200 herrings. John rushed home with the trout stuck up his shirt.

"In those days we got around by bike, and we covered plenty of territory. We'd go to Day's Bay, the Ngauranga Gorge, Haywards Hill. One day we biked all the way to Seatoun. We had the southerly against us on the way in and a northerly against us on the way back!"

Bill Fraser says that the young Reid geared his life around sport. "We were all fairly quiet guys, John more so than most. He enjoyed himself, but didn't drink or smoke, or really get up to much mischief. But whenever sport was involved, he was very determined."

It didn't take long for Reid to stand out at college. "We held him in awe," says Nightingale. "He was scoring centuries while we were scratching to make 10. John was built like a gorilla. He was twice as strong as the rest of us. Not only did he make huge scores, but he bowled fast and fielded brilliantly."

One big day for the cricketers at Hutt Valley High was in early 1946 when Australian cricketers Ray Lindwall, Colin McCool and Arthur Mailey, who were touring New Zealand, visited the school to do a spot of coaching and have some practice in the nets. Reid hammered the ageing Mailey, who was touring as a journalist, but played more respectfully when fast bowler Lindwall wheeled down a few deliveries. "That was a big thrill," says Fraser. "They were already famous names. I remember when Australia played New Zealand in the test match at the Basin, John and I, and probably some others, too, got time off school and went to the Basin both days. We took our scorebooks and kept the score."

Though he was quickly spotted as a budding cricketer of immense talent, Reid feels he was a better rugby player at college. In a backline of young stars, he stood out at first five-eighth and also did the team's goal-kicking. Fraser: "He was big, but very quick on his feet, very talented."

The sports-mad youngsters at Hutt Valley High School were probably more fortunate than most as regards the support and coaching they received. The headmaster was Norman Millard, one of the great men of Wellington rugby (and the person after whom the Millard Stand at Athletic Park was named). He didn't coach the First XV, but his presence must have helped. Craig McKenzie and Wellington rep Stan Ramson coached the First XV at times. All Black back Graham Delamore was a PE teacher at the college and he would often take part in the First XV training sessions. He would play for the First XV's opposition and position himself at first or second-five, where Reid would delight in tackling him and trying to run through him. The cricket coach was Ted Aim, an able player himself and the father of a first class cricketer.

It would be pointless reciting all Reid's many sporting deeds at school. He once scored 189, including 116 in boundaries against Wairarapa College; another time he took 9-11 against Dannevirke High School. There were many such golden days. The only cricketer who approached him for ability was Trevor Meale, the First XI captain the year ahead of him. But Meale, while a good batsman, did not bowl and certainly did not have the charisma of Reid. The cricket ball throw was a constant source of amusement with Reid consistently the second-longest thrower at college, bettered only by one Bob Lockett, who, as the tallest boy in the school, generated exceptionally good leverage.

Even as a schoolboy, Reid was welcomed by the seniors at the Hutt Cricket Club. Where most youngsters at the nets were generally consigned to bowling and fielding, Reid did plenty of batting, and came under the influence of Ken James, the great New Zealand wicketkeeper before the war. James had returned from England, where he played county cricket with success, and proved a good coach and a mentor to the enthusiastic group of young cricketers from Hutt Valley High School.

During Reid's early years as the New Zealand test captain, he gained a reputation as being somewhat intolerant of other players' deficiencies. His attitude seemed to be: if you can't do it, give me the ball and I'll do it myself. Therefore, it's surprising to learn that as the First XI captain, he was nothing like that. "John was far ahead of everyone else in the cricket team," says Fraser, "but he was a good schoolboy captain. He was very thoughtful and considerate. We all looked up to him and tried our best, but none of us was anywhere near as good as him. He didn't seem to mind. He encouraged us and really did his best for us. We were very proud of John, and proud to be his team-mate. Within a short time, he was in the New Zealand team, so that was exciting for us, too.

"Later on, when he captained New Zealand, he had very high expectations of his players, but he wasn't like that at college. Maybe by the time he was captaining New Zealand he knew what was required to succeed at test level and so was demanding more of his players."

Reid's school sports career was cut short by two bouts of rheumatic fever, which eventually led to a long spell in hospital, then at home resting. He was first hit by the illness in 1944, and again late in 1946. Ironically, it was the rheumatic fever which shaped his life. Most importantly, while in hospital he was looked after by one young nurse, Norli Le Fevre of Wadestown. By 1949, he was so taken with her that whenever her name was mentioned by a team-mate on tour, he would reply, "Gee, she's nice."

The rheumatic fever, and the resulting heart murmur, altered his life in other ways, too. Because of the severity of the illness, especially back in the 1940s, he was told he would have to greatly reduce the amount of sport he was playing. This must have been terribly difficult for a young man of Reid's ability. As far as cricket went, he largely gave away bowling and took up wicketkeeping, the move hastened by a dislocated shoulder that was sustained in virtually the last college match of the 1946 season. James provided some useful wicketkeeping tips. In 1946, when he captained the First XI, he was the team's premier batsman and their wicketkeeper.

By the end of 1946 he was in hospital and recalls having the Hobbs Bat, the school batting prize, presented to him by the Australian High Commissioner, Sir Roden Cutler, at hospital. "I met Sir Roden many years later in Sydney when I was refereeing and introduced myself. I reminded him about the presentation he'd made to me in hospital and he remembered the occasion. He said he'd felt very sorry for me, a boy who was so keen on his sport looking so ill in hospital."

However, the wicketkeeping that Reid did at college stood him in good stead. Because of his experience behind the stumps, he was selected as Frank Mooney's wicketkeeping understudy on the 1949 tour of England and for the rest of his career was a useful reserve wicketkeeper, even at test level.

It seems odd now, when we think of Reid with his formidable strength, to imagine that he needed nursing. But when he broke into the Wellington Plunket Shield while still a teenager, his mother rang Wellington selector Hugh Duncan and told him she did not want John doing any bowling. She was most concerned about the possibility of a relapse. In England, Hadlee also used Reid very sparingly as a bowler until the final fortnight of the tour, even though he could have done with an extra bowler of Reid's pace.

Any aspirations Reid had of being an All Black also vanished with the second bout of rheumatic fever. His last big match was in 1946 when the Hutt Valley High School First XV played Dannevirke High in the curtain-raiser to the Kiwis v Wellington game at Athletic Park. At the time New Zealand was starved of top-quality sport. The Kiwis, under Charlie Saxton, had built a fantastic reputation in Europe and there was massive interest in the team when they played a few matches in New Zealand on their return. And unlike these days, the curtain-raiser, too, was played before a fairly full house.

Hutt Valley High had some tremendous schoolboy rugby players. Besides Reid and Fitzgerald, Colin Loader, Don Jowett, Lionel Smith and Peter Osborne were all extremely talented and, waiting in the wings a year or so younger, was Ron Jarden. Hutt Valley High had beaten both Wellington College and St Pat's Silverstream, who played third grade open rugby, and the match with Dannevirke High was eagerly anticipated. It turned out to be a beauty. Hutt High led 10-0 at half time, but were outplayed by Dannevirke in the second spell and eventually lost 17-10. Reid and Fitzgerald were identified by rugby critics as players of rare talent. Fitzgerald went on to become a good All Black. But for Reid, this was virtually his last game of rugby. It was decided it would be better for his health if he played just one main sport, and though initially he had favoured rugby even ahead of cricket, he opted for cricket because it was less taxing physically. Also there was less likelihood of picking up a chill that might lead to another bout of rheumatic fever.

"I really enjoyed my rugby," he says, "but I didn't really look upon the top players then as heroes. I suppose the closest to a rugby hero I had was Bob Scott. I used to love the way he played, and I was infatuated by his ability to kick goals from halfway in bare feet. Not being able to play rugby really hurt me. I felt like something had been taken away and for quite a while I couldn't bring myself to watch rugby matches, especially if the players were the boys I had played with at school."

He has maintained an interest in rugby throughout his life. In the late 1950s he took up squash and rugby refereeing, first in Oamaru, then in Wellington, as means of keeping fit during the winter. He'd have made a good, authoritative referee, too – who was going to argue with him? But after two or three seasons, he became frustrated that he was unable to make much progress up the ranks of referees and gave it away.

"I enjoyed refereeing initially, but in the end I got sick of being assigned to lower grade games at all four corners of Wellington. If I could have seen some appointments with more responsibility on the horizon I might have stuck with it longer."

Like so many New Zealanders, Reid retains a strong interest in rugby. One of his better friends was his old schoolmate Ron Jarden, who was one of the legendary All Black wingers. Reid and Jarden were regular squash partners. He had other links with rugby. While he was New Zealand cricket captain, he got to know Wilson Whineray and other rugby identities while attending and speaking at various sports functions. Some, like Don Clarke, were first class cricketers, a further link.

Another effect of the illness was to alter Reid's employment ambitions. "I had hoped to specialise in physical education, and had been accepted to enter training college in Wellington, but once that was ruled out, I became a slipper designer and clicker. I can't say I particularly enjoyed it, but I did it until the early 1950s when I became a cricket coach and began playing league cricket in England."

Before leaving these early years of Reid's life, we should deal with the birth of Bogo, his nickname. It was Nightingale who bestowed upon Reid the nickname that has stayed with him since. "Initially I called him Umbogobogo," says Nightingale, "but that got shortened to Bogo Boy, then Bogo. It suited him. It had an African sound to it, and brought visions of an immensely powerful, hairy animal from deep in the jungle."

2 | BRIT BATS AND ENGLISH BOUQUETS

In 1999 New Zealand, labelled "boring" and "lacking star quality" when they arrived in London, beat England 2-1 in the test series, thus consigning England to the bottom of the world test cricket rankings. The country which produced W.G. Grace, Jack Hobbs, Sydney Barnes, Len Hutton, Denis Compton, Fred Trueman, Jim Laker and other legends was now rated behind test newcomers Sri Lanka and Zimbabwe and even the New Zealand team the English media had so enjoyed deriding.

But even at this, the lowest point in its cricket history, England still remains the home of cricket. When John Reid, Bill Fraser, Ming Nightingale and their mates were playing their imaginary games of cricket along the street in the early 1940s, when it was Larwood or O'Reilly bowling to Bradman or Hammond, the venue wasn't the Adelaide Oval or Ellis Park. It was Lord's. The game began in England and has spread throughout the world. Despite its current lowly status, England remains the place to tour. It was even more so in 1949, when New Zealand's links with the Mother Country were so much stronger. There was no talk in those days of New Zealand becoming a republic, and England tended to treat New Zealand as would a parent watching over a teenager who has just left home.

The New Zealand team's tour of England in 1949 was perfectly timed for Reid. He made his first class debut on New Year's Day, 1948, for Wellington against Canterbury, at the age of 19 and, even in those days when players operated on a restricted programme of just three or four first class games a season, had the time to earn a place in the side. If the tour had have been scheduled a year or two earlier, he would have missed out.

Instead, he not only got the opportunity to undertake the favourite tour of most cricketers, but he was able to play alongside and watch such mature cricketers as Walter Hadlee, Merv Wallace, Martin Donnelly, Verdun Scott, Jack Cowie and Tom Burtt. How much quicker would Chris Cairns and Adam Parore have matured in the 1990s if they'd had those sorts of role models?

"That 1949 tour was my introduction to many ideas which I use in my refereeing," says Reid. "I learned about how to play cricket according to the rules, but also within the spirit of the game. I learned about cricket on and off the field. I realised it was a game to be played hard, but to be enjoyed.

These things might sound fairly mundane, but they were an important part of my cricket education." Reid, only 20, was described as the baby of the 1949 team, but as Martin Donnelly said, "He was a bloody strong baby."

Reid was to make three tours of England with New Zealand sides. He captained the touring teams in 1958 and 1965, but without question the 1949 tour, which gave us the legacy of the Forty-Niners, was the best. In that wonderful summer, Hadlee's men, so ably managed by Jack Phillipps, played 32 first class matches and lost just one, to Oxford University on a rain-damaged pitch. In those days counties fielded their strongest sides against touring teams and New Zealand won a series of thrilling matches on the last afternoon, usually as a result of good declarations and hectic run-chases.

The four-test series was drawn 0-0, with honours about evenly shared. Put simply, both batting sides (Donnelly, Sutcliffe and co against Hutton, Compton and co) were far too good for the bowlers and there was little prospect of any test being completed within three days. It was ironic that New Zealand's fine showing in 1949 led to a full five-test series, with each match set down for five days, being scheduled for 1958. That was a vastly different New Zealand side and they were battered mercilessly by a formidably strong England combination.

Reid's reputation was such that well before the 1949 side was picked, his selection was assured.

After leaving school at the end of 1946, he walked straight into the Hutt Cricket Club's senior side, a powerful, aggressively minded young batsman who had the added attribute of being able to keep wickets. Besides various minor rep games for the Hutt Valley and Brabin Shield fixtures, Reid was pulled into the Wellington Plunket Shield squad and told by sole selector Hugh Duncan that he was there for at least three matches, a huge vote of confidence for a lad just out of college.

It was a seasoned Wellington team with wise old heads like Stewie Dempster, the captain, Eric Tindill, Joe Ongley, Peg O'Neill and Stewie Wilson. "John's fame preceded him," recalls Tindill. "Even as a college boy John had made quite an impression. He came with a reputation and quickly lived up to it."

Frank Mooney, busy trying to cement his place in the Wellington team at that time, agrees: "John always had a big name, even at college. He was as well-known for his rugby as his cricket. Whatever he did attracted attention. As soon as I first saw him play, I could see he was something special. He was a natural. He was like a great racehorse that stands out immediately. But apart from his ability, he was just a normal young fellow who was especially keen to learn."

Reid scored 79 against Canterbury in his first class debut – "He hit the ball with youthful fury," said one writer – and made two further half-centuries during the season, finishing with 244 runs at 48.8 an innings.

Don Neely, just a schoolboy, watched that innings of 79 and was one of many youngsters who lined up later to get his autograph. "My over-riding memory of that innings is of John's big backlift. He generated a lot of power, which impressed me, and I decided it was because of that big backlift. I tried it out afterwards and kept having my stumps knocked out of the ground."

Reid made such an impact in his first season that he was chosen for the inter-island match at Dunedin, playing alongside Merv Wallace, Bert Sutcliffe, Verdun Scott and against Walter Hadlee, Tom Burtt and the Australian Ray Robinson. It hadn't taken Reid long to make his mark. He confirmed he belonged in that company by scoring 66 and adding 146 in 103 minutes with Wallace.

Considering his youth and attacking style, Reid put together massive scores. In a game for Hutt Valley Colts against their Canterbury equivalents, he reached 216 and hit 97 in the return fixture.

As the 1948-49 season arrived, everyone's thoughts were turning to the tour of England. Reid batted consistently well. He made 194 at a run-a-minute for Hutt Valley against Nelson, then 89 and 135 against Wanganui, whose attack included Harry Cave and Don Beard. In the first class arena, Reid's scores of 17, 46, 32, 88 not out, 19, 13, 117 and 25 indicated a precocious ability. Not only did he score consistently, but he made his runs with power and poise. During his unbeaten 88 against Canterbury at the Basin Reserve, he hammered seven 4s and four 6s, all the more impressive as he opened the batting that day. There was one particularly spectacular 6, over cover off left-arm spinner Tom Burtt. Jack Phillipps, watching the game, and already named as the touring team manager, said: "That was a great innings. He'll be on the boat and I don't know if he'll be ahead of me or behind me on the gangway."

Geoff Rabone, who played for Wellington that season, recalls the match against Otago at Carisbrook. "John was brought on before tea by our captain, Joe Ongley, to tickle up Lankford Smith who had proved most obdurate, and bowled him a sharp bouncer which crashed into his shoulder. Full of concern, John rushed down the pitch to tend to Smith and was told rather brusquely to get back to his bowling mark and give Smith more of the same. At tea, Joe Ongley had a talk to John and said, 'When you're brought on to ruffle a batsman, you don't apologise to him when you hit him.'"

By the time of the final trial match, at Christchurch at the end of January 1949, Reid had so impressed national selectors Walter Hadlee, Jack Kerr and Merv Wallace that Hadlee, captaining The Rest, asked Reid to open the innings with him. "With my co-selectors' approval," recalls Hadlee, "I told John that he would be selected for the team, not to worry and to go out and show how he could bat. He made 117 and left no doubt about his quality or his future."

Besides his batting, Reid offered other strengths. "John had not long recovered from rheumatic fever," says Hadlee. "At that stage he was not

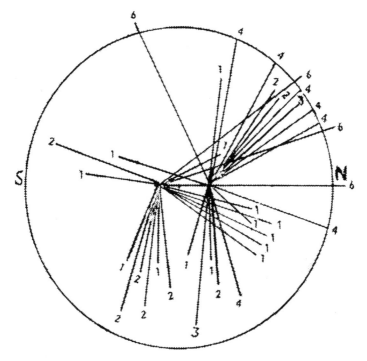

The wagon wheel of Reid's 88 not out against Canterbury at the Basin Reserve in 1949. Note the 6 over cover. This spectacular innings marked Reid, then 20, as a cricketer of special talent.

bowling more than the occasional short spell, though he was capable of mustering lively pace. He was known to be a part-time wicketkeeper and was obviously agile and energetic: an automatic selection."

Interestingly, Reid himself was far from convinced he would be selected, and in scanning the names of potential candidates, he felt Doug St John, the stylish Otago batsman, was a major rival for a middle-order place. "I hoped that because I could bowl, and with my wicketkeeping thrown in, the balance might tip my way, but I was not confident."

There was much speculation about the makeup of the team. Donnelly, whose form for Oxford University and Warwickshire, had so impressed the English critics, was a certainty, but there were any number of candidates jostling for the other places. Wicketkeepers Eric Tindill, Frank Mooney and George Mills all had their backers. With Mills failing a medical test, Mooney was given the nod. Arthur Cresswell, the Wellington pace bowler, took the most wickets during the season, but missed selection, though his brother Fen was included. Auckland opening batsman Don Taylor, who averaged 60 with the bat that season, also missed. He was unfortunate to be vying with Sutcliffe, Hadlee and Scott for opening positions. Geoff Rabone was brought into the picture late, and John Hayes was included as the young fast bowler.

Opening bowler Tom Pritchard, Donnelly's team-mate at Warwickshire, was also spoken of as a contender and with his pace and stamina would certainly have been an asset in Hadlee's team. However, he ruled himself out because he was keen to stay on with Warwickshire to earn himself a benefit match. "Not having Tom was a pity," says Reid. "He was a really good fast bowler. As a schoolboy I'd watched him take all 10 wickets in an innings in a North-South Army match at the Basin Reserve. He bowled nine batsmen and had the 10th, Alf Postles, lbw."

These selection decisions all provoked much comment, but no one quibbled at Reid's inclusion. He was the youngest player in the side, but was there on merit.

Merv Wallace has vivid memories of the young John Reid. "I remember playing against him for Auckland. He was just a youngster then. Someone mentioned to me that he bowled slowish off-cutters, but that he had a quicker ball which was quite good. Soon enough, I was batting when John came on to bowl. The first over presented no particular problem. He wheeled down some brisk off-cutters. But in the next over he bowled a couple of quicker ones, and they were really quick. If the first one had been straight, it would have cleaned me out properly. In those days, John would have been a very quick bowler, but for the effects of the rheumatic fever. He had very strong shoulders."

Wallace was even more taken with Reid the batsman. "He always showed a lot of promise, especially since before we went away he had hardly played any Plunket Shield cricket. I am a great believer in encouraging youth, but I would never put a young fellow into a team just on promise. He has to be there on merit. He has to be able to perform better than the players he is replacing. That was the case with John."

If he was to be the junior member of any side, Reid was fortunate it was the Forty-Niners. Whereas, the 1937 team had split into cliques, it is obvious from reading about the 1949 tour and talking to team members, that there were no divisions. Hadlee was fair, if serious, and understood the social requirements of a touring captain in England. Wallace, Donnelly and other senior members could not have been more helpful. In this environment, Reid thrived. "John took advantage of being in that 1949 side," says Wallace. "He was the youngest player in the team, but he fitted in well. He was always confident, but not so much back then. He was suddenly a team-mate of players like Squib Donnelly and Wally Hadlee, players he'd looked up to, and he obviously loved the experience. John spent a lot of time with me. He was always prepared to listen and learn.

"It's a funny thing on tour, how you become mates with people. John was interested in sightseeing and one of his hobbies was photography.

But I always got the impression that he was extremely cricket-orientated. That's all he wanted to talk about."

Different personalities suit different people. Walter Hadlee, as captain of the Forty-Niners, clearly had a huge influence on the young John Reid. Reading Reid's tour diary, it is obvious how much he respected his captain. But there is also no doubt that Wallace's softer personality struck more of an empathy with Reid. There would be few people whose knowledge of cricket was deeper than Hadlee's, but Reid tended to seek Wallace's views first. Hadlee and Reid, two giant figures of New Zealand cricket, are men of strong opinions, both steeped in the game. Hadlee is more of a planner and is meticulous in this respect. Reid as a player was more spontaneous, though he, too, had a fine appreciation of cricket tactics and technique.

The two retain a strong mutual respect. Hadlee was the manager of the team Reid led on tour in 1965. He was also a leading administrator when Reid was the New Zealand captain. When Hadlee wrote his autobiography, *The Innings of a Lifetime*, he called one chapter "The John Reid Era" and he is unstinting in his praise of Reid as a cricketer. "If a team had three John Reids, they would never lose," he says.

But having said that, their personalities did not always gel. Wallace has watched all this. "In 1949 John respected Wally. He looked up to him. Later on, as John progressed, there was sometimes a bit of a clash. I never found that with John. He would always come to me. If he brought a Wellington side to Auckland, he'd ask me to come down to the nets to have a look at a young player. We always worked very well together. He took advice very well."

The 1949 tour has been well covered. Alan Mitchell, the New Zealand Press Association correspondent, wrote a most appropriately titled book *Cricket Companions*, which captured the spirit well. Don Neely's *Men in White* covered it factually and Walter Hadlee gave an insider's view, full of wit and wisdom, in *The Innings of a Lifetime*.

Nevertheless, it is important to recount events from the tour in some detail, especially when they involve Reid. After all, it was his experiences in England in 1949 that helped shape John Reid as a cricketer and push him a long way along the path towards the player he became.

Hadlee's side began with a draw against Yorkshire, during which Hutton made 167. "A lovely bat, but not the style of Merv," was Reid's diary entry. Reid made his debut for New Zealand against Worcestershire. He batted at No 6, having watched Scott and Wallace make centuries and Hadlee 97. "I batted badly for eight and was caught at mid on, following through when I shouldn't have." In the second innings, he got to 23 before being lbw to Jackson. "A Plunket Shield shot" was how Reid described it. This is an intriguing reference that occurs several times in his diary. It could be seen as rather critical of New Zealand's domestic competition, but I take it as an indication of Reid's determination to raise his batting to another level in England.

In Reid's next match, against Leicestershire, he ran into Australian left-arm googly merchant Jack Walsh. Half a century later, Reid still shakes his head when he thinks about Walsh. "I made 45 in an hour, but Walsh had me in all sorts of trouble. He was such a good bowler. That innings was an education." Reid was eventually out when he trod on his wicket facing Lester, trying to sneak a single at the end of the over. There would have been further education watching the partnership of 299 between Wallace and Donnelly. It was in this match that Reid picked up his first wicket for New Zealand, when he had the Leicester opener Berry caught by Sutcliffe in the slips.

Then it was on to Cambridge University, where Reid and Wallace put on 324 for the fourth wicket. Wallace hit 197 and Reid, who batted for six hours, scored an unbeaten 188, including 23 4s. "It was pretty slow, but I enjoyed it very much," his diary notes. Reid's work wasn't finished, for he also kept wickets in this match, making two catches and two stumpings.

Wallace recalls that Cambridge match well. "It was the first time I'd batted with John for any length of time. I remember looking up the wicket at him and he'd be grinning at me, all hair and teeth."

Though the tour was only in its early stages, Wallace had already got through a power of work, having scored 82, 126, 108, 26, 8, 9, 171 and 197. He had already spent hour upon hour in the middle and was looking to conserve his energy where possible. "John was batting very well, and kept stroking the ball right to the boundary edge. We ran a succession of threes, until finally I went down to him and asked him to hit it a little harder. He was running me into the ground. I figured if he hit more boundaries, I wouldn't have to do as much running! As it was, I'd already lost a lot of weight by then and had my trousers pinned with safety pins. I was running holding my bat in one hand and my trousers up with the other!"

The big century obviously put Reid in line for a place in the test side, especially as he was an equally brilliant fieldsman in the covers or the slips. However, he did his cause little good with a first ball duck against the M.C.C. on his first appearance at Lord's. "I was very conscious that it was Lord's, and was quite nervous when it was my turn to bat. I was in quite early. I walked down the stairs, through the Long Room and the glass doors and then down the few steps towards the picket fence and on to the field. You can feel the slope when you walk out. I was very conscious of where I was. The first ball I received was a half-volley from Trevor Bailey and I played over it and was bowled. It was pretty quiet on the way back with the M.C.C. members in the Long Room perhaps wondering if this young fellow had urgent business elsewhere."

An indication of how different tours were in those days can be seen by Reid's diary entry during the next match, against Oxford University, when he mentions that the team had now been away from New Zealand three months. These days that would be considered an exceptionally long tour, but the Oxford match was only the seventh of a 32-match programme.

Another aspect of the tour so different from today was the team's non-cricket activities. There was no first class cricket on Sundays and the team took the opportunity for sightseeing, or meeting friends and relations. They visited Windsor Castle, Eton College, Wembley, Wimbledon, St Paul's, the B.B.C. headquarters, the Bradford mills, the Waterman pen factory, various bat factories, any number of churches and castles and dozens of other tourist sights. In London, a favourite spot was the Gay Nineties Club. There were boat trips up the Thames and drives into the countryside. During most evenings they would attend a movie or the theatre, go for a walk around the town they were in, or converge on one of their team-mates' rooms where a long and informal debrief would take place. It all sounds fairly tame by today's standards, but it is clear the team got a thorough look at Britain, which modern sides could not claim. Like several of the team, Reid was a tee totaller, and there was certainly far less alcohol drunk than in recent times.

The 1949 team was not a young one. Four players had toured England 12 years earlier. Several of the side had served in the Second World War. They had gone to England to play good cricket and support each other and took their enjoyment from being in each other's company in the best of cricket surroundings.

One of Reid's passions was photography. He was appointed to a three-man photo committee and spent much time having good photos copied and passed on to other team members. On the boat home he sifted through more than 700 photos, some of which are reproduced in this book.

Wallace feels it would be difficult for a modern team to match the camaraderie evident in 1949. "We spent six weeks together on a boat and got to know each other very well. Then we had quite a few days in Eastbourne practising. All this time together builds up very good spirit. Now the boys hop on a plane, talk to the fellow next to them, then get off in London, and are into the tour within a couple of days. Back in 1949, life was a lot simpler. We were happy to do things as a team. Now they all have cars and money. They go to parties and have different interests. Everyone in the 1949 side wanted to learn about cricket. It was just the way it was. They enjoyed everyone else's company. They were quite happy sitting around in one of the fellows' rooms, chatting about the cricket, perhaps ordering a cup of tea later in the evening."

Neil Harvey, who was the baby of Don Bradman's wonderful 1948 team to England, said recently that he learned a vast amount that had nothing to do with cricket on that tour. Reid feels the same about his experiences in 1949. "We all took our dinner suits with us and at least once a week we attended functions where a dinner suit was required. We mixed with dignitaries and learned about protocol. I recall dining at the Lord Mayor of London's Mansion House and being very careful that I was using the correct knife and fork. We got to see England and parts of Europe. It was a tremendous learning experience for me, not long out of college."

But back to the cricket...

The New Zealanders were unlucky at Oxford to have to bat on the second day on what umpire Frank Chester described as one of the worst pitches he'd ever seen. In a low-scoring game, New Zealand was left needing 210 to win and by stumps on the second day was 45-5. There was hope, though, with Reid and Cave not out and Wallace, Donnelly and Brun Smith still to bat. The next morning Reid was caught first ball slashing a ball into the gully. With New Zealand fighting to avoid defeat, it was not a stroke which particularly enthused captain Hadlee. "I suppose it didn't look too good," says Reid, "but the shot was on. I hit the ball in the middle of the bat and it crashed into the gully fieldsman, hitting him in the chest and knocking him over. Unfortunately the ball rebounded to second slip and I was on my way. It was a piece of pure bad luck."

At Hove against Sussex, Merv Wallace's hopes of scoring 1000 runs by the end of May finally evaporated. He finished with 910 at an average of 70. With Sutcliffe struggling for runs early in the tour, Wallace's contribution was immense. However, Sutcliffe, who scored just 295 runs in the first month, showed signs that he was beginning to find his feet. "Against Sussex on a run chase, Bert made 56 and Martin 88," Reid recalls. "They were both at their best and it was really something to see. I opened and made 82, and had good partnerships with both. Bert hit the first ball for 6 straight over the bowler, a shot I'll never forget. We were chasing 247 in just over three hours and got them with five wickets in hand."

Reid celebrated his 21st birthday during the next match, at Taunton, though not with any special success, being dismissed for four. His team-mates asked him to pick two books for his birthday and he chose one by Len Hutton and another about England. The team then signed them for him.

The tour selectors – Hadlee, Wallace, Donnelly and Cowie – decided to include Brun Smith ahead of Reid for the first test, naming Reid 12th man. It must have been close. At this stage Reid was not being used as a bowler – he had bowled just 32 overs in brief spells – but his batting was developing fast. However, Smith had scored 92, 73 and 41 in his last three innings and got the nod.

The games rolled by... an exciting run chase against Hampshire when New Zealand scored 109-3 in 28 minutes to win on the last afternoon, the second test, with Reid again 12th man ("I watched Martin Donnelly make a double century and give Trevor Bailey a real pasting"), and then the game against Derbyshire. "I had a good knock in that game, scoring 66. I'd heard they had an England bowler, Copson, in their attack. I'd been batting a while and giving them a whack when I asked Frank Mooney which one was Copson. In those days you had to buy a scorecard at the ground to find out who was who. Frank pointed out Copson, and after that I became much more cautious. It was a good lesson for me: you should play the ball, not the name. He bowled me for three in the second innings. Perhaps I was still thinking about his reputation."

People were a lot more matter-of-fact in those days. Hadlee, who scored a blazing 43 to help New Zealand scamper to victory, collapsed in the dressing room afterwards. The temperature on that last day had reached 104°F. Reid's diary entry: "Wal fainted in the dressing room after the match – heat and too much worry." These days there would be team meetings, addresses by the team psychologist, huge media coverage... the works. Back then, Hadlee was attended to, recovered and played the next match, against Northamptonshire.

Reid confirmed his good form with a double of 107 not out and 72 in the Northants match. "I was hitting them well by this stage and scored my 107 in 115 minutes, with 15 4s. In the second innings, when we were chasing quick runs, I made 72, which included seven 4s and two 6s."

It was obvious the selectors faced a tricky problem going into the third test. Brun Smith had played superbly in the first two tests, averaging 86.5. In his last innings, against Scotland, he had made 68. Hadlee explains: "Eventually we included John and left out Brun. It was disappointing for Brun, who had batted really well. It was, however, always hoped John would get some test experience and I was keen he should get the chance. By then he had made more than 770 runs, averaging 38, and was looking strong. We felt his time had come."

Reid's diary: "Had a practice at Old Trafford in the morning and wrote some letters in the afternoon. At 7pm the third test team was announced and I am taking Brun's place! Went to a Lord Mayor's dinner – Walter Nash was there. In bed at 10.15pm."

Wallace, another of the tour selectors, explains the situation: "John was technically a bit better than Brun, who used to give everyone heart attacks the way he batted. He didn't use his feet well and slashed outside the off stump, often hitting the ball in the air. The county sides worked him out fairly soon. John was a useful bowler and a top class fieldsman who could catch brilliantly either in the outfield or the slips and turn a game. As one of the aims of the tour was to bring on the younger players, and John was so dedicated, he deserved his chance."

England captain Freddie Brown put New Zealand into bat and at lunch New Zealand was 84-4. When Hadlee was dismissed by Bailey, Reid was left with two balls to face before lunch. An edge to leg gave him his first runs in test cricket. Reid noted: "After lunch, Martin and I dug our toes in and put on 116 before I was lbw to Jackson in the last over before tea. I managed to get 50 – a few snicks here and there, but they all count!" Esteemed English critic Neville Cardus was a good deal more complimentary, describing Reid as "a club cricketer in excelsis. I do not mean that he is not endowed technically, but only that he combines with common-sense against a good ball an unashamed appetite for a brawny blow against a bad one". Reid scored a solid 25 in the second innings as New Zealand played out time.

"After the test," Hadlee recalls, "the team was in an exuberant mood, particularly Bogo Reid, who had something to celebrate with his first test behind him. Nearly everyone had made a good contribution and the bad moments had been overcome by determination and commitment. So we went through our repertoire of songs, led by the better voices of Mooney, Sutcliffe and Rabone, and the falsetto of Thomas Browning Burtt."

It was interesting how teams mixed in those days. After the second day's play, several of the New Zealanders went to Broughton House and talked with some disabled servicemen. They were joined by England's star player, Denis Compton.

A fortnight later, Reid played spectacularly for an unbeaten 151 against Warwickshire, during which he reached his 1000 runs for the tour. "They had a good attack, with Eric Hollies, who was famous for bowling Bradman for a duck in his final test innings the previous year, and New Zealander Tom Pritchard. Hollies bowled me for one in the first innings. I suppose I could console myself that that was better than Bradman! In the second innings I hit 22 4s and a 6. The message had gone around the counties that I could hook, but that I hooked in the air. Pritchard was the quickest bowler in England and tried me out with a lot of bouncers. I hooked him repeatedly and one of them ended up in the bleachers."

Reid's good form continued with another powerful innings in the next match, against Nottinghamshire. He hammered 155, reaching his century in three hours and then scoring his next 55 (10 4s and a 6) in less than half an hour. Reid and Rabone, who made 120, put on 246 in 250 minutes.

The fourth test loomed, and it was to be a busy one for Reid because wicketkeeper Mooney was ruled out with an injured finger. After scoring just five before missing a full toss from Douglas Wright and being lbw, Reid had to work overtime keeping while England made 482 off 117 overs. He made two catches and noted: "Kept quite well, but missed a stumping off Reg Simpson."

New Zealand was in trouble in their second innings, which they began 137 behind. They were 131-4 when Reid joined Wallace. While Wallace stroked a pleasant 58, Reid was more aggressive. He reached his half-century in 80 minutes and then greeted the second new ball by slamming 14 runs off Bailey. Finally Reid mis-timed a shot of Laker and was caught in the covers for 93. "That was a really fine innings," says Hadlee. "The ball was spinning viciously because the top had gone off the pitch, but John showed maturity and composure."

So after two tests, Reid could point to a batting average of 43.2. He'd bowled a couple of overs and kept throughout one test. "A promising start to an outstanding test career," was Hadlee's summation.

Geoff Rabone says: "John ended the test series coming in at No 6 after Donnelly. Even in those days, he was a tremendous bloke to have coming in at No 6. His technique wasn't as tight as it became, but he was always a hard hitter."

Reviewing Reid's play on tour, Wallace says it was his batting that lifted him out of the ordinary. "He improved as a bowler, but because he was only young, and had been ill, he didn't get much bowling to do, though he was always handy. His wicketkeeping was adequate. He got by on natural ability and did a reasonably good job. His fielding was always superb. But it was his batting that really improved."

Near the end of the tour, with Cowie, Hayes and Cresswell all suffering injuries, Reid got more bowling. With Hayes unavailable so often, Reid was often the team's quickest bowler. Against the South of England, he opened the bowling with Cowie and not only dismissed Compton and Bailey in both innings, but ruined England opener Harold Gimblett's match. "I was probably a bit quicker than he thought, and when I bowled him a bouncer, it got through and hit him in the mouth. There was blood and teeth everywhere. It looked awful and I felt bad. I know fast bowlers are supposed to be tough and uncaring, but I went up and helped him out."

The tour ended with the traditional match against H. D. G. Leveson-Gower's XI at Scarborough, when, appropriately enough, New Zealand embarked on a successful last-afternoon run chase, scoring 213 in 120 minutes. Reid's memories of this feat involve the batting of Martin Donnelly. "Martin scored 145 not out and 53 not out in this match, a typical effort from him. In the first innings he pulled us together when we were struggling. In the second, he finished off the run chase. I batted with him for a while and marvelled at his control. Just when we were falling behind, Martin smashed Alec Bedser for four consecutive boundaries through the on. The first went through mid-on. Bedser bowled each successive ball progressively wider of the off and each time, Martin belted him between mid-on and mid-wicket. Merv finished the match with his favourite drop-kick shot over square leg for 6."

The Forty-Niners have become one of New Zealand's more famous sports teams. Names like Sutcliffe, Hadlee, Donnelly, Wallace, Reid, Scott, Mooney, Cowie, Rabone, Cave and Burtt hold pride of place in New Zealand cricket history. Five of them are in the New Zealand Sports Hall of Fame. Eight of the team – a record – scored 1000 runs during the tour. Two made 2000 runs. There were 29 centuries scored. Burtt led the bowling with 128 wickets, and five bowlers took at least 50 wickets. Frank Mooney claimed 66 victims on tour, a record for a wicketkeeper from any country on an England tour. The test series was squared, a fair result, and one which put an end to the absurdity of three-day tests, and 13 matches were won. The tour returned a profit of £16,700, which laid a strong financial base for the New Zealand Cricket Council and helped fund future tours.

For Reid, the tour had been a wonderful opportunity. He scored four centuries, three in excess of 150, and totalled 1488 runs. His average of 41.33 placed him fourth behind Donnelly, Sutcliffe and Wallace. "Bert

Sutcliffe and I were two of the younger players in the team. We were very lucky to have senior players so keen to help us. We were eager to learn, to talk cricket whenever we could. But those senior players were very caring and knew a tremendous amount about cricket. When I look at the makeup of some New Zealand teams over the years, I realise how fortunate I was to tour in that group."

Reid says it was just as well the more experienced New Zealand players were so willing to help and so knowledgeable because he got precious little help from the English pros. "I would innocently ask a question like, 'What is the best way to play an off-spinner?' and would be met by a stony silence and usually a quick change of subject. The pros, it seemed, gave you nothing for nothing. I also noticed another strange thing. If a young batsman like myself got a few runs, but in the process played uppishly through mid-wicket or hit a hook shot in the air, there would be a fieldsman in those positions for the catch in the very next county match. Talk about news travelling along the grapevine! The pros passed on this information from county to county, but offered no help in return, their technical secrets being kept under wraps.

"Obviously there were notable exceptions. I remember Joe Hardstaff, the veteran Notts pro, fielding at short leg and watching me play around my front foot for the 20th time. 'Get bloody foot outside ball,' he growled, which I did to the very next ball, and almost knocked off his head. 'That's better, lad,' and the game carried on."

Wisden, reviewing the tour, commented on Reid's "bristling aggression" and said he made the greatest advance of any player in the side during the tour. "Long before the end of the summer, Reid was established as the leading all-rounder. Learning rapidly by experience, he improved his batting by adding solidity to his punishing strokes. He was always the best of a superb fielding side, showed himself a good deputy in the last test for the injured wicketkeeper Mooney and, though Hadlee resisted the temptation to use him much, he could deliver as fast a ball as anyone in English cricket."

Hadlee describes Reid as a good team member who mixed well: "He was the junior member of the team, but everyone enjoyed his company. He was always a lot of fun and quite spontaneous. I don't think even John would describe himself as contemplative! By the end of the tour, he was a very good cricketer. I hardly bowled him until well into August. His mother asked me before the tour to look out for his health. It would have suited us to have John bowling because he was very quick and two of our pace bowlers, Cowie and Hayes, had injury problems. But I was more concerned with John's batting and he improved tremendously. Before we left, we could all see John's potential and I was pleased that by the time we returned he had a definite long-term future. He had become a real cricketer."

∼

1958

If the 1949 tour was one long triumph, the 1958 tour was the reverse. New Zealand was accorded the honour of a full five-test series. But English cricket was as strong as it has ever been, and New Zealand sent over a sub-standard batting side. They lost four of the tests heavily and were probably saved from defeat by rain in the fifth.

"I've often since described that team as a kindergarten side," says Reid. "They were not well chosen. Some good, experienced players, especially batsmen, were left behind. The selectors – Giff Vivian, Lankford Smith and Harry Cave – sent some very young, green players to England, and expected them to improve and bat with confidence against bowlers like Trueman, Statham, Tyson, Laker and Lock. It was ridiculous."

Before the tour, Reid made a strong plea to have Merv Wallace accompany the side as player-coach. "I looked around New Zealand and could see that we were desperately short of experienced batsmen of class. In 1949, Donnelly, Hadlee and Wallace had all been to England before and all were top batsmen. In addition, there were several other batsmen who had the ability to score heavily. It wasn't the case in 1958.

"I knew Merv well. I had total faith in his cricket knowledge. I'd seen it first hand during the 1949 tour when he was like the team coach or senior pro. Merv and I had worked well together when he'd been appointed coach of the New Zealand team in 1956 and '57. I was very keen to have him with me in England. In fact, it was vital. I even offered to step down from the captaincy and play under Merv if it meant having Merv make the trip. Not only did the selectors not include Merv, who was still a good batsman, but they chose a very poor team. Merv and I were brought in as advisors to the selectors, but absolutely no notice was taken of our views. For instance, I'd been to school with Trevor Meale and knew him well. I'd seen him playing in Wellington for years. I advised against his selection, but he was still sent. He played two tests and scored 25 runs at an average of 5.25 and for the full tour scored 502 runs at 21.8. Again against my advice, we sent two wrist-spinners when it is well-known that the best spinner to take to England is an orthodox left-armer. Tom Burtt had done well in 1949 and Hedley Howarth was also to shine in 1969. We had no left-arm spinner in 1958.

"It was pathetic, really. To see Jack Darcy opening the batting against Trueman and Loader in the Lord's test when he'd made just two half-centuries on tour and had never made more than 89 in a first class match was very disheartening. Jack fought as hard as anyone could fight, and made 14 and 33. His 33 was more than double any other score in our second innings. But what a task he was set, facing vastly more experienced England bowlers on their home patch with virtually no top-class batting under his belt. I felt sorry for him."

Wallace says he feels he and Reid would have worked well together in

1958. "It was a pity the way things worked out. I could have gone as player-coach, and I think I could have helped. I'd only had a short time as coach and felt I could have done more. One member of the New Zealand Cricket Council said to me at Eden Park, 'We can't send players just for perks.' I told him he didn't have much understanding of a big tour if he thought that travelling as a coach or a captain was a perk."

Reid: "It was after that experience that I insisted I become part of the selection panel. I was the captain, but I wasn't getting the players I needed. After the 1958 experience, the selections became a lot more consistent. We picked a much more sensible team to tour South Africa in 1961-62 and went over there and drew the series 2-2."

During the 1958 England tour, Reid also gained some appreciation for the social demands on a touring captain. "I realised in 1958 what a good job Wal Hadlee had done in 1949 as far as the public speaking and other responsibilities of the captain went. Touring England is unlike any other country. There are a lot more functions and much more speaking is required. Wal had more than I did in 1958, and the responsibility these days is a lot less, but in 1958 the speeches were quite a worry for someone like me, who was still quite shy of speaking in public. Until then I had avoided public speaking where I could, though being an oil company rep had involved me more in making speeches. In England, I found myself in some daunting situations, including addressing the Sportsman's Lunch at the Savoy in London. I looked around a room of more than 500 guests and saw many people who were famous in their own fields. As the captain of New Zealand, you are intensely aware that many of those listening will be judging the team by the quality of the speech the captain gives – a perturbing thought. I was fortunate during the 1958 tour that Jack Phillipps did a lot of the speech-making for me.

"At the Sportsman's Lunch, I sat next to the Duke of Norfolk, who was at that time the President of the M.C.C., and Lord Birkett, both confident and supremely talented speakers. I was busy nervously writing things down on the back of the menu in preparation for my speech when the Duke leaned over and asked me if I wanted him to say anything on my behalf. I said that would be most helpful, and mentioned that the wickets we were striking were generally diabolical, worse than many club pitches back in New Zealand. He then suggested that I should just introduce my players. So Lord Birkett spoke first, then the Duke, and then Jack and me. I ran through our players and told a story about each one. That was fine. I was very appreciative of the Duke's understanding of the situation. In the end I got better at speech-making, but it was a struggle at first. By 1965, the number of speeches a captain was required to make had dropped away noticeably."

Strangely, the 1958 New Zealand team, despite their poor final record, began their tour brilliantly. They drew with Worcester, then beat Leicestershire, Essex, Cambridge University and the M.C.C. A draw with

Oxford University was followed by victories over Glamorgan and Somerset and a draw with Hampshire. Only the Surrey match of the early fixtures was lost. You had to go back to Don Bradman's 1948 side to find a touring team with a better record going into the first test.

But that was about the end of it. England won the first four tests by 205 runs, an innings and 148 runs, an innings and 71 runs and an innings and 13 runs, with the rain-spoiled fifth test drawn. Outside the tests, the weather dominated proceedings. Only six of the 33 matches were not affected by weather and, incredibly, the team lost 17 complete days because of rain. "It even got to the point," says Reid, "that when we arrived in Leeds we went to the local rugby league ground and threw the ball around among ourselves, just to have a bit of a run out in the open." With many matches ruined by the weather, there was a succession of draws outside the tests, though the return Surrey match was also lost. The final match, against T. N. Pearce's XI, was tied.

"There was a combination of factors contributing to our results," says Reid. "The weather was horrific, especially compared to 1949, when it was a long, hot summer. The pitches were not hard and fast, as they had been in 1949. England had some big-name batsmen like Graveney, Cowdrey, Dexter and May, but May was the one who really hurt us. He hit the ball so powerfully he could murder an attack and he made runs against us wherever we went that year. Our batsmen generally weren't good enough to handle the conditions. Bowlers like Laker, Lock and Trueman were just too good." In the damp, miserable conditions the tests were a bleak time for the New Zealand batsmen and the popular refrain went:

Ashes to ashes,
Dust to dust,
If Laker doesn't get you,
Lockie must.

Lock took 34 wickets at 7.47 each during the tests. Laker's 17 wickets cost 10.17 each.

"On paper we had quite a good bowling attack. Tony MacGibbon was outstanding throughout, but Johnny Hayes, Bob Blair and Harry Cave lacked penetration. We had two wrist-spinners, Jack Alabaster and Alex Moir, but I couldn't use them properly because our batsmen never scored enough runs to give them a target to bowl at.

"All in all, it was an unsatisfactory experience. Our batsmen weren't up to it. Our best two batsmen were Bert and me, but we failed in the tests. Lawrie Miller, a heavy scorer at home, got found out in England, where the leading bowlers there soon sorted out how to counter his front foot technique. Some of our younger batsmen had little idea."

The figures support Reid. Only four batsmen reached 1000 runs on tour,

Reid being highest with 1429, and only three averaged even 30. Reid's overall figures were good. He finished fourth in the English seasonal averages for 1958 and, as he wryly reflected, none of the English batsmen had to face an attack comprising Laker and Lock, plus two of Trueman, Statham, Loader and Tyson once, let along six or seven times. Several batsmen, including Meale, Darcy, Miller and Noel Harford never played for New Zealand again. Only seven centuries were scored by New Zealanders during the summer, compared with 29 in 1949. MacGibbon, with 73 wickets, was the top wicket-taker. Wicketkeeper Eric Petrie had a good tour and was honoured with selection in the Gentlemen's team (against the Players) near the end of the season.

Reid probably fell into the trap of trying to do too much. "During this tour and in fact quite often in the 1950s, there was often only Bert and me – and when Bert retired, only me – who had scored a test century. I felt a tremendous weight knowing that if I got out, our batting would be extremely brittle. There's a big difference walking in to bat with the score 12-2 and 165-2. If a team gets early wickets, it can set attacking fields and bowl aggressively.

"Sometimes I tried to shield other players from difficult bowlers and it cost me my wicket. That was bad cricket on my part. I realised it in England in 1958. I was out once trying to chip Tony Lock over the infield for a single to keep the strike. The next day I was walking down towards Piccadilly Circus and got to thinking about it. I decided it wouldn't happen any more. I'd play for the team, but I wouldn't throw my wicket away like that, trying to protect a lesser batsman when at that stage my wicket was important."

~

1965

It required a good deal of soul-searching before Reid decided to make the long overseas tour in 1965. "I really did wonder if I should make myself available. I would turn 37 during the tour, I had a knee injury that was getting worse all the time, I had my squash centre to run, and it was still in the days when there was very little money forthcoming from the New Zealand Cricket Council to help cover costs. There was another aspect, too. I'd always loved cricket with a passion, but by 1965, I think I had begun to fall out of love with some aspects of playing cricket. I was a different generation to most of the team. On that 1965 tour, I found that except for Bert Sutcliffe, I was much older than most of them, and really it was only my Wellington team-mates, Artie Dick and Barry Sinclair, that I felt I had much in common with. Five players were 21 or younger and eight were making their first tour.

"I still loved cricket as a game – once a cricketer, always a cricketer – but the appeal of playing was starting to diminish. I didn't have any doubt that

I was still fit enough. I was playing A grade interclub squash and, in fact, was spending more time on the squash court than in the cricket nets. However, in the end, despite my reservations, I couldn't turn down such a trip as was on offer. We were to go to India and Pakistan, travel overland through Europe to England, stop off in Scotland and Ireland, then have a week each in Bermuda and Los Angeles. In the days when cricketers travelled so much less than they do now, it was very enticing."

So Reid made his last tour as a player. He duly had a knee operation on his return and was forced into retirement by the injury. That meant his last first class innings in New Zealand had been those against Pakistan in the test series at home in early 1965. The first test was to be his farewell to the Basin Reserve and he parted in style, smashing 97 in 130 minutes, including 16 boundaries. His figures for the three-test series were good – 229 runs at 38.16 an innings – but it wasn't exactly the sort of blazing exit, with all the attendant publicity, that a Hollywood scriptwriter would have demanded.

When Reid wrote *A Million Miles of Cricket*, he was not overly enthusiastic about the 1965 tour. "We made no material progress, nor did we slip back," he felt. In hindsight, he is more positive about the tour. "As it turned out, a lot of players were introduced to international cricket and they served New Zealand well over the next decade or so."

The tour of England – a short tour that encompassed three test matches and 16 other matches (including one each in Scotland and Ireland) was preceded by a rugged tour of India and Pakistan. It was an absurd itinerary. There was no time to blood young players on the first leg of the tour and some, such as Terry Jarvis, were still in poor health when they reached England.

Bevan Congdon, Barry Sinclair, Vic Pollard, Ross Morgan, Graham Vivian, Bruce Taylor, Terry Jarvis and Richard Collinge all made their first New Zealand tours. In addition, Bryan Yuile, Dick Motz and Graham Dowling still had at least four seasons of international cricket ahead of them. Only Reid, Sutcliffe, Artie Dick, John Ward and Frank Cameron were at or near the end of their careers.

It was a team in which investments paid off. Bruce Taylor and Bevan Congdon went on to play outstandingly for New Zealand in the West Indies in 1972. Congdon also scored two 170s in the 1973 test series against England. Taylor became the New Zealand record-holder for test wickets. Later Collinge topped Taylor's mark and helped New Zealand beat England for the first time when he bowled Geoff Boycott with a peach of a delivery at the Basin Reserve in 1978. Vic Pollard, despite restricted availability because of his decision not to play on Sundays, had some great days. He was to win both the Winsor and Redpath Cups, to bowl well against Australia B in 1967, and to score two test centuries in England in 1973.

Sinclair vied with Dowling as New Zealand's best batsman until he bowed out of test cricket in 1970. Jarvis, Vivian and Morgan all became leading provincial cricketers who were still sometimes representing New Zealand in 1972.

But all that was ahead. In 1965, Reid's team was young and inexperienced. "I don't think the team was as well selected as it might have been. The selectors were Merv Wallace, Gordon Leggat and myself, so there was plenty of experience there. I still can't believe we overlooked a proven world class leg-spinner in Jack Alabaster to take a gamble on an 18-year-old in Graham Vivian. That was poor selecting and to some extent was a repeat of the mistakes made in 1958 when promising players were chosen at the expense of experienced players. We could have done with more experience in the batting. Noel McGregor, Paul Barton, Murray Chapple and John Sparling had been in fairly good form during the New Zealand season, but none made the tour. Sparling was unavailable; the others were overlooked when they would have offered experience. We did select Gary Bartlett, but he failed the medical, which allowed Bruce Taylor into the side. Taylor turned out to be one of our better players on that tour."

The team's fielding, especially the catching, was surprisingly mediocre, the batting disappointing and the spin bowling almost non-existent. Only the pace bowlers – Motz, Cameron, Taylor and Collinge, distinguished themselves.

"For the first time, England tried a split season," says Reid. "We toured during the first half of their summer, and the South Africans had the second half. The weather was not particularly good while we were there, from May to mid-July, and the pitches were very poor. I even lodged a complaint with the M.C.C. and noticed that the wickets improved markedly from that point."

The best of the New Zealand batsmen were Pollard, who went on to win the Redpath Cup as Batsman of the Season, and Sinclair. But Sinclair, despite finding good form in the county games, managed only one half-century in the tests. Pollard, strong and vital, reminded English critics of the young Reid. He scored 4, 81 not out, 55, 55, 33, 53 in the test series, and two of his dismissals were run outs. New Zealand performed creditably in the first two tests. At Edgbaston they fought back by scoring 413 in the second innings, with seven batsmen reaching 40. At Lord's they scored 347 in their second innings and set England a second innings target of 218. However, in the third test, at Leeds, they were hammered into submission by John Edrich (310) and Ken Barrington (163) and lost by an innings and 187.

One of the delights of the England segment of the tour was following the batting average of Frank Cameron, who threatened to emulate Australian Bill Johnston's effort of 1953. Johnston, a genuine tail-ender, was dismissed only once in 17 innings on tour and finished with a Bradman-like batting average of 102. ("Class always tells," he joked afterwards.) Cameron, with few pretensions to batting, scored 29 not out, 1 not out, 10 not out, 5 not out, 4 not out, 4 not out, 0 (bowled Trueman in the first test), 1 not out, 14 not out, 3 not out, 9 not out, and 10 not out, by which time his average was 90. Then he spoiled it by making a duck against Warwickshire. This left him with a final tour batting average of 45, still good enough to proudly head the list.

Reid struggled in Britain. He had a run of poor scores, broken only by a half-century against Glamorgan. "I'd been making a start quite often," he says, "but had been unable to go on and build big scores. Then near the end of the tour I spent a few days with Peter May and his wife, Virginia. Our discussions at one stage turned to what a batsman should do when he was out of form. There are various theories, but Peter's advice was new to me. I told him I'd been getting out bowled and lbw quite often and he suggested I might be hitting across the line. His advice was to try to hit the stumps at the bowler's end. The idea was to encourage the playing of the stroke down the line. In my next match, against Kent, I scored 165 and hit the stumps at the other end four times. On one occasion, Barry Sinclair was very nearly run out by a straight drive which just missed the stumps after the bowler had touched the ball." After his punishing century against Kent, whose attack included Derek Underwood, Reid had innings of 84 against Warwickshire and 54 in the third test. Still, an England tour return of 799 runs at an average of 31.96 was less than he had hoped for. Handicapped by a worsening knee, he bowled just 73 overs, fewer than Ross Morgan or Congdon.

"It was difficult for John on that tour," recalls Walter Hadlee, who managed the side. "His knee was causing him a lot of problems. However he was a classy player right to the end. He was a murderous hitter who was always likely to hammer an attack."

～

JOHN REID'S VIEW
ENGLAND – THE PLAYERS

Sir Leonard Hutton: I rated Len and Denis Compton as the best batsmen we struck in 1949. They were among the all-time greats, but entirely different. Len, with that Yorkshire conservatism, played within himself all the time, Denis with inventiveness and ingenuity. Len's footwork was flawless. He had some magnificent shots and could score all around the wicket, but except for the second half of his double century against us in the Oval test, he never really let himself go. He was the first professional to captain England for any length of time, and made ruthless use of his fast bowlers. The strain of being his team's best batsman and captain showed towards the end, but we made his departure from test cricket a memorable one. After England had looked to be in trouble against us at Auckland in 1955, they bowled us out in our second innings for 26 and won by an innings!

Denis Compton: Denis was a law unto himself, always improvising. He used to somehow drive the ball straight at leg slip off Fen Cresswell. He used the sweep a lot, but played it in such a manner that he was virtually playing with a straight bat. He was very unorthodox. He often never bothered to get his feet near the ball, except that when he defended, he was very tight. He could dance down the track and played Tom Burtt better than anyone, because he was so inventive. Denis was a great character. There was still food rationing in England in 1949, but, typical Denis, he turned up at our hotel one day with a whole fillet of steak. Though his knee was giving him trouble by 1949, Denis was still a leading soccer player, and won an F.A. Cup-winner's medal with Arsenal in 1950.

Bill Edrich: After their famous season in 1947, Compton and Edrich were invariably paired together in the public mind, but I was not overly impressed with Edrich in 1949. He was a gritty batsman, who concentrated well and kept his head down, but I felt he was past his best. By 1949, Bill wasn't doing too much bowling, which surprised us somewhat as we had looked upon him as a genuine all-rounder. He could bowl quickly on occasions, but perhaps he found bowling as well as batting drained him of too much energy on the county cricket circuit.

Godfrey Evans: Evans was the best wicketkeeper I've seen. He was amazingly acrobatic, and was so full of life that he must have helped keep his fieldsmen on the alert during long afternoons. The way he stood up to Bedser and his work against him on the leg side was incredible. He was so intimidating in this respect that he became a separate attacking force for England. Godfrey was always a character. Until his death in 1999, he was a regular sight around the test venues in England, big mutton chops whiskers, and was the odds-setter for Ladbrokes. Through the 1990s, Ian Healy of Australia was regarded as the world's No 1 wicketkeeper – certainly in the record book – but when I compare him with Evans, I feel Evans had an extra dimension to his keeping. Standing back, they were both athletic and safe, but Evans was in another class standing up to quickish bowling. Healy, of course, distinguished himself with his work standing up to Shane Warne's spin.

Sir Alec Bedser: When we arrived in England in 1949, Bedser was the big name in the England attack. He'd had a very successful time against Bradman the previous year, and we were a bit wary of him. But we didn't find him as lethal as we thought we might. He was still a good bowler, no question, with a really awkward leg-cutter, all the more devastating because you were looking for his in-swing. He was helped immensely by having Godfrey Evans stand up to him. This became very restrictive for the batsman. Bedser, a big man with huge hands, had a lumbering run-up and was about the pace of Cave and Chatfield.

Bob Appleyard: A very under-rated bowler who often had to battle with Johnny Wardle to get a good run in the Yorkshire team, let alone England. He bowled off-spin or off-cutters at a nippy medium pace and could be devastating. His health wasn't always the best and he didn't have a long career, but he cleaned us out in 1955. Appleyard doesn't get the credit his bowling deserved.

Fred Trueman: One of the finest fast bowlers ever and the first bowler to claim 300 test wickets. His strike rate of a wicket every 49 balls compared more than favourably even with Michael Holding (51), Richard Hadlee (51) and Dennis Lillee (52). He was fast, lethal and able to move the ball both ways, with an especially good outswinger. Fred was very aggressive when he was bowling, but he was a nice enough guy and I liked him. He wasn't popular in England in his early days, and was often omitted from test and touring teams when he should have been in. He used to mouth off a bit, but it was never nasty and often humorous. We both had a memorable test at Christchurch in 1963. I got a 74 in the first innings and 100 in the second, and Fred took seven wickets in the first innings and another two in the second. It was a good battle. Fred closed out his test career against us in 1965. He was 34 by then and took just six wickets at an average of nearly 40 in the series, but was still quick enough to hit Bert Sutcliffe a nasty blow to the head during the Edgbaston test.

Brian Statham: I found Statham easier to play than Trueman, not that I ever scored particularly well against him. He got the ball to come in off the seam and was extremely accurate, but at least you knew where it was going. He had a similar action to Adcock, and was about the same pace, but wasn't nearly as nasty a bowler. In fact, he was probably the most easy-going fast bowler I ever encountered.

Frank Tyson: He wasn't nicknamed "Typhoon Tyson" for nothing. He was easily the quickest bowler I faced and lethal because you didn't know where it was going. I recall batting against him at Auckland in 1955. He hit the bicep of my arm and actually paralysed it. I lost all feeling. Tyson had me ducking and diving. Then Bailey came on, intending to give me more of the same treatment, but he wasn't as quick. I had the feeling back in my arm by then, but didn't let on and put his first ball over the old clock tower. Batsmen were always concerned facing Tyson because he was all over the place. I first faced him in a test after having played a series of club matches in Dunedin. We had to do that back then because our first class season was so short. By the time I lifted up my bat, my off stump was already gone. My reaction time just wasn't quick enough. He was in a different league. After that experience, I got some of the boys to throw me some bouncers from halfway down the track. That helped, and I managed a few runs in the next test. In terms of pure speed, Tyson and Jeff Thomson might have been the fastest since the Second World War, with Pakistani Shaoib Akhtar threatening to break into that category.

Trevor Bailey: I didn't rate Bailey too highly. I liked positive cricket, and he was a defensive, negative type of player, someone to help you avoid defeat, rather than to win. He was a reasonable all-rounder, and in 1949 was their quickest bowler. I do remember Trevor bowling me first ball in my first innings at Lord's, in 1949. Martin Donnelly, who had gone to Oxford University, used to like to get after Bailey, who had gone to Cambridge, and took special satisfaction in scoring 206 against him in the test at Lord's and more runs at Scarborough at the end of the tour.

Peter May: Peter was one of the best batsmen I ever played against, on the same level as Hutton and Compton. To give today's cricket followers an idea, I would rate him about on a par with Sachin Tendulkar, though entirely different in methods. Peter is still regarded as the finest batsman produced by England since the war. His on-driving was truly formidable, and it was necessary to place two mid-ons for him, as he hit the ball so hard and straight. He really punished us in 1958, scoring five centuries in 10 innings. His 165 for Surrey on a poor wicket, when the next best score was 25, was the sort of innings you never forget. The wicket was a dullish grey and looked sick. Yet Peter played some magnificent shots off the back foot over extra cover for 6 off Tony MacGibbon. Tony was bowling fast-medium, and Peter smacking them straight at the gasometer. What impressed me about Peter was that unlike Hutton and Colin Cowdrey, he always set out to dominate the bowlers. I played against him fairly regularly and enjoyed captaining teams against him. He was a tough but fair cricketer and a very nice person.

The Lord Cowdrey of Tonbridge: Colin (initials M.C.C.) was a very competent, controlled batsman, technically efficient, with plenty of time to play his shots. But he was not as dominating as May. Even so, he had a great technique and always seemed in charge. Like May and Hutton, Colin never committed himself to play forward or back in advance. Rather, he got into a half-cock position like a golfer about to hit the ball doing a "press" – a slight forward weight adjustment. Colin has always loved cricket and has contributed to it in a huge number of ways. Besides being a test star, he has been president of the M.C.C., chairman of the I.C.C. and has held many other cricket posts over the past few years.

Tom Graveney: Tom was a little unusual. He was definitely a front foot player, using his height to get well forward, but he also hooked well. He liked to drive and could play the quicks well. I rated him just under

Cowdrey. Like all class batsmen, he had time to play his shots, and I recall him giving Bob Blair a pasting, when New Zealand batsmen had struggled with Blair's pace.

Ted Dexter: Though he didn't have a long test career, Ted was one of the classic batsmen, on a par with Cowdrey and just behind May. Ted had all the shots and stood tall, not unlike Mark Waugh. With his power and majestic style, Ted used to draw comparisons with Walter Hammond of the previous generation, a compliment in any company. Like Hammond, Ted was also a useful medium-pace bowler. Some said he was inclined to be aloof, but I found Ted very approachable. He captained the England team in New Zealand in 1963 and I then sat next to him for 16 hours as we travelled to Bombay and on to Nairobi to join up with Ron Roberts' International Cavaliers side. I got to know him a lot better on that trip. That was about the time when Ted was having trouble with the M.C.C. about his wife, an international model, travelling in the same country as the England team. How times have changed!

Jim Laker: There were three great off-spinners during my career – Laker, Hugh Tayfield and Lance Gibbs. As New Zealand seldom played the West Indies, I never saw much of Gibbs, but Laker was the bowler who spun the ball the most. He was a bit quicker than Tayfield and had a brilliant straight ball, the "toppie" which caught countless batsmen unawares and brought him any number of wickets either bowled or caught behind. Jim spent a couple of seasons coaching in Auckland, where he was very popular. He was a friendly character who enjoyed chatting with the opposition after play, even to the extent of disclosing a few professional secrets. He'll be forever remembered for taking 19 wickets against Australia in the Old Trafford test in 1956.

Tony Lock: It was Harry Cave's film and my lounge that exposed Tony's bent arm. At a time when there wasn't much cricket on television, one of Harry's hobbies was taking cricket films. He happened to film Lock bowling against us in England in 1958 and when we played the film one evening early in 1959 during a party at my place, it was plain for all to see – Lock's faster ball was as fast as anything you'd see in cricket and he clearly threw it. Both teams were watching. I think Lock was shocked by what he saw. He was getting tremendous whip with that action and could turn the ball a huge amount. He went away and redesigned his action so that he bowled with a straight arm, but I'm not sure he was ever as effective again.

Ken Barrington: In a perverse way, I suppose New Zealand could claim some success against Barrington. In 1965 he scored 137 against us in the first test and was subsequently dropped for slow play, his innings having taken 437 minutes. Ken had an exaggerated two-eyed stance, so never played an off-drive, even to half-volleys fed up by us outside the off. He had a good defence and could bat for hours, but despite his test average of 58.6, I don't put him in the top rank as he was never likely to collar an attack. Ken was an unselfish, brave batsman, just the sort of person a captain wants in his team. In addition, he was a good friend and I was very saddened to hear of his sudden death from a heart attack in 1981, when he was just 50.

Fred Titmus: One of the few cricketers whose careers have spanned five decades (from the 1940s to the 1980s). He was an England regular for a number of years, a useful off-spinner, a handy batsman and a heady cricketer. Though Fred never caused us the problems that Laker and Tayfield did, I rated him well up the ranks of off-spinners, and not only because he bowled me "through the gate" for 97 on my last appearance for New Zealand at Lord's!

Geoff Boycott: Everything was for Geoff Boycott, no matter what the situation of the game. He was one of the most selfish batsmen that I have ever encountered, about on a par with our own Glenn Turner. That meant that Boycott often scored heavily, but it took him hours, to the detriment of his team. He did not help his team win matches. You have to be able to score quickly enough to enable your team to force a win. But Boycott would never take a risk. He was not an entertainer. He lost further lustre by making himself unavailable for test cricket for three years in the mid-1970s for what seemed like no particularly compelling reason. I have since come across Geoff in the course of my refereeing. Geoff and other television commentators were pushing a key into the pitch on a length, and I objected. The I.C.C. eventually brought in a rule outlawing the practice. I could imagine what he would have said if someone had used a key on a pitch he was about to bat on.

Derek Underwood: An awkward customer. On good wickets, he was a defensive bowler, pushing the ball through much quicker than most spinners, and concentrating on pinning the batsman down on leg stick. However, on a wet or crumbling wicket, he was a different proposition. His control, pace and turn made him very difficult to combat and he became a match-winner.

John Edrich: This will sound absurd, but he made a triple-century against us in the Leeds test in 1965, and I reckoned he was lucky. How can you be lucky when you make more than 300? It was my 58th test, and in all those games, I'd never seen anyone bat so long and play and miss so many times. The frustrating aspect for us was that just when he seemed to be in all sorts of trouble, he'd belt a series of boundaries, usually lofted on-drives or cover drives. When I meet him these days, we joke about that innings. He was a good, gutsy left-handed batsman – you don't score more than 100 centuries without having a lot of strengths.

Graham Gooch: I still say he had the cricket world conned. Everyone used to remark on his high backlift. And he did have his bat back high above his shoulder, like a baseballer, as he waited for the bowler to approach the wicket. But when the ball was bowled, that bat was back down. There were a lot of imitators of Gooch, but they'd get themselves bowled because they didn't get their bat down as quickly. Gooch developed into a very sturdy opening batsman, a good player, especially of pace bowling, and I'd rate him on about the same level as Ken Barrington. Gooch began his test career with a pair against Australia, but as he aged, even into his 40s, was still the best batsman in England.

Ian Botham: There can be no doubt that Botham was one of the great cricketers of the century. His presence and reputation are evident at all the venues I visit in my capacity as an I.C.C. referee. To the cricket public, Botham is a huge figure. He was primarily responsible for dragging English cricket out of a lean patch in the early 1980s. His play in the last three tests of the 1981 Ashes series was sublime. However, it must be said that in the late 1970s, when Botham made such a startling entry onto the world stage, a large percentage of the top stars had been bought off by Kerry Packer's World Series Cricket, leaving the way clear for those left, such as Botham, to record some incredible performances.

One of a referee's code of conduct jobs is to protect the spirit in which the game is played and to penalise anything that brings the game into disrepute. Cricket heroes need to be squeaky clean and role models for young, easily impressed fans. These stars have a responsibility to their public. I'm afraid Ian has let them down in this respect. On the field he was generally fine, but some of his antics off the field at the height of his career were unfortunate. Today I enjoy his television commentaries and he could be positioning himself for a role selecting England's team.

Mike Gatting: While his name is inevitably linked with that of Pakistani umpire Shakoor Rana, with whom he had a famous on-field confrontation, I recall Gatting for other reasons. He led the England rebel team that toured South Africa in 1989-90 and showed courage beyond the call of duty when he accompanied Ali Bacher, the South African cricket chief, among the thousands of people demonstrating against his team's tour. Gatting knew he could be attacked at any moment, but agreed to announce the abandonment of the tour, a brave, but sensible, decision.

As a batsman, Gatting was equally brave. His figures – 79 tests, 10 centuries, an average of 35.5 – indicate he fell below the very best level, but

I retain memories of him batting against the fearsome West Indian pace quartet with a broken nose and black eyes.

Alec Stewart: I've been a fan of his. I was the referee one time when he scored a century in each innings against the West Indies, and they were two brave and composed innings. For some years he was the most dangerous batsman in the England team, a back foot player who got behind the ball well. I thought his technique was pretty complete and he invariably sought to bat positively. He ran into a lean patch early in 1999, which I attributed to too much responsibility. He was the captain, wicketkeeper and opening bat, which is too much to ask of anyone. As the England captain, he brought a lot more panache to the role than his predecessor. I admired the way he took care over his captain's report on the umpires. Looking back, my impression was that Alec suffered from the various divisions that were apparent in England teams through the 1990s.

Michael Atherton: One of the few England batsmen of the recent crop who would bear comparison to some of the bigger names of the past. I have seen Michael play some very fine, gutsy innings when the rest of the house was falling around him. His back injury placed his career in jeopardy, but at his best he revealed similar strengths to Ken Barrington, and that put him on a fairly high level.

I wasn't as impressed with his test captaincy. He wasn't captain of his county, so his experience in this area was limited to a couple of seasons at university. Natural leadership is something some people are born with, but cricket captaincy requires practice and lots of it. Picking a batsman's weak points and setting the appropriate field has to be learned. Balancing bowlers and restricting runs in a one-day international is hard work and very taxing. It goes way beyond simple leadership flair.

Graeme Hick: With Hick, figures are deceiving. He absolutely murders average bowling, and has raced past his century of centuries. But his output in tests has been relatively poor. He doesn't get behind the ball and quick bowlers around the world didn't take long to work him out. They bang it into his body, or look to have him nick the ball into the slips. Having said that, Hick is an attractive batsman with all the shots. He is a good one-day player because fast bowlers cannot bowl short in that style of cricket and there are very few fieldsmen positioned in the slips and at gully. It's difficult to know what the future holds for Hick. He was dropped from the England test side after their defeat by New Zealand at the Oval in 1999. It was the eighth time he'd been dropped, and you do wonder how many more times he can be recalled. However he is still part of England's one-day squad, and there is always the chance that good form in the one-day game by Hick will persuade the selectors to bring him back into the test side.

Without wanting to sound like an old-timer, I find it hard to compare Stewart, Atherton and Hick favourably with many of the fine England batsmen of previous decades. They fall far below the Hutton-Compton-May level, which is understandable. But all three are inferior by some distance to Cowdrey, Graveney and Dexter. Perhaps the demise in the batting standards of England's test players is reflected by the team's tumble down the world rankings.

Darren Gough: A very likeable and lively, hard-working fast bowler. He has plenty of natural ability and isn't afraid to bend his back. When I've seen him, I'd say he has been rather unlucky. He has a lot of catches dropped off his bowling. I suppose I'd put him about on a par with Statham and Bob Willis in terms of pace and effectiveness. One of the things I like about him is that he will come back late in the day and bowl just as fast as earlier. He must be disappointed with his batting. It seemed for a while as if he might develop into a genuine all-rounder, but his batting has really gone, and he now has the batting attitude of a real tail-ender.

3 | OFF TO LEAGUE

A county cricket career was never an option for John Reid, for the simple reason that it would have meant an end to his days of playing test cricket for his country. Not surprisingly, Reid drew the attention of various counties' talent scouts after his encouraging tour of England in 1949. A young man who could hit powerfully and play long innings, a bowler who was as quick as anyone in the country, a superb fieldsman anywhere, a handy reserve wicketkeeper – it was no wonder Reid found himself the target of some generous offers.

Warwickshire, a county which had a history of employing New Zealanders, inquired if Reid would be interested in joining its ranks. If he had done so, Reid would not have lacked for company. At or about that time, Tom Pritchard, Martin Donnelly, Don Taylor and Ray Hitchcock, all New Zealanders, were wearing Warwickshire colours. In 1949, Tom Dollery, who proved a popular coach in New Zealand for some seasons, was appointed Warwickshire captain, the first professional to lead a county side full-time.

Reid also received an offer from Worcestershire, and, if he had chased vigorously, would no doubt have attracted interest from other counties. But he never gave any of these approaches long consideration. "At that time an overseas player could not play county cricket and also represent his country," says Reid. "The lure of test cricket and the opportunity to represent New Zealand was far too strong to be given up in return for a county contract."

A surprising number of New Zealanders had been county players. Before the First World War, Arthur Sims and Daniel Reese played alongside the immortal W.G. Grace in his London County team. In addition, Reese played eight matches for Essex as an amateur.

Between the wars, a number of New Zealand's greatest players, including Bill Merritt, Stewie Dempster, Ken James and Ces Dacre, played county cricket. Others, such as Roger Blunt and Giff Vivian, played for Nottinghamshire furniture magnate Sir Julien Cahn's team. Ian Cromb, the Canterbury all-rounder, had a spell of league cricket in 1933 and Tom Lowry, the W.G. Grace of New Zealand cricket, represented Cambridge

University, the Gentlemen of England and Somerset during the early 1920s. Legend has it that he chose Somerset because he was born close to Wellington. The English authorities didn't realise that by Wellington he meant the New Zealand capital, not the English town.

Dempster moved to England at Cahn's invitation, stayed and qualified for Leicestershire and for six straight seasons averaged more than 40 with the bat. From 1935 to 1939, he played 108 matches for his county, scored 4659 runs at 49.04 and hit 18 centuries. He represented Warwickshire briefly after the war, then returned to Wellington. James threw in his lot with Northamptonshire in 1935. His stylish wicketkeeping drew much praise and he eventually claimed 220 victims and scored 3500 runs for Northants. Merritt, the brilliant leg-spinner of the 1927 and '31 touring teams, played in the Lancashire league for Rishton for two years, for East Lancashire for a further five, and then for Dudley in the Birmingham league from 1940 to 1955. He also had three seasons of county cricket with Northants, resuming his lethal combination with keeper James. Dacre, a dashing batsman, qualified for Gloucestershire in the early 1930s and, batting alongside Walter Hammond, achieved some prodigious feats. In six successive seasons he topped 1000 runs, always batting at a frenetic pace. He smashed his first ball in county cricket onto the pavilion roof.

After the Second World War, Pritchard was the most prominent New Zealander in county cricket. He represented Warwickshire from 1946 to 1955, had a dozen games for Kent and then played in the leagues.

Strangely, no more New Zealanders played county cricket until Glenn Turner arrived at Worcestershire in 1967. He was followed to England by the likes of Geoff Howarth, David O'Sullivan, John Parker, John Wright, Richard Hadlee, Martin Crowe, Chris Cairns, Dion Nash and Danny Morrison.

"The players of the modern era were able to combine county and test careers, but that wasn't an option for those in my generation," says Reid. "Therefore a few really good players, such as Australians George Tribe and Jack Walsh, and West Indian Roy Marshall, virtually ruled themselves out of international cricket by becoming county players. Most, though, opted to play league cricket. The Lancashire and Yorkshire leagues were the strongest and drew the best overseas players. In Lancashire, you could see stars like Ray Lindwall, Frank Worrell, Charles Barnett, Vijay Hazare, Everton Weekes, Ces Pepper, Bruce Dooland, Polly Umrigar, Alf Valentine, Clyde Walcott, Vinoo Mankad and Colin McCool. They were able to earn some money playing cricket in their off-season and, for those still with test ambitions, gained useful experience playing in English conditions."

Reid joined the Heywood Cricket Club, 25km north of Manchester, and very much enjoyed the warm-hearted people of the cotton mill towns in Lancashire. "Initially it was quite eye-opening for me. I stayed with some of the locals, who lived in Coronation Street-type houses. The people I stayed with were very proud of having a bathroom and they might well have owned the only house on the street with its own bathroom. Most of the people in the area used a bath-house at the end of the road and paid a shilling for a bath.

"The status of the club pro astonished me. Opening the vegetable show, presenting prizes at the local soccer club, at schools, for a band competition, speech-making (which horrified me)... I was always in demand. Perhaps my greatest coup was to kick off at a women's soccer match!"

Not surprisingly, Reid proved a huge success on the cricket field. The standard of play was not high, probably only the equivalent of a second grade New Zealand club side, with generally sub-standard fielding. A league season comprised 20 Saturday matches and another six midweek fixtures. "Games often boiled down to a duel between the two test-class pros opposing each other. Games were one-dayers, but not limited-overs. The team batting first declared at tea."

Reid discovered a whole new culture in league cricket, and he quickly came to appreciate the importance of collections. A hat would be taken around the ground for a five-wicket bag at six runs apiece (5-30 or better), and for every 50 runs scored. "The club took 10 per cent of the take for a team excursion to Blackpool at the end of the season. My largest 'take' was £23, which was a substantial sum in the 1950s. My smallest collection was sixpence. The circumstances surrounding that sixpence still make me smile. We were playing away at Oldham and I had just completed my best-ever bowling analysis of 10-17. A bowler can go through his whole career without taking all ten, so I was naturally very pleased, but there was a downside. As the Oldham wickets fell, the home crowd departed in droves. Traditionally the collection has to be made by the players, who managed to catch only one unlucky patron before he could get away: hence the sixpence."

During his three years at Heywood, Reid returned fabulous figures:

1952: 982 runs at 44.6 and 114 wickets at 10.2
1953: 868 runs at 58.2 and 85 wickets at 13.9
1954: 1373 runs at 76.27 and 100 wickets at 18.5

He was only the fifth cricketer in the history of the Central Lancashire league to do the double, the previous four being Leslie Warburton, Ces Pepper, Vinoo Mankad and Charles Barnett. By reaching his 1000 runs in his 16th innings, he equalled Frank Worrell's league batting record.

Some of his individual performances were incredible. Because there was little time to build an innings with the bat, Reid often shone even more with the ball. Besides his 10-17 against Oldham (off 16 overs), he had 9-27 against Stockport. This feat included a hat-trick and a spell of 6-0.

He was compared with the best cricketers playing league cricket at the time, the West Indians Walcott and Worrell, and was just as popular. Cricket writers were glowing in their praise of the man who, for some obscure reason, was often called "Jack Reid" in the local press. Besides his league commitments, Reid took part in a good number of other fixtures, for the London New Zealand club, for Commonwealth selections, and in charity and benefit matches.

One he especially remembers was a two-day match at Colwyn Bay, north Wales, in 1952, when he played for Charles Barnett's XI against a West Indian XI. "The West Indian team included the legendary George Headley and it was a thrill to play against him. But the best batting in their team came from Clyde Walcott who hit with astonishing power." Barnett's team included a famous Indian batsman, B. B. Nimbalkar, who once went within a whisker of breaking Don Bradman's then world record of 452 not out. Playing for Maharashtra at Poona in 1948-49, Nimbalkar was 443 not out at lunch and a world record seemed certain. But the fielding side, Kathiawar, had had enough and refused to come out after the break, conceding the match. Reid recalls Nimbalkar as a delightful batsman, but has equally strong memories of another Indian test player, Cottari (C.S.) Nayudu. Reid opened the second innings with Nayudu, and it must have been a batting feast. They raised the century in 40 minutes and put on 190 in 75 minutes. For once in his career, Reid was outscored. He made 68 at nearly a run-a-minute while Nayudu scored a blistering century.

Reid drew renewed interest from county cricket officials and in 1954 he turned down approaches from Northants, Warwickshire, Leicestershire, Gloucestershire and Worcestershire. In addition, former England wicketkeeper George Duckworth, representing Enfield, led the approaches from various league clubs seeking his services. Though Reid and his wife, Norli, had enjoyed their time in England, he decided enough was enough and it was time to return to New Zealand permanently.

During the course of a long article on Reid, the *Manchester Guardian* described him as "the cheerful buccaneer of cricket", a phrase which, happily, was to remain applicable throughout his career.

Reid says his spell at Heywood' did teach him at least four valuable cricket lessons:

"1. Don't throw away your wicket with a rash stroke as that ensured there would be no collection.

"2. I quickly came to realise there would be no test class slip catching, or even good fielding, so instead of persevering with my normal fast-medium outswingers, I learned to bowl medium-paced off-cutters, my logic being that if the batsman missed, I'd knock down his castle.

"3. I overcame my problems of playing Sonny Ramadhin during my time with Heywood. He played very successfully for the Werneth side and one day we played him on a very slow, damp pitch. If I made a mistake in picking the turn, I had time to change my stroke, which was a great help.

I broke the pavilion window in the process of making a reasonable score, and found he never troubled me again. I generally played him as an off-spinner and worked out that if he beat me with a really good leg-spinner, the ball would probably miss the bat and the stumps.

"4. The importance of entertainment was brought home to me. I'd always played my cricket positively and aggressively, and I could see how popular that attitude was in league cricket. On a nice day a reasonably big crowd turns up and they expect to enjoy their day in the sun. Too often we see this aspect of cricket ignored by selfish cricket. For instance, declarations are always loaded on the defensive side, overlooking the fact that to win, the risk of losing should be present because the carrot must be offered to the team chasing runs."

4 | PLAYING TO THE AFRICAN BEAT

Veteran Australian sports writer Dick Whitington saw a lot of big cricket. He played Sheffield Shield for South Australia before the Second World War, playing under Vic Richardson and Don Bradman, and immediately after it toured with the brilliant Australian Services team led by Lindsay Hassett, and including players like Keith Miller and Cecil Pepper.

Whitington, a particularly close friend of Miller, saw all the great batsmen in those post-war years – Bradman, Morris, Barnes, Hammond, Compton, Hutton, Weekes, Worrell, Walcott, May, Harvey and so on. By the time he was assigned to cover the New Zealand team's tour of South Africa in 1961-62, he was as astute a judge of a cricketer as one would find anywhere. Yet Whitington, hard-bitten and healthily cynical, was amazed by the cricket John Reid played in South Africa.

"The greatest batsman in cricket today," was how he described Reid in *John Reid's Kiwis*. "I suggest you visualise the 1961-62 tour without Reid and reflect that he, batting at a considerably faster and more brilliant rate than any others, scored 1981 runs, compared to 1781 by Compton, 1526 by Harvey, 1489 by Hobbs, 1477 by Hutton and 1411 by Morris on their best tours of South Africa. I suggest also to you that you compare the calibre of batting support enjoyed by Compton, Harvey, Hobbs, Hutton and Morris to that accorded Reid. Then consider that Reid alone of the six had, in addition to scoring runs galore, to lead the team."

The greatest batsman in the world? That's a generous assessment, especially coming from a non-New Zealander. But Artie Dick, one of the more analytical members of the New Zealand team that season, says he can understand what Whitington meant. "I would think some of the innings John played over there would be up there with the best any player in the world could produce. The South Africans had a number of lethal fast bowlers – Adcock, Pollock, Heine, Lawrence. It would be a very good attack today. But John tore them apart. Even at Johannesburg, where we were well beaten, he played a lone hand. It wasn't grim defence, either. It was spectacular, powerful attack."

Reid made two tours of South Africa, in 1953-54 and in 1961-62. On the first he was outstanding, on the second sublime. It is small wonder that so many of his happiest cricket memories involve playing in South Africa. "There was something about the country which helped me produce my best," he says. "The light was really clear, the pitches true. I was able to concentrate on my cricket and play up to my best form."

The first tour of South Africa was disappointing for New Zealand. Geoff Rabone led a poorly selected team that was hammered 4-0 by a much superior South African combination. But the second tour was a triumph for Reid's New Zealanders, who won two tests and drew the five-match series 2-2. These were only New Zealand's second and third test wins and the first away from home.

~

1953-54

Geoff Rabone was given a difficult assignment, for the team he took away was sadly lacking in experience. There were just four survivors from the famous 1949 team to England – Rabone himself, Reid, Bert Sutcliffe and wicketkeeper Frank Mooney. Experienced campaigners like Tom Burtt and Gordon Leggat were overlooked. Instead international novices John Beck, Bill Bell, Ian Leggat and Guy Overton were chosen. Others, such as Murray Chapple, Bob Blair, Eric Dempster, Lawrie Miller and Matt Poore had just one or two tests behind them. There was a suggestion that Merv Wallace (one of the national selectors that season) or Walter Hadlee might be named to lead the side, but nothing came of the idea and in the end the chosen 15 looked rather ill-equipped to take on a South African side that not long before had split a five-test series in Australia.

Rabone didn't have an easy time of it. Normally manager Jack Kerr's genial methods would have been fine. But this was a team in which some players lacked self-discipline. "It was a hard team to captain," says Rabone. "Eleven of the players had never been away before. That meant we'd had a very big turnover in four years."

One of the problems for Rabone was that several of the players did not know what was meant by reasonable bedtime. "Yes, that made it hard, and I don't think I was the most popular bloke when I tried to deal with it," says Rabone. "Our fielding was deteriorating badly, so I called a fielding practice at 6.30 in the morning. The taxis arrived at 6.15. That didn't go down too well. I figured if they couldn't get themselves off to bed at a decent hour, they could get up early in the morning. They all turned up, of course, but two or three of them wore their pyjama tops – a form of protest.

"It was so different to the 1949 tour. Back then, we were a close-knit group. We'd converge in somebody's room each evening and discuss cricket. At about 9.30 someone would call up for a dozen cups of tea. We enjoyed each other's company. All had lived through a war. We were all self-disciplined and several had been overseas before. In South Africa, when the day's play was over, you didn't see some of the players for dust. Cliques developed. It was apparently the same problem Curly Page had had in England in 1937."

Despite the difficulties, Rabone and Reid emerged with respect for each other enhanced. Reid says, "Geoff did not have an easy job, but he never stopped trying. He knew the team needed discipline and he tried his best to instil it. Sometimes I agreed with his methods, sometimes I didn't. But I appreciated how much effort he put in and know how frustrating it must have been for him when not everyone's attitude measured up."

Rabone says he wishes everyone had applied himself as did Reid. "John was very, very well-performed throughout the tour. He couldn't have been more strongly behind the team management and was a great team bloke... great. I never got anything but strong support from him and I relied on that. John had his own ideas and as always he was not slow to come out with his opinions, but I had no problems with that at all. I wish they'd all given me as much support."

Reid did not sail to South Africa with the New Zealanders, instead travelling from England, where he had been playing league cricket. He showed immediately he was in fine form, smashing a match-saving century in just over two hours against West Province. Thereafter he did not produce runs consistently, but between his low scores was dotted the odd magnificent innings. Hugh Tayfield took eight wickets in an innings for Natal, but Reid thrashed him during a masterful four-hour effort that produced 175, including 22 4s and three 6s. Tayfield's 48 overs cost him 170 and while he could claim a moral ascendancy over most of the New Zealand team, Reid had treated his bowling with disdain.

The most famous match of the tour – and perhaps in the history of New Zealand cricket – was the second test at Johannesburg. It is a match which even now stirs much emotion in those who played. There were two factors. Before the second day's play, Boxing Day, news reached the team of the Tangiwai rail disaster, in which 151 people were killed. Among the dead was 19-year-old Nerissa Love, the fiancée of Bob Blair. The young Wellingtonian withdrew from the match while his grieving team-mates returned to the battle.

And a battle it was, for the Ellis Park pitch on that second day was one of the most spiteful imaginable. After South Africa had been dismissed for 271, New Zealand faced a nightmarish time as they bore the brunt of a hostile attack from fast bowler Neil Adcock. With the ball kicking and rearing, the New Zealanders took a pounding. Rabone was caught at slip. Then a bouncer from Adcock deflected off Chapple's gloves into his chest and onto his wickets. Three balls later, Sutcliffe was struck on the ear by an Adcock delivery. The lobe was split and he was taken to hospital. In 25 minutes Reid was hit five times before he was caught for three. Miller received a fierce blow on the chest and staggered from the field coughing blood. He, too, was taken to hospital. Another Adcock bouncer hit Poore and broke the wicket. It was in these calamitous circumstances that Beck made his test debut. New Zealand was 35-4 and had two batsmen in hospital, with another back at the hotel mourning the death of his fiancée.

In the afternoon New Zealand fought back gallantly. Miller was cheered when he returned to the wicket and helped add another 24. Beck and Mooney batted bravely. And then Sutcliffe emerged, head swathed in a turban of bandages.

"I'd had several stiff whiskys in the dressing room, then I went back out there to see if I could help," says Sutcliffe. "I decided not to muck around." So Sutcliffe launched a glorious onslaught, hitting the third ball he received for a 6 over square leg. He took to Tayfield and hit him for two 6s in one over and, with Mooney, added 50 in 39 madcap minutes.

While Sutcliffe continued to blaze away, Mooney, MacGibbon and Overton came and went. When New Zealand's ninth wicket fell, the players turned to leave the field, but stopped when the stricken figure of Blair emerged from the tunnel. The huge crowd rose in overwhelming silence as Sutcliffe, blood seeping through his bandage, went to meet his team-mate, placed his arm around Blair's shoulders and accompanied him to the wicket.

Sutcliffe smashed three 6s from Tayfield's next over and then Blair swung mightily at the last ball of the over and lifted another 6, over mid-wicket. In the next over there were two more 6s before Blair was stumped. The last pair had added 33 in 10 minutes and left the field with their arms around each other's shoulders.

There was such drama and emotion that the statistics seem irrelevant. But Sutcliffe had played one of the great test innings, his 80 not out in 112 minutes containing only 28 scoring shots. His seven 6s had been bettered in test cricket only by Walter Hammond, who hit 10 against New Zealand in 1933.

New Zealand went on to lose the match by 132 runs, but this was one occasion when the result paled into insignificance. I have spoken to Sutcliffe several times about that Boxing Day, and he is unable to describe the events without being choked by emotion. And it's not just Sutcliffe. I recall doing a video interview with Reid for the New Zealand Sports Hall of Fame. Tears filled his eyes as he recalled that dramatic Boxing Day and we had to stop the camera while he composed himself. When I asked Blair about it in 1999, he said, "I can't talk about it. It's still too raw."

Rabone says: "There was no more emotional day in cricket history. Blair was a character who took a bit of getting through to and the girl he had met was one who had a big influence on him. He was deeply in love with her and was totally knocked over when news of her death came through. He was back at the hotel in a bad way. We all got hit. Adcock was 6ft 6in and had long arms and the pitch suited him perfectly. It was green and fiery. Adcock was bowling very quick in-duckers to the right-hander. Bert was hit badly. Miller was bringing up blood. It was mayhem."

It's not just the New Zealanders who have strong memories of the Ellis Park test. Roy McLean, one of South Africa's leading batsmen, recalls being told early in the morning of the Tangiwai train disaster. "I was rooming with Ken Funston," says McLean, "and Dick Brittenden, who was along the corridor of the hotel, knocked on our door and told us of the tragedy. It made the occasion very sombre.

"Then when play started, New Zealand had to bat on a really vicious wicket. The Kiwis took a real battering. But the moment I most recall is of Bob Blair walking out to bat. I was fielding at square leg and when he passed me on his way to the wicket, he had tears running down his cheeks. We all felt the same."

The match was important to Reid in another way, too. He watched the South Africans play the New Zealand pacemen with relative ease while his own team was constantly worried by Adcock. Former South African test player Eric Rowan, speaking to Reid, suggested the difference was that the New Zealanders tended to look to get forward, while the South Africans were back foot players. "That advice led to me altering my technique. I became a back foot player, and over the years I refined the technique until I felt I could take on any bowler in the world with confidence. I might still get myself out, but I would at least know I was equipped with the proper technique."

Reid got an early opportunity to try out his revised technique, for the third test began at Newlands just two days after the Ellis Park massacre. It was at Newlands that Reid played one of his great innings. Entering the match, his test scores since 1951, when he made a 50 against England, had been 11, 11, 0, 3, 6, 1, 9, 7, 6, 0, 3, 1. He had sometimes batted as low as No 8 in the order. There was no suggestion he be dropped. He was still scoring runs aplenty in other first class matches and his class was evident. Besides, he often opened the test bowling attack.

In cricket parlance, by the time he got to Newlands, he was overdue for "a big one". He went to the wicket with New Zealand, having batted slowly on the first day, 239-3. "It was a nice batting track," says Rabone. "Chapple, Sutcliffe and I got fifties, so the platform was set. John cashed in with a magnificent innings. That was his value. He smashed Tayfield out of the park a few times and really dominated." Beck made 99 and with Reid put on 176 in 147 minutes. Reid took more than an hour to hit his first boundary, but his fifty came up in 102 minutes and his maiden test century just 57 minutes later. He scored a century between lunch and tea and in all hit 18 4s and two 6s. "Very few of John's innings weren't good, but this one was especially explosive," says Rabone. "He wasn't interested in pushing for ones and twos. In those days he tended to block or hit boundaries. Later on he developed the ability more to build an innings, the taking of ones and twos playing a greater part in his play."

New Zealand eventually reached 505, their highest test score, then bowled out South Africa for 326. In the second innings South Africa, following on, had lost five wickets and had still not reached New Zealand's total when stumps were drawn. That was really the end of the glory for New Zealand, who lost the last two tests rather comfortably. In the end, South Africa simply had more weapons. Players such as McGlew, McLean, Cheetham, Waite, Endean, Ironside, Adcock, Murray, Tayfield and van Ryneveld were a class above most of the New Zealand team.

Reid accompanied the New Zealand side as far as Australia on the return journey. He batted well in all three matches against the state sides, his 160 against a Victorian attack that contained Australian test off-spinner Ian Johnson being scored at nearly a run a minute and enthralling the locals.

The South African tour averages made sobering reading. Only three of the team, Sutcliffe, Reid and Rabone, managed to average more than 30 with the bat. Reid's 1347 runs were scored at 42.09 an innings, a good return, considering he was also a leading bowler. Reid took 56 wickets at 21.33, only MacGibbon, 57 at 21.17, shading him. Reid thus became the only overseas player to have performed the double of 1000 runs and 50 wickets on a tour of South Africa. It was a feat which defied great all-rounders like Wilfred Rhodes, Frank Woolley, Walter Hammond, Richie Benaud, Charles Macartney, Keith Miller and Alan Davidson on their tours of South Africa.

~

1961-62

Martin Donnelly would say simply: "I think John Reid's performance on his second tour of South Africa was the equal of any New Zealander at home or abroad." On the face of it, it's a fairly bold statement. Was he better than Stewie Dempster, Jack Cowie, Bert Sutcliffe and Donnelly himself on their best tours of England, better than Glenn Turner in the West Indies, better than Martin Crowe at home against the West Indies in 1987? Donnelly, in that gentlemanly manner of his, was emphatic. "From talking to Dick Whitington, who reported the tour, and to some of John's team-mates, it is obvious he reached heights seldom if ever matched."

The figures certainly support such a generous assessment. In the five-match test series, Reid topped the batting averages and aggregates, scoring 546 runs at 60.64. The next best was Zin Harris' 284 runs at 31.55. He also led the test bowling averages, taking his 11 wickets at 19.72. For the full tour of South Africa, he scored 1915 runs at 68.39. The next highest average was Murray Chapple's 31.94. The next highest aggregate was Graham Dowling's 714. He scored seven centuries; no one else scored more than two. As a bowler, Reid finished fourth on the averages and aggregates, with 27 wickets at 25.80. In 1986 Mike Gatting made the statement that playing a New Zealand team including Richard Hadlee was like playing the World XI at one end and the Ilford Second XI at the other. The South Africans must have felt a little like that when confronted with Reid's brilliant play that season.

"It was the highest point of my career," says Reid. "The aim of every cricketer is to reach the top of his form when playing for his country, and that's what I did that year." The strange thing about it was that Reid badly hurt his knee on the journey to South Africa. "We played a match against Western Australia at Perth on the way over. I was fielding on the boundary and dived for a ball and did a cartilage. I didn't miss any games, and it was not diagnosed as a cartilage complaint at the time. The attitude back then was that you battled through as best you could. It was never right on the tour. I was given cortisone injections with a huge needle, a case of the remedy being worse than the complaint. Throughout the tour, I bowled only when I had to."

One of the differences between this team and the side Reid took to England in 1958 was the selection process. "I ended up with the team I wanted. I had players like Murray Chapple, Noel McGregor, Jack Alabaster, Zin Harris, John Sparling, John Guy and John Ward, who had toured with New Zealand teams before. There was a solid nucleus of experience. I'd love to have had Barry Sinclair in the team, but he had a horror run the previous season. He just couldn't get going and in the end he had to passed over in favour of players who had scored heavily.

"I pushed for Murray Chapple as my vice-captain. There had been some talk about a strong rivalry between Murray and me, and there was, when he was leading Canterbury and I was captaining Wellington. But I felt Murray would make a good vice-captain. He might not always be in the test team, but he was a useful player. Besides that, he had a good cricket brain and had the respect of the players. So I rang him late one night and asked if he'd like to do the job. He accepted immediately, and proved a big success. One area he handled well was organising net practices. This took a load off me, and enabled me to spend more time on my own batting."

Reid was also well-served by having Gordon Leggat as the team manager. "Gordon was superb. In fact, he emerged as one of the stars of our team. He was a brilliant speaker, was well-organised and offered me tremendous support. He had been a test player himself not long before, so brought a good insight into top cricket into his decision-making."

The African segment of the tour began with a match against Rhodesia at Bulawayo. These days the game would be allocated an extra couple of days and be labelled a test match against Zimbabwe. "My chief memory of that game," says Reid, "is that we ran into Geoff Griffin for the first time. I was batting with John Guy when he came on. Immediately I got hit on the shoulder. I went down to Guy and said, 'He pinged that one.' A batsman can tell if a bowler has thrown a delivery. It slips through lower. I just didn't get hit by short balls. I was a hooker and either I got out, or the ball ended up on the road. But Griffin hit me. Of course, he'd toured England in 1960 and run into trouble with their umpires. In this case, I think the umpires were correct." Despite Griffin's attention, Reid turned on a memorable display of fireworks, smashing 97 in even time, including 18 4s and a 6.

The next big match was against Transvaal at Johannesburg. "This was where we struck Hugh Tayfield, who, with Jim Laker's retirement, was regarded as the best off-spinner in the world. He had troubled Peter May's England touring team and obviously would be featuring in the South African test plans. But Hugh had not had a great tour of England in 1960, so we felt if we showed we could handle him easily, the South African selectors might lose faith in him. At a pre-tour meeting, Gordon Leggat and I had discussed Tayfield and decided I would get stuck into him. On top of that, it was decided that come what may, no one would get out to him. As it turned out, I made 49 and 56. But Paul Barton and Noel McGregor made centuries and Zin Harris got a fifty. Tayfield finished the match having bowled 53 overs and took 2-141. We were on top of him the whole time. He was not selected for any of the tests, so it was a good team effort of ours."

Reid remained in solid form, but really struck it rich against Western Province at Cape Town, when he scored a devastating double-century. "Newlands was a favourite ground for me. On the previous tour, I'd made two centuries there. This time I saw the ball right from the start and really got on top of the attack." Reid and Chapple, who made 96, put on 244 runs in just 152 minutes. Reid was eventually stumped for 203, scored in just 224 minutes. He hit 25 4s and four 6s and drew effusive praise from Herb Taylor in the *Cape Times*. Taylor, the greatest batsman in South African history until then, wrote: "In John Reid, the New Zealanders have a player in the Wally Hammond and Dudley Nourse class... The most important feature from the tourists' point of view is that Reid's shining example is bringing out the best in the other Kiwi players. They are trying not only to emulate his success, but also his aggression. Reid's presence in the side seems certain to make a difference to the tour, and draw crowds in the same way as Wally Hammond, Denis Compton and other world class batsmen have done on similar tours of South Africa."

Reid's double-century must have been truly spectacular. Tom Reddick wrote in the *Cape Times*, "John Reid is a batsman of world class. I have seen Macartney, Bradman and McCabe and not one of them ever showed greater mastery over an attack than Reid did over the Western Province bowlers. This power box on legs played every stroke in the book with incredible violence. One shot I have never seen bettered – the drive through the covers off the back foot. Until this match, I thought Peter May's innings of 170 runs was the best I had seen at Newlands, but this 200 mph holocaust that hit us on Saturday was even more exciting."

Reid (in white) chases hard during a college rugby match in 1946.

Lifelong friends Bill Fraser (left) and John Reid, on bikes carrying cricket gear – a common sight around Hutt Valley in the 1940s.

The Famous Forty-Niners about to depart for England.

Stewie Dempster leads out the Wellington team at Eden Park in 1948. This was Reid's first season in first class cricket. From left: Reid, Ron Murray, Jim Kemp, Peggy O'Neill, Dempster, Rex Challies, Eric Dempster, Eric Tindill, Doug Dumbleton.

Happy travellers. Geoff Rabone (left), John Reid and Brun Smith bid bon voyage in 1949.

Left-hander John Dewes is caught at first slip by Reid off Jack Cowie in the match against the M.C.C. at Lord's in 1949.

A powerful Reid cover drive during his brilliant 135 against South Africa at Newlands in 1954.

New Zealand Prime Minister Sid Holland hosts a Parliamentary function for Wellington captain John Reid (centre) and M.C.C. captain Len Hutton in 1955.

Bert Sutcliffe (left), John Reid, Morrie Mackenzie and Ron Jarden examine the New Zealand Sportsman of the Year Trophy in 1955. Mackenzie edited the *New Zealand Sportsman*, which co-ordinated the voting process in those days. Sutcliffe won the trophy in 1949, Jarden in 1951 and Reid in 1955.

Nevile Lodge of the *Sports Post* captured the euphoria of cricket followers after the historic win over the West Indies in 1956.

It rained so much during New Zealand's tour of England in 1958 that at times the cricketers seemed more at home turning out in these rugby league outfits they borrowed from the Leeds club. Back row, from left: Alan Mitchell (N.Z.P.A. correspondent), Bert Sutcliffe, Harry Cave, John Ward, Bill Playle, Trevor Meale, Alex Moir, John Sparling, Jack Alabaster, Lawrie Miller, George Duckworth (baggage man). Front row: Jack Darcy, Bob Blair, Tony MacGibbon, John Reid, Johnny Hayes, Noel Harford, Eric Petrie.

The Reid family. John holds Richard, Norli holds Ann and Alison stands to the right.

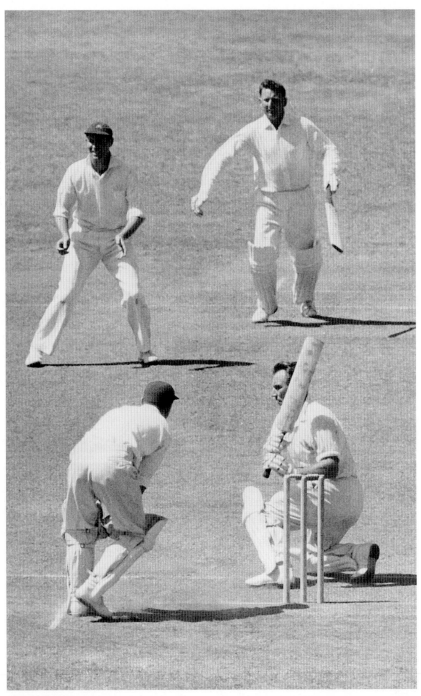

Reid sweeps against Western Province at Newlands in 1961. Murray Chapple is the other batsman.

By the time the New Zealanders got to Durban for the first test, they had reason to be confident. The batsmen were in good form, Bartlett, Motz and Cameron were a decidedly useful pace trio and Alabaster was proving an unusually accurate leg-spinner. Sparling and Reid were batsmen who provided an off-spinning option.

"It was a match we should have won. In the end we lost by 30 runs, after needing 197 to win. I had a very bad bout of flu and was never with it. I shouldn't have played, and batted below my best, scoring 13 and 16. Peter Pollock opened their bowling and took nine wickets in the match, and that's what won it for them, along with a century by Jackie McGlew. But even so, Paul Barton, Zin Harris and Noel McGregor got fifties for us. The game was there to win."

The second test was drawn, after McGlew set New Zealand 278 to make on the final afternoon. Reid was unbeaten on 75, but the target was too severe. However, again the New Zealanders had shown they could compete on level terms.

This was illustrated by the third test which began a few days later. Harris scored 101, Reid 92, Chapple 69 and McGregor 68 as New Zealand reached 385, a winning score. Cameron and Alabaster ran through the South Africans in the first innings and then Reid declared the New Zealand second innings. A fighting unbeaten half-century by Artie Dick enabled Reid to make what now seems a generous declaration – 408 runs required in a day plus a session. In today's terms that would have left South Africa with 118 overs to bat, or needing 3.45 an over. But back in 1962, when bowlers were less tardy about their over-rates, and especially with a New Zealand attack boasting spinners Alabaster, Reid and Sparling, South Africa received more than 142 overs.

The New Zealanders found it tough going, as McLean scored a century and McGlew reached 63. "Jack Alabaster did a marvellous job, bowling 50 overs and taking 4-119, but it was Gary Bartlett who really rocked South Africa," says Reid. "His 2-40 doesn't look marvellous on paper, but he dismissed both McGlew and McLean and did them both for pace. McGlew was caught behind and McLean was caught hooking when the ball came onto him much faster than he'd expected and he was caught at mid-off. That was what Bartlett offered. At any stage he could be brought into the attack and could beat even a well-set batsman through sheer pace."

After a week off, Reid rejoined the team at Bloemfontein for the game against Orange Free State. "I flew up to Bloemfontein in a thunderstorm. We were flying under a ceiling of black cloud with lightning jagging across the sky. I thought I'd never make it. It was the worst flight I'd ever had.

"I was really mad when I went into bat. We were 23-4 and I thought the guys just weren't taking on enough responsibility themselves. I was batting a little lower in the order because I hadn't had any recent practice, and I got stuck in and hit 101 in 112 minutes. Murray Chapple made 150 and we put on 131 runs in not much more than an hour." This spectacular innings induced Whitington to write: "Reid's century included just about every kind of stroke I have seen Bradman play. His late cuts, square cuts, cover and off drives, on drives, hooks and sweeps, all struck with tremendous power and graphic crispness, ringed the green ground and transformed the match."

Artie Dick remembers that match fondly. "I wasn't playing in that game, and I was happy about that once we started to collapse. I was sitting with John and he was getting wilder and wilder. He had an expression on tour that he wanted to deliver 'a thousand words', which meant he wanted to put the heat on someone who wasn't performing. I sensed there might be a few thousand words delivered at the end of the New Zealand innings and was very pleased his anger was directed at other players! Then he went out to bat and he smashed the first five balls for boundaries. The sixth one would have gone for four as well, but instead it nearly broke mid-off's leg."

Amazingly, Reid scored another century in the second innings with an exhibition that was even more devastating than the first. He passed 50 in 25 minutes and 100 in 68 minutes. In all he made 118 in 81 minutes of frenetic activity, smashing five boundaries in one over and four in another.

Next up was a match against a South African Colts XI that included such future stars as Ali Bacher, Denis Lindsay, Tiger Lance and Graeme Pollock. The Colts team thrashed the New Zealand bowlers, making 318-4, then New Zealand dipped to 46-3. Enter Reid, who unleashed a furious, sustained assault on a fairly useful attack. He scored at a run-a-minute and finished with 165, including 26 4s and four 6s. At this point, Reid was in the best form of his career. His last three innings, all centuries, had aggregated 384 runs in 383 minutes with 290 coming in boundaries.

"The Colts team included Jackie Botten, who bowled big in-swingers. He bowled me when I'd made 165, and the story went round that I might be weak against in-swing. My next four innings were 112, 60, 142, 107, so I think I well and truly put that story to rest. I made the 112 against Natal, whose attack included Neil Adcock. At the close of the first day I was 96 not out. The next morning Adcock bowled me a half-volley first ball and I hit it for 6 over mid-wicket. It was the best shot I remember playing, but that was the sort of form I was in by then."

New Zealand was disappointed to lose the fourth test by an innings and 51 runs. South Africa selected Adcock and Peter Heine as their quick bowlers and with Godfrey Lawrence taking nine wickets in the match, they were just too good. Reid, though, continued his cracking form. "I'd reached 60 in the first innings and was then out to the best catch I've ever seen. Colin Bland was in the covers and like all good cover fieldsmen, he edged to his left, because generally that's where the ball is sliced. I really got onto a drive and hit it between mid-off and cover. Bland, who was going left, stopped, and dived to his right and took it with two hands about six inches off the ground. Even I applauded that one. I knew how hard I'd hit it."

In the second innings, Reid reached his highest test score, 142, but only two of his team-mates got to double figures. "This was the match in which I had a bit of a verbal sparring session with Heine. He took the second new ball after I'd passed my century. I must have missed one because he said with some feeling, 'You aren't good enough to get a touch.' I pointed across the ground and said, 'Have a look at the scoreboard.' Heine then made a derogatory comment after each ball he delivered for about three overs. At that stage I complained to Jackie McGlew and Heine was briefly withdrawn from the attack. That was as close as players back then ever got to what is now called sledging."

Reid warmed up for the crucial fifth test with a century against Border, his sixth in eight innings.

"We were down 2-1 going into the fifth test, but felt like we had a real show of winning. We took a gamble playing Paul Barton, who had dislocated his shoulder during the fourth test. It was one of those punts which really paid off. Paul, with his shoulder strapped, made a magnificent century in our first innings and saw us through to a total of 275. We bowled them out for 190 and knew we were in with a chance."

The New Zealand second innings began an hour before stumps and the batsmen were subjected to a brutal barrage of short-pitched bowling by Adcock and Pollock. Sparling had two ribs broken before being given out caught in the gully when the New Zealanders thought it had been a bump ball. Reid then promoted Harris to first drop. Harris and Graham Dowling stuck it out until stumps. "I really admired Harris and Dowling that evening. Dowling had a more complete technique, but Zin really didn't have the equipment to face that sort of barrage. He got by on guts and nothing else. I'd seen Bob Blair break his cheekbone back in New Zealand, and that memory must have been with him. But he never flinched. Adcock and Pollock gave it everything they had. Today they would be called for intimidatory bowling. It mightn't look much in the scorebook, but Dowling and Harris seeing us through to stumps only one down set us up for the chance of victory."

The next day only Reid, with 69, got going and New Zealand struggled through to 228, giving South Africa an hour plus the whole final day to score 314.

The New Zealand players, riled at the intimidatory tactics of the South African speedsters, wanted to reply in kind. "I had fought against getting into that sort of a battle the whole series," says Reid. "For a start they had three quicks and we had two. And Bartlett, while he was blisteringly quick, often didn't know where the ball was going. So I didn't let them bowl short, except in this match. I waited until the vital moment. The game was getting close. South Africa had gone from 199-8 to 259-8 and time was running out. So I called up Dick Motz to bowl at Adcock, making it loud and clear that it was 'catch-up time'. Then I put in a couple of short legs and a silly mid-off. The signal was clear. By the time Motz bowled the ball, Adcock was back on the square leg umpire's toes. Motz whipped down a half-volley and bowled him. That was the breakthrough we were after.

"Motz bowled very bravely in this game. He had strained ribs which had been bandaged. The plaster was initially strapped around his chest. By the time he finished, it was in a roll around his waist."

The final day was a gripping battle and it was the spin of Alabaster and Reid which really set up the New Zealand win. Alabaster bowled 52 overs and took 2-96 and Reid, sore knee and all, took 4-44 from 45 overs. "It was my best bowling ever, a very long spell. Alabaster bowled exceptionally well. We had the runs on the board to enable him to bowl for long spells and he had by then developed into a world class spinner. He could move the ball both ways just enough to get an edge."

Alabaster says he enjoyed bowling under Reid's captaincy in South Africa. "If I was being objective, I might say I was bowled too soon sometimes, and sometimes for too long. But I wasn't complaining. I loved getting the opportunity. Often I'd be bowling before lunch. It was encouraging to see the captain had so much faith in me. I was very proud of my bowling in that fifth test. It was my most important spell in test cricket."

Reid's attitude to bowling his spinners contrasted to that of South African captain McGlew, who often went entire days without giving the ball to his off-spinner Harry Bromfield. The suggestion was he was fearful of what Reid might do to Bromfield, but this was defeatist thinking: it wasn't as if the South African quicker bowlers were having much success against Reid anyway.

Reid's forceful captaincy was one of the features of the season. "John was demanding as a captain," says Dick. "He was aggressive and he expected a lot from his players, sometimes perhaps too much. By 1961 he had been the New Zealand captain for quite a few years and had mellowed somewhat, but it's a relative term. He still let people know if he felt they weren't performing. John was fortunate to have a manager like Gordon Leggat. Sometimes once John was finished with a player, Gordon would come in and pick up the pieces. John and Gordon gelled perfectly; they were an ideal partnership."

So the series ended in triumph for New Zealand, a win in the final test by 40 runs with 20 minutes to spare.

The teams were closely matched, with South Africa's top order of McGlew, Barlow, Waite, Bland and McLean looking a little more solid overall than Reid, McGregor, Barton, Dowling and Harris. Both teams had good pace attacks, with Bartlett, Motz and Cameron in their own diverse ways as effective, if not as hostile, as any three of Pollock, Adcock, Heine, Burke and Lawrence. Perhaps New Zealand's biggest advantages were in the aggressive captaincy of Reid and his use of spin bowlers. Alabaster's 22 wickets were 16 more than South Africa's main spinner, Bromfield. Even

Reid, with his gammy knee, took three more wickets than Bromfield.

It remains one of the most successful tours undertaken by a New Zealand team. It's interesting, looking through the scoreboards, to see how many of the players contributed at vital times. Reid dominated the show. But most of his team-mates, even those without big reputations, chipped in. Harris and Barton scored test centuries. Chapple scored 69 when selected for the third test. Dowling was a consistent scorer, McGregor reached 20 six times in his 10 innings, often giving the New Zealand effort impetus. Artie Dick, taken as reserve wicketkeeper, ended up playing all five tests after John Ward was injured, and excelled. Though the first test was only the seventh match in which he had ever kept, he finished the series with 23 wickets, 21 catches and two stumpings. His total would have equalled the world record, but for the fact that South African John Waite stretched the world mark to 26 during the series.

The pace bowlers, Motz, Bartlett and Cameron, all played their part. Bartlett remained a constant threat to the South Africans because of his extreme pace. Motz finished with 81 wickets on tour and was used as both shock and stock bowler. Cameron wasn't the luckiest of bowlers, but was always reliable, intelligent and brave. By the end of the tour, he was proving a constant threat as an opening bowler. Jack Alabaster had a magnificent tour. Not only was he one of the players Reid constantly turned to for a second opinion, but he got through a formidable amount of work. Including the matches in Australia on the way home, he bowled 787 overs, and claimed 88 wickets at 27.14. He not only gave Reid a potent wicket-taker because of his deceptive wrist-spin, but he was as accurate as any finger spinner.

Reid says two other reasons for the team's success were the fielding and the team spirit. "I'd been overseas with good fielding teams, as we had in 1949, and with teams where a lot of chances were missed. I knew how vital fielding would be and I constantly stressed it. By the end of the tour, we had taken more than 75 per cent of our catches, and that percentage rose to 93 per cent in the tests. Their batsmen weren't getting extra innings all the time, courtesy of our generosity.

"As a team, we got on very well. Gordon was truly a magnificent manager, and Murray Chapple was the ideal vice-captain. The feeling and camaraderie in the side was terrific. I'm always very pleased when I see the fellows from that tour. We have very enjoyable team reunions and it's as if we finished the tour only yesterday."

Artie Dick says it was his happiest time in cricket. "It was the best five and a half months a person could have. The guys got on well, we played well and we were successful. I have fabulous memories of that tour."

So ended Reid's best tour as a batsman. Dick Whitington, struggling to find words to express his admiration for Reid's batting, wrote that he was tempted to describe Reid as "another Stan McCabe" but felt that would not do the New Zealand captain justice and settled instead for "a Compton-McCabe combined". As well as Reid batted, this does seem rather effusive, but the intent behind the words is clear. Jack Cheetham, convener of the South African selectors, said: "My task and that of my selectors would have been very simple this summer but for the batting of John Reid."

John Waite, an outstanding wicketkeeper-batsman, played against New Zealand on both Reid's South African tours. He said in *John Reid's Kiwis* that by 1961, Reid had developed into a world class batsman. "He was one of the strongest, if not the strongest batsman I ever played against, and the finest hard-hitting batsman I kept to. He lofted the ball more frequently than any top class batsman I watched and at first we thought this might be a weakness. But later we realised his strength made it a good proposition for him and increased his calibre and stature. Even John's mis-hits carried the field, sometimes even the outfield. John backed his strength to beat the field and usually he won. He was unique among good batsmen because of his willingness to loft all brands of bowler in the interests of fast scoring.

"On defence he was not as impregnable as, for example, Len Hutton. You did occasionally see a bit of ball from behind the stumps when John was batting; you saw nothing of it when Len was in. But John was sound when he wanted to be sound."

Waite rated Reid the finest New Zealand batsman he played against, considerably better even that the Bert Sutcliffe, who toured South Africa in 1953-54.

Reid's team-mates knew they'd witnessed something special – a great player at his absolute peak. Graham Dowling says: "People who watched John bat only at home saw a very good player, but they can have no idea of what he did in South Africa that season. In all my years of playing and watching test cricket, I have never seen such magnificent batting."

Jack Alabaster says Reid's batting in South Africa was as good as anything he's seen from a New Zealander, except Bert Sutcliffe at his best. "The South Africans had good quick bowlers and seamed the ball around a bit. But they didn't have a lot of variety in their attack. Once a batsman like John Reid got into form and was then fed the same attack for match after match, he became consistently dynamic. He thrashed Adcock when we played Natal and against Orange Free State he arrived at the wicket when we had lost four wickets for almost nothing and two hours later had smashed a century. He never showed that form in New Zealand, except for the occasional innings. That's not to say he didn't bat well here. He made a wonderful hundred against England at Christchurch in 1963, a real fighting innings when the next highest score was 22. In its own way that century was as good even as his big scores in South Africa. It's just that in South Africa, he was consistently commanding and always dominating. I'd never really seen anything like it from him back home."

Artie Dick voices similar feelings. "There is no question about it. His batting over there was astonishing. He did it back home occasionally, but for aggression and dominance, it was just sensational. In John's batting, and in Gary Bartlett's bowling, we had two weapons we could fire back at South Africa. Gary didn't always bowl accurately, but his extreme pace unsettled even the best batsman. And John was a constant threat as a batsman. The opposition knew that he was quite capable of transforming the match in two hours of blazing attack, and he did it many times that season. Having John in our batting lineup was a huge source of confidence for the team."

The South Africans also acknowledge the impact of Reid's presence. "John, or Bogo as we called him, carried the whole New Zealand team," says Roy McLean. "He had some useful cricketers backing him up, but he was the real menace. We all knew that. Our problem was that we didn't know how to attack him. He got right into line and played pace bowling very well, and we did have Adcock, Heine and Pollock, after all. And he really punished spin bowling. He would use his feet and dictate to the bowlers. The trouble was we couldn't even keep him quiet; he was always looking to dominate.

"It was a very useful New Zealand team, and they drew the series against a strong South African side. But without Bogo, they'd never have stood a chance. He was so positive. When his team-mates were around him, you could see them start believing they could do it. He gave his entire team confidence because of his own magnificent play and his attitude."

⟿

JOHN REID'S VIEW
SOUTH AFRICA – THE PLAYERS

Jackie McGlew: A gutsy opening batsman who played some magnificent innings against us. He had to be rated one of the best openers of his time, but was inclined to be on the slow side. I enjoyed captaining New Zealand against South Africa under Jackie in 1961-62. He had a broken thumb going into the Cape Town test during that series – we found out when one of our team was receiving medical attention at the same time as him – and he wondered why our fast bowlers showed such interest in his condition during the game. But there was no way a minor detail like a broken finger was going to prevent Jackie from playing. Jackie was as good an opening batsman as South Africa have had in my time, perhaps on a par with recent Australian captain Mark Taylor, another tenacious player with excellent concentration. They came under the "not flashy but gritty" heading.

Roy McLean: My favourite South African batsman and one of the better cricketers I played against. He wasn't altogether correct, but he could turn a game. He had powerful attacking shots off the front and back feet and always scored quickly. He was a delightful person who was never treated kindly by the South African selectors, being dropped regularly, despite his match-winning ability. "Roysie" has remained a true friend for nearly 50 years. We correspond regularly about the state of international cricket, his new home in Durban, my fishing successes and which overseas visitors he is expecting. Roy and his wife, Barbara, are wonderfully hospitable hosts.

Hugh Tayfield: I rated him alongside Jim Laker, and you can't get higher praise for an off-spinner. He bowled very well against us in South Africa in 1953-54 and throughout the rest of the 1950s had tremendous success, even against England and Australia. Tayfield was the sort of bowler you never quite got to. He had deceptive flight and was a fantastic fieldsman off his own bowling.

Johnny Waite: The best wicketkeeper-batsman of my era. How he could keep for two days and then often open the batting was beyond me. He was a good, correct batsman who hit the ball hard, a genuine No 3. Johnny was on the tall side, but despite that was an excellent wicketkeeper. He really was the ideal player to have in any side. Johnny has also remained a good friend over the years, even though Johannesburg and Taupo are so far apart that regular contact is difficult.

Peter Heine: One of the most aggressive fast bowlers of his time. He was about on a par with Neil Adcock for pace, but didn't use it as well. Heine had a windmill action and wasn't adverse to giving the batsman a few bouncers and words, sometimes at the same time!

Neil Adcock: A consistently hostile and accurate fast bowler. When the pitch offered him assistance, he was lethal. He could move the ball, particularly off the seam. If I was to compare him, I'd say he was similar but slightly better than Brian Statham, though not as good as Fred Trueman. For today's cricket followers, he was about on a par with Glenn McGrath for pace, and every bit as intimidating.

Peter Pollock: Another of the intimidating South African pace bowlers of the early 1960s. He was a bit of a bully – he didn't do a lot with the ball, but rushed in and bowled fast. When we toured South Africa in 1961-62, he was their third-string pace bowler, but he improved considerably after that. He was a quicker bowler than his son Shaun, but not as good a batsman. He was the convener of the South African selection panel for some years.

Eddie Barlow: In the early days of Eddie's career, he was a very frustrating man to bowl to. We found during the 1961-62 series that he used to great effect the unintentional snick over the slips! Yet he ended up third in the South African test averages for the series with a figure of 36.6. As his top score was just 67, it is obvious he was consistently getting South Africa off to a good start. Like so many South African cricketers, Eddie made the most of his ability, his competitiveness and determination compensating for any technical shortcomings. Eddie went on to become a very good batsman and also turned himself into a handy medium-pace bowler until his career, like so many others of his era, was cut short by South Africa's exclusion from the world stage. Eddie also had a busy and varied domestic career in South Africa, being director of cricket in several provinces and coach of Transvaal (now called Gauteng).

Graeme Pollock: A most interesting player. He made 78 against us at Port Elizabeth when he was only 17 and we could see then that he was a player of unusual promise. Like all leading South Africans of his generation, his test career was decimated by his country's exclusion from international cricket, but he still averaged 61 in his 23 tests. I saw a lot of him at Northern Transvaal and even two decades after his test debut, he was still scoring very heavily in that unflustered manner of his. He was a tall left-hander who had a really good eye and a fascinating technique. He had a wide stance and would simply widen his feet further, and then play one of four shots, one to each corner of the ground. He really clubbed the ball, and relied on his eye. His feet were never too close to the ball, but with Pollock it didn't seem to matter.

Barry Richards: The thing that struck you about Richards was the time he had to play his shots. He was a complete batsman, a master, and is way up the top of any list of batsmen. He had so much class that sometimes it looked a bit easy for him, and he'd get bored.

Mike Procter: "Proccie" is one of the former greats I run into regularly on my trips around the cricket world on I.C.C. referee duty. We first met when he was director of cricket at Natal and was still playing occasionally in the early 1980s. Later he became a South African selector and team coach and now he is in demand as a television commentator.

From what I saw of Procter as a player and the brief snatches of footage that are sometimes shown, I regard Procter as one of the most special players of his era. He was a genuinely fast bowler and delivered the ball off the "wrong" foot with a chest-on action that produced big inswing. On his day he produced some unplayable deliveries. He was also a massive hitter who performed prodigious deeds for Gloucestershire in county cricket. And let's not forget, he did once score six successive first class centuries, so we are talking about a genuine batsman, not a tail-ender who swung lustily. The pity of it is that because of South Africa's ban from international cricket, he played just seven tests. Even in that brief period, he hinted at his class by taking 41 wickets at 15 runs each. Procter's first class cricket exploits suggest that given the opportunity, he might have gone on to build an all-round test record worthy of comparison with Keith Miller.

Clive Rice: A genuine all-rounder, but a much better bowler than a batsman. He could be a lethal bowler and, in partnership with Richard Hadlee at Notts, on wickets prepared for pace bowling, formed a deadly combination. I had a lot of time for Rice as a cricketer. He was a very good fast bowler, an effective batsman and fieldsman and a thinking captain.

Hanse Cronje: I coached him in South Africa back in 1988, when I would describe him as a useful player. He has an excellent temperament and has got the most out of his ability and become an effective test player who has worked hard on his batting. I'd rate him about the same standard as Colin Bland as a batsman. South Africa has been a hard-to-beat and generally well-disciplined team under Hanse's captaincy.

Allan Donald: The great white hope of the South African side. He is a very aggressive fast bowler who can move the ball and bowls with good accuracy. In terms of pace, I'd put him ahead of Ambrose and behind Waqar, probably on a par with Neil Adcock. With his height and hostility, he has been a handful for the best batsmen around, and has improved since he learned to keep better control of his emotions. Donald was the key figure in South Africa's success after their re-emergence in international cricket in the early 1990s because he was such a match-winner.

Lance Klusener: What an exciting contribution Klusener is making to cricket. He was a deserving winner of the Player of the Tournament award at the 1999 World Cup. Klusener is a genuine all-rounder. He bowls right-arm fast-medium (almost off the "wrong" foot, it seems) with plenty of energy, though not a great deal of movement of the ball. His powerful left-handed batting is guaranteed to cause a stir in any crowd, the more so as he is good enough technically to come off regularly. "Zulu", as his team-mates call him (I imagine because he was brought up in Kwazulu-Natal and speaks the native language), is also a delightful character, full of fun and with a ready smile which can turn quizzical if a batsman snicks him over slips or between his legs for four.

The South African team is a solid unit with skills in all departments. They have a no-nonsense attitude to winning, which is fine by me. But Klusener, Jonty Rhodes and Shaun Pollock are a talented trio who bring some lighter moments to their team's otherwise serious outlook.

Jacques Kallis: Another top-flight all-rounder who will be around the first class scene for many years. He bats at the top of the order and sometimes opens the bowling at a very slippery fast-medium, so he carries a burden of responsibility in the South African side. At No 3, Kallis is a very correct player who handles pace well and can give the slow bowlers a bit of stick when required. As a bowler, his tall, strong physique enables him to generate pace to accompany his deceptive outswing and change of pace. Like virtually all his team-mates, he is an outstanding fieldsman. To my mind, Kallis is on a par with Darryl Cullinan as the best batsman in the South African side and on occasions can also be the best strike bowler – a quality cricketer.

Shaun Pollock: Another of the outstanding South African all-rounders of recent years. Shaun has more than lived up to the fine traditions of this famous South African cricket family. He is a lively and at times hostile fast-medium bowler, a great fieldsman and a hard-hitting No 7 batsman who would be welcomed in any international side. Pollock is possibly the finest bowling all-rounder of his time, though still one notch below the likes of Kapil Dev, Imran Khan and Richard Hadlee.

5 | HOW LOW CAN YOU GO?

Twenty-six. It's a number that haunts New Zealand cricket, a figure that sits staring out of the pages of *Wisden*, an annual reminder of the grimmest day in our test history. On March 28, 1955, Geoff Rabone's New Zealanders were bowled out by England for 26, setting a world test record low that might well last forever.

The amazing thing was that New Zealand began their second innings of that Eden Park test in good spirits. They trailed on the first innings by just 46 and felt that if things went well, they might set England a tough fourth-innings target and perhaps grab an historic victory.

Such optimism was soon shattered.

"It was a good England side," says Reid. "They'd just come from Australia, where they'd overwhelmed the Aussies and comfortably held onto the Ashes. They had superb batsmen like Tom Graveney, Reg Simpson, Peter May, Colin Cowdrey and Len Hutton. Godfrey Evans, then at the peak of his powers, was their wicketkeeper. Trevor Bailey was their all-rounder. Their bowlers were Frank Tyson, Brian Statham, Bob Appleyard and Johnny Wardle. There wasn't a weak player in the whole eleven and Tyson, of course, was in his prime, having just blitzed the Aussies with his pace and ferocity.

"Against that, we went into the two-test series in late March not having had any first class cricket for several weeks. We had a trial match in February and for most of us, that was it. In the first test, at Dunedin, we were outgunned, and could score just 125 and 132. Tyson took seven wickets and was just too quick for us.

"But we looked better for most of the second test, in Auckland. We got to 200 in the first innings. I was pretty happy with my 73, Bert Sutcliffe reached 40 and Rabone chipped in with 29. Tyson and Statham were still a handful, and so was Bob Appleyard, who took three wickets with his very brisk off-cutters, but we definitely looked more solid. Then England batted and Alex Moir ran through them. Johnny Hayes did a good job by picking up Graveney and May and then Alex struck a good patch. In the end he took 5-62 off 25 overs. We'd have restricted them further if Tyson and Statham hadn't put on 28 for the last wicket, but even so, we felt we were in with a genuine chance."

The New Zealand second innings began at 3pm on the third afternoon, Sutcliffe and Gordon Leggat taking on Tyson and Statham. Within minutes, the procession started when Leggat was caught by Hutton off Tyson. It was a disappointing start – six runs for one wicket. Soon the disappointment turned into a disaster. By tea, New Zealand was 13-3. The situation deteriorated further into a nightmare and finally a calamity.

The scoreboard bears sad testimony to a truly pathetic batting display. Only Sutcliffe, who was fourth out, reached double figures. He was on 11 when he swung hopefully at left-arm spinner Wardle and was bowled. Usually in these sorts of situations, there is some sort of fightback. Perhaps a couple of the tail-enders will come together, swing lustily and raise the total towards 100. Not this time. Wickets kept tumbling. At 22-8, Rabone appealed against the light, which drew jeers from the shocked crowd, and a shake of the head from the umpires. Minutes later it was all over when Hayes was bowled by Statham.

Amazingly, New Zealand had batted 105 minutes and faced 27 overs in edging excruciatingly to their 26. Only one player (Cave) hit a boundary. Five batsmen failed to score. Even extras offered no help.

Rabone takes questions about the occasion with typical good humour. "Yes," he says, "it still comes up fairly often.

"It was so unexpected. We had restricted England to a small lead, and considering their team was stacked with good players, we were quite happy. When I look back now, I wonder if a reaction set in, that we thought we had already done well. Then a few things went wrong and the rot set in."

There were other factors, such as the pitch, and the England attack, but they cannot explain a team total of just 26. "The wicket wasn't brilliant. It had rained overnight," says Rabone. "And the England attack was outstanding. A chap like Bob Appleyard isn't spoken of much today, but he was a fantastic bowler, sending down quick off-cutters. He had the ball rearing up at the batsmen."

Rabone says the realisation of what was happening gradually dawned on the team. "I was trying to hang around out there, but none of us lasted too long. I couldn't believe we were getting knocked over the way we were. We all felt pretty numb afterwards in the dressing room. I'll put it this way: I've been in more hilarious situations.

"In cricket, one batsman will often have a bad day, or even several batsmen. It's very rare for the whole 11 batsmen to have a bad day together. But that's the thing about cricket. I often compare it to tennis where if a player makes a bad shot, it's love-fifteen. In cricket, he's out and back in the hutch for the rest of the afternoon. A tennis player can win a match having made a lot of errors. But a batsman pays a heavy price for just one. We certainly paid a heavy price that day in Auckland."

The critics were scathing. Arthur Mailey, the Australian spinner of the 1920s, and usually a friend of New Zealand cricket, described the batting as "too pathetic for words... Merely holding a negative bat at the ball is not batting at all".

One of the spectators at Eden Park was Arthur Gilligan, who had been commentating the Ashes series in Australia. Gilligan had led England against the 1924 South Africans when that team was dismissed for 30 at Birmingham. Now he got to see that record low eclipsed.

"It was a freak occasion," says Reid. "We thought we had a sniff of a victory and ended up being beaten by an innings! Tyson was the really intimidating bowler. Trueman was a master bowler, with all sorts of subtleties. Tyson just steamed in and let it go at you at frightening pace. We'd never been subjected to that sort of pace. But let's not forget, he had destroyed the Australian batting, too, that summer.

"We were all very quiet and sombre afterwards. We were as shocked as the New Zealand cricket supporters who followed the game. We had batted woefully and there had been a total lack of application. Once a landslide starts, it is very difficult to stop. We felt we had let down New Zealand cricket. It was a low ebb for us, and we were shocked. I knew we were not world-beaters, but we weren't that bad. We had to go out and prove it."

Ironically, almost precisely a year later at the same venue, the New Zealanders, having plunged to an all-time low, rebounded to provide New Zealand cricket with its greatest moment – its first test victory. Of the players who suffered the abject humiliation in 1955, four – Reid, McGregor, Cave and MacGibbon – were there to enjoy the triumph the following year.

And Rabone? That best-forgotten test at Eden Park was the last time he captained New Zealand. But there was no suggestion he was demoted, or held responsible for his team's black day. He was a young man with many diverse non-cricket responsibilities back in the early 1950s, and was not always available for test cricket. He declined an invitation to tour Pakistan and India in 1955-56 and went on to represent New Zealand on and off until 1957, but by then Reid was firmly in place as the test captain.

NEW ZEALAND

First innings		Second innings	
B Sutcliffe c Bailey b Statham	49	b Wardle	11
JG Leggat lbw Tyson	4	c Hutton b Tyson	1
MB Poore c Evans b Tyson	0	b Tyson	0
JR Reid c Statham v Wardle	73	b Statham	1
GO Rabone c Evans b Statham	29	lbw Statham	7
SN McGregor not out	15	c May b Appleyard	1
HB Cave c Bailey b Appleyard	6	c Graveney b Appleyard	5
AR MacGibbon b Appleyard	9	lbw Appleyard	0
IA Colquhoun c sub b Appleyard	0	c Graveney b Appleyard	0
AM Moir lbw Statham	0	not out	0
JA Hayes b Statham	0	b Statham	0
Extras: b 3, lb 6, no 2, w 4	15	Extras	0
Total	200	Total	26

Fall of wickets: 13, 13, 76, 154, 171, 189, 199, 199, 200, 200.

Fall of wickets: 6, 8, 9, 14, 14, 22, 22, 22, 26, 26.

Bowling	O	M	R	W	O	M	R	W
Tyson	11	2	41	2	7	2	10	2
Statham	17.4	7	28	4	9	3	9	3
Bailey	13	2	34	0				
Appleyard	16	4	38	3	6	3	7	4
Wardle	31	19	44	1	5	5	0	1

ENGLAND

TW Graveney c Rabone b Hayes	13
RT Simpson c and b Moir	23
PBH May b Hayes	48
MC Cowdrey b Moir	22
L Hutton b MacGibbon	53
TE Bailey c Colquhoun b Cave	18
TG Evans c Reid b Moir	0
JH Wardle c Reid b Moir	0
FH Tyson not out	27
R Appleyard c Colquhoun b Hayes	6
JB Statham c Reid b Moir	13
Extras: b 12, lb 3, no 8	23
Total	246

Fall of wickets: 21, 56, 112, 112, 163, 164, 164, 201, 218, 246.

Bowling:	O	M	R	W
Hayes	23	7	71	3
MacGibbon	20	7	33	1
Reid	25	15	28	0
Cave	24	10	25	1
Moir	25.1	3	62	5
Rabone	2	0	4	0

6 | INDIAN SUMMERS

The image of Gordon Leggat, his ample frame crumpled into a tub better suited to rinsing a shirt in, has endured in New Zealand cricket history. Leggat, nicknamed Tubby, was an opening batsman in Harry Cave's New Zealand team to Pakistan and India in 1955-56. The team faced conditions that cricketers today would not countenance. Primitive hotels, lack of hygiene, food poisoning, and serious disease and illness were just some of the off-the-field menaces. And that's not to mention a relentlessly tough itinerary, matting wickets, intense heat and umpiring few would suggest was impartial.

It's doubtful if any New Zealand cricketers have embarked on a tour where the odds were so stacked against them. Worse, they went with unsuitable clothing (heavy wool-based trousers and viyella shirts), no medical support and only the vaguest notion of the conditions they would encounter. If players are drawn together in adversity, then this team was as tight as a drum. All 15 tourists returned with their own horror stories of the 13-week tour, but it is the picture of Leggat, squashed in that utterly unsuitable tiny portable bath – using the term "bath" broadly – that seems to sum up what the team faced. "The bath served eight of us who were assigned to one room at our hotel in Peshawar," says Reid, who was Cave's vice-captain. "It was our only means of bathing either at the hotel or the cricket pavilion. We were playing in temperatures of more than 100, so at the end of the day's play all we wanted was a shower. Instead we had to wait to get back to the hotel where eight of us would queue up for the ridiculous little tub. The novelty soon wore off."

Touring the Indian sub-continent even these days is not easy. Precautions must be taken to avoid food poisoning, and the conditions are unlike those cricketers experience anywhere else in the world. But players now know what to expect. Forewarned is forearmed. In addition, the standard of accommodation is often superb.

It most certainly wasn't in 1955. "We didn't enjoy the tour," says Reid. "How could you? It was a tragi-comedy all the way. We usually had more players who were unfit than fit. Team selections were often meaningless because it was a case of counting the players who turned up at breakfast. If they were able to get to breakfast, they were selected. It wasn't until well into the second leg of the tour that we were able to field the team selected the night before. We suffered a feeling of futility."

The New Zealanders returned home looking like they had endured lengthy spells in prisoner of war camps. Harry Cave, gaunt at the best of times, was now 12kg lighter and virtually transparent. He had to miss some of the next series, against the West Indies, which cost him the test captaincy. Jack Alabaster was 79kg when he left New Zealand and under 63kg on his return. Bert Sutcliffe was so weak and sick that he was unable to play the final two tests against the West Indies. He lost 10kg and was a thin 63kg when in the pink of health. Johnny Hayes contracted hepatitis and, little more than a shell, went straight into hospital on his return, playing no more cricket that season. Tony MacGibbon contracted dengue fever and amoebic dysentery and has never really shaken off the effects. He lost 10kg and, as he says, "I didn't have much to come and go on in the first place."

The stories they brought back defied belief. MacGibbon spent an entire night on the toilet, his suffering fractionally alleviated because his team-mates brought him a couple of pillows for "comfort". Matt Poore, who contracted a stomach infection early in the tour, spent several days fearing he would die and not knowing if that would be so bad. Alex Moir sat with him for three nights. One player, whose dysentery never really went away, batted wearing a towel tied as a three-cornered nappy.

It is amazing how unprepared the New Zealanders were. Imagine a team travelling to the Indian sub-continent now without a doctor or even a physio. "The alarm bells began ringing when we met a New Zealand doctor resident in Karachi, a Dr Butterfield," says Reid. "He told us to drink whisky and water, with more whisky than water, and to ensure all water we drank was bottled. Otherwise, he warned us, we must stick to soft drinks. He also gave us an opium concoction to use as a 'cork'. And, for the benefit of the curious, we didn't smoke it; we ate it!

"The illness started straight away. If we ate the local food – an enticing curry, for instance – we would pay for it. We tended to stick to chicken at the many functions we attended. We couldn't eat green salads, which would have been washed in water. But there were traps everywhere. The oranges over there were sold by weight, so overnight they were soaked in water to build up their moisture and weight. You'd peel an orange thinking you were safe, and not know about the water in it."

Reid says that of all the memories he retains of players suffering during the tour, Hayes stands out. "I felt terribly sorry for Johnny. On his previous tour, to England in 1949, he'd been injured and missed a lot of our games. He felt he had a lot to prove this time. And he tried as hard as any cricketer has ever tried, usually on pitches that offered him absolutely nothing. Poor old Johnny. He was very often very sick. I remember him at Ahmedabad bowling against an All India XI. He let a bouncer go and as the ball flew past the wicketkeeper, Johnny pounded after it. He sprinted past the cowering batsman, past the keeper, past fine leg, up the pavilion steps and into the dressing room. We didn't see him for the rest of the day!"

At Bangalore, Poore, carrying a dog off the ground, was bitten and had to be treated for rabies. This necessitated a daily stomach injection for the next two weeks.

The team developed a black humour about their plight, inventing names for their ailments – Lahore Looseness, Delhi Belly, Karachi Cork, Bangalore Bowels.

These days Sutcliffe smiles when he reads of the trials and tribulations of teams in that section of the world. "I smile because I'm not there!" he says. "We were guinea pigs in 1955. The only medication we had was Halizone tablets which you dropped into your carafe of water in the morning so that by evening the water was as pure as it could be without being boiled. Apart from the day we arrived, there was only one other day on which every player stood upright. That was the day the third test against India started. Of course, by the time the test finished we were struggling to find a 12th man who could field. Our trouble was that we were beaten, so we really couldn't say too much when we came back. It would have sounded like excuses.

"I'd never have gone if I'd known what it was going to be like. We had a child due any day and I was very reluctant to go anyhow. But it was a tricky time politically and when I was being persuaded, against my will, to make the tour, Commonwealth relations were frequently mentioned. My state of mind can be gauged by the fact that I didn't pack until the night before we left. Long before the end, I deeply regretted my decision. It wasn't even remotely worthwhile."

The trouble, says Sutcliffe, was that no matter how careful players were, they couldn't avoid sickness. "Even if you were careful with what you ate at the hotel, you couldn't control how the food at the ground was prepared. You'd get a banana and peel it with one hand and have to be careful not to touch the edible part with the other. That's how easily the disease spread."

Reid recalls that while he was having a sprained ankle attended to in the pavilion at Bombay, he saw local officials preparing the iced water for the next drinks break. "A huge block of ice was thrown onto the floor, attacked with a hammer and smashed into pieces, then picked up and thrown into the water container. After I'd told the rest of the team, we went off water and restricted ourselves to hot Milo for on-field refreshment."

Under such conditions, the New Zealanders played 16 matches, including eight tests.

In 1955, the umpiring, especially in India, was a constant concern. An overall lbw count in India of 25-6 against New Zealand suggested some of the problems in that area. Players and local umpires, fluent in English, having hurried conversations in Hindu, did not make the New Zealanders feel any more at ease. Sutcliffe recalls the time he was given out caught behind after he had withdrawn his bat "as far as humanly possible".

MacGibbon remembers one Indian batsman being so obviously caught at first slip that the New Zealanders didn't even appeal. But when he didn't move and the question was finally posed, the batsman was given not out.

New Zealand team manager Henry Cooper, in his end-of-tour report, wrote: "Umpiring in India is not good by international standards, and could well cause dissatisfaction among visiting players. Bad decisions (and some were so bad as to be almost ludicrous) were so frequent and so very often of such great advantage to the local side that it was hard to believe they were all due to lack of concentration and judgement, or even incompetence."

The New Zealanders had to learn about matting wickets, not only how to bat on them, but about how to monitor the angle the pegs were inserted. Reid says: "We learned the hard way. If you are batting, you want a tight mat, so you want the pins knocked in on the angle. If you are bowling, you want the mat loosened, so you want the pins in straight. What we had to avoid was batting on loose matting that favoured their spinners."

The tour got under way in an unsatisfactory manner when, after being unable to buy bats in Karachi, the team cabled Gray Nicholls in England with an order for 14 new bats. The bats arrived promptly, but were not released by customs until the Pakistan leg of the tour was completed. In the meantime, the New Zealanders had to beg and borrow to find bats to use in the tests.

Another aspect of touring, especially in India, that proved a burden was the large number of official team functions. In the last 29 days of the tour, the New Zealanders attended 35 official functions. Good public relations is one thing; that was absurd.

Not surprisingly the New Zealanders' results were mixed. They played six matches in Pakistan, lost three and won one. They lost the three-match test series 2-0. In India, the team played 10 matches, and won two and lost two. They lost a well-fought five-match test series 1-0.

Even if conditions had been in the New Zealanders' favour, they would not have found life easy against the high-quality opposition. It was early days for Pakistan as a nation. The partition had occurred in 1948, with the Muslims moving north and the Hindus remaining in India. But there were plenty of capable cricketers. Pakistan's ranks included Khan Mohammad, Fazal Mahmood, Zulfiqar Ahmed, all fine bowlers, an all-rounder like Abdul Hafeez Kardar and batsmen like Imtiaz Ahmed, the wicketkeeper, Hanif Mohammad and Hassan. India's batting was led by Mankad, Singh, Manjrekar, Roy, Umrigar and Ramchand, who all scored at least one century in the tests and averaged more than 58. Their bowling relied heavily on the beguiling spin of Subhash Gupte, who bowled 356 overs in the series, nearly 200 more than any other Indian, and took 34 wickets.

The best New Zealand batsmen were clearly Reid and Sutcliffe. Reid finished the tour with 1024 runs at 52.89 each, and Sutcliffe, who struggled for runs in Pakistan, scored 1031 runs at 42.95. No one else even approached 700 runs.

Sutcliffe and Reid had a great time of it in the tests in India where Sutcliffe scored 611 runs at 87.28 and Reid 493 at 70.42. Both made two test centuries against India, the highlight being their brilliant partnership of 222 in three hours at New Delhi. Sutcliffe set a New Zealand record with 230 not out while Reid smashed an unbeaten 119. The slaughter was stopped only because Cave declared with New Zealand 450-2 in the hope of forcing victory. Instead, India replied with 531-7.

The New Zealand bowlers really struggled. The pacemen got little from the wickets and Jack Alabaster and Alex Moir, the spinners, lacked the penetration and accuracy to test the best Indian and Pakistani batsmen. Reid was the leading bowler on tour, his 39 wickets taken at a cost of 23.87. All the pacemen – Reid, Cave, MacGibbon and Hayes – bowled with tremendous guts and grit. But the spinners must have winced when they glanced at their tour figures – Alabaster had 19 wickets at 41.89 and Moir 12 at 63.83.

Again, though, it must be stressed that this is a case where the record book tells very little. It doesn't tell, for example, of the Indian spectators' atomic bomb trick. A cracker would go off inside a bottle, causing a shattering noise. When New Zealand batted, the really clever bombers timed their explosions for just before the moment of impact of bat on ball, causing the batsman to flinch. During the Bombay test, Sutcliffe was batting beautifully and was on 73 when he was undone by a bottle bomb. When India batted, the bombings were timed differently, and instead the bombs celebrated a local player reaching 50 or 100. The New Zealanders also had to get used to the massive crowds and the noise they generated. When New Zealand batted, the home team's pace bowlers would be assisted by the crowd noise. It would be a low hum as the bowler began his run and would gain in volume during the run-up until at the moment of delivery it reached a howling screech. Reid, batting at Bombay, became incensed by this noise. He withdrew from his batting stance at the last moment several times in succession, trying to quell the crowd noise. When play eventually resumed, he lost his cool, tried to hit one into the stands and was given out lbw. "I learned a valuable lesson that day – never under any circumstances allow a crowd to get to you when you're batting."

~

1965

When New Zealand next travelled to India and Pakistan, in 1965, the side contained two survivors from the hellish 1955-56 tour – Reid and Sutcliffe – both of whom had vowed they would never return as players.

Sutcliffe's inclusion was one of the talking points when the team was named. He had been out of international cricket for five years, but had agreed to make himself available for test cricket again. "I was very keen to tour England," says Sutcliffe. "I would not have put up my hand if the tour was just to India and Pakistan. The memories of the first tour were too horrific."

Reid, too, was hardly bursting to get back to the Indian sub continent. "I can't say I was really looking forward to that part of the tour. I was the New Zealand captain and there was never any question of making myself unavailable, but I knew what a brutal tour it could be."

At least in 1965, Dr Bill Treadwell of Wellington was included in the touring party. "We still ran into health problems, but they were much less regular and less severe because we had Bill on hand," says Reid. "I'd recommended to the Cricket Council that we must take a doctor and I think they'd followed the example of the Australians who had been there not long before and had been much better off with a doctor in the team. We still always had a couple of players ill and for the last match, the test at Karachi, we were in bad shape with a long list of unfit players. But compared to the first tour, we were all in the first flush of health!"

The team selection was interesting. In 1955 the selectors had taken a punt on Jack Alabaster, a leg-spinner who had no first class experience. Alabaster had a gruelling tour, bowling to batsmen who handled his leg-spin with ease. But the tour benefited him greatly and he went on to become one of the great New Zealand spin bowlers. In 1965, the selectors, including Reid, gambled on another unknown leg-spinner, Graham Vivian of Auckland. The decision backfired. Vivian proved to be no more than a part-time spinner, and the team was left one frontline spinner short.

Sutcliffe was picked primarily because of his ability to play spin bowling. "The tour was beginning with seven consecutive test matches in India and Pakistan. With the spinners we would encounter there, we felt we needed Bert's experience and ability to play spin, especially as many of our batsmen were relatively new to test cricket. Bert soon justified his selection. He made 56 in the first test against India, at Madras, and 151 not out in the next test, at Calcutta. He did his job."

Conditions were better in 1965 than they had been a decade earlier. "Yes, they were better," says Sutcliffe, "but they still weren't great. We were mobbed everywhere. If you suffered from claustrophobia, then India wasn't the place to be. And the noise! If you were batting you were fair game. Crackers, chanting, anything to distract a batsman. The hotels were much better. They had a Hilton at Karachi. I nearly dropped over when I saw that. The cleanest place was the Brabourne Stadium, the Indian Cricket Board's headquarters in Bombay [now called Mumbai]. We slept in the rooms above the ground and they were first class."

The itinerary in 1965 was unbelievable. Why would a team be scheduled to play seven straight tests, especially in such torrid conditions? "Not only that," asks Reid, "but why would we then agree to begin the tour at Madras, which was the hottest, most humid place in the country? The decisions were made by our board and I suppose it came down to money, but it made things far too difficult for the team. I couldn't help wondering if the reports of our manager and captain from the 1955 tour had even been read."

Reid stresses that unlike a tourist, or even a businessman, cricketers cannot generally take a day off because they feel off colour, especially when test matches are being played. "We had batsmen like Barry Sinclair and Terry Jarvis, who were terribly sick. They should have been confined to bed, but they battled on. It's frustrating for cricketers when they know they are trying as hard as they can but not doing themselves justice because of ill-health. They play because they are thinking of their team, but they know they will be judged back home and in the record books by cold statistics."

Water was again a problem. "We were assured at every hotel we used in India and Pakistan that the water was boiled, but it was nearly always merely filtered. At the Intercontinental Hotel in Karachi, some of our team ordered milk shakes and they were great, except it turned out they'd been made with milk powder and water. Those players paid dearly for letting their guard down. My temperature reached 105. I should have been dead, and that's what it felt like! At Calcutta, we found provision had been made to keep the butter firm and palatable-looking – by having it float about in a tub full of unboiled water and ice tossed in by hand after it had been broken up on the floor." To circumvent the water problem, Reid's players resorted to a couple of soft drinks that had been cleared by Dr Treadwell, even using them when brushing their teeth. "Even today," says Reid, "I can't drink Seven-up!"

While Reid and Sutcliffe pointed out conditions had improved since 1955, their team-mates could only smile grimly. At Delhi, where Sutcliffe, Collinge, Pollard, Ward, Cameron, Reid, Jarvis and Sinclair were all ill or injured, the tiny dressing room contained just one toilet which seized up on the first morning. For the rest of the match, Dr Treadwell was a one-man bucket brigade, not the most enjoyable of tasks.

Besides heat and hygiene worries, Reid's team faced the usual problem with umpires, especially in India. One of the worst decisions of the tour involved Reid himself, when he was given out lbw to Nadkarni at Madras. He was on 42 and going well when he was sent packing. "That decision actually helped us," says Reid. "It riled our team. When we went out to field, we were genuinely angry and fighting mad. We bowled out India for 88, the lowest score they had ever recorded at home at that time."

At times the umpiring was comical, providing you weren't involved. During the third test at Bombay the umpires walked for three days in sombre fashion between square leg and their position at the bowler's end. On the last afternoon, when New Zealand collapsed and a win for India seemed possible, they fair scuttled into position to give the home team every chance to bowl as many overs as possible. "In the end," says Reid, "with the crowd roaring and baying, they were actually running into position."

A CRICKETING LIFE

As in 1955, the New Zealanders were again unable to record a test victory during the tour. In India, the first three tests were drawn and the fourth lost by seven wickets. In Pakistan the first and third tests were lost, the second drawn. There were some individual highlights. At Calcutta, Bruce Taylor scored a century and took five wickets in an innings on his test debut. It was there that Sutcliffe scored his last test century and Reid, playing his 50th test, hammered 82. He showed a fine lack of inhibition for the test match stage when he hammered four 6s in just 10 deliveries, lifting Desai (twice), Durani and Jaisimha over the ropes. How many batsmen today would contemplate hitting four 6s on the first morning of a test? Dowling scored a century in the third test, at Bombay, where Taylor again took five wickets.

But the Indians, playing at home, were difficult to beat. Sardesai, Manjrekar, Borde and Pataudi provided plenty of runs while Venkataraghavan, Chandraesekhar and Nadkarni were world class spinners.

By the time the New Zealanders got to Pakistan, they were starting to be worn down. They struck a unique wicket in the first test, at Rawalpindi, where Reid set a world record with his 53rd consecutive test match. Left-arm spinner Pervez took eight wickets as New Zealand was bowled out quickly twice and lost by an innings. "This was the only test wicket I played on where I could honestly say it was deteriorating before the game began. Artie Dick had just arrived as a replacement for our injured wicketkeeper, John Ward, and bagged a pair. The whole stay at Rawalpindi was unsatisfactory. The Flashman Hotel was a dingy little place and the cricket venue was no more than a club ground. It was a world record test for me, but also one of my least memorable."

The New Zealanders batted well in the second test, at Lahore, where Dowling (83), Jarvis (55), Sinclair (130), Reid (88) and Morgan (50) got among the runs. A double century by Hanif Mohammad ensured a draw for Pakistan.

In the third test, at Karachi, Reid batted up to his best form, scoring 128 in 268 minutes. He hit three 6s and 15 4s and really punished Pervez, the spinning danger for Pakistan. Reid was equally dominant in the second innings, top-scoring with 76, but couldn't prevent an eight-wicket loss. What was amazing about Reid's century was that he was batting with a dangerously high temperature. "I was about 80 not out at tea and apparently during the break I was on the table raving. I must have got to the century on automatic pilot. I don't remember it.

"The 1965 tour was much better than the first one," says Reid, "but when we flew out I still looked back on it as an unsatisfactory experience. You get physically drained and there's frustration because you know the dice are loaded against you. I didn't score enough runs and the rest of the batsmen performed only intermittently. Taylor, Motz, Cameron and Collinge bowled well, but our spinners weren't good enough. I didn't bowl as much as I would have normally because by then my knee was really causing me trouble. Vivian wasn't anywhere near test class as a spinner, and Pollard and Yuile did not trouble batsmen who were used to dealing with top class spin bowling."

∽

The Indian sub-continent, says Reid, is a much more palatable place to play cricket these days. "Today the Taj group of hotels are as good as anywhere in the world, with swimming pools and other up-market facilities, and good European food available. The only way you know you are in a third world country is by the vast crowds on the streets and in the markets. Security is well-organised, as it needs to be. There are still huge crowds at most matches and everywhere you can see cricket being played. Of the one billion people, a large proportion are fanatical about their cricket and it would be a gross understatement to say they like to see India win. When I've refereed in India, there has generally been a security officer allocated, plus car and driver. Missiles on the field are still a problem, but moats or ditches and barbed wire restrict a pitch invasion on the main grounds."

Reid says that problems which arise now in India generally occur at the lesser-known cities where the hotels and facilities are often of more questionable quality.

In Pakistan, touring itineraries are generally restricted to the main centres, where cricket facilities and hotel accommodation are excellent. "Pakistan has become an enjoyable place to tour, and in 1955, I never thought I'd say that. I've refereed in Pakistan several times in the past few years and been impressed with the progress. It isn't obvious that the problems of a third world population are just outside the hotel foyer.

"The population explosion has to be seen to be believed. In 1965 the population of Pakistan was 60 million. It is now 120 million. Security is very good for the I.C.C. officials as a fleet of cars is made available, and a liaison officer is on hand at all times. The crowds are as volatile as they are in India, but they much prefer the one-day matches. Relatively few turn up to test matches."

Sri Lanka is the third test-playing country on the Indian sub-continent. As it made its test debut only in the early 1980s, Reid never played there. However, he has come to know the country well through his refereeing commitments. "My first real visit to Sri Lanka nearly didn't happen," says Reid. "Apart from a stopover at Colombo on a voyage to England during my playing days, I'd never been to Sri Lanka, or Ceylon as we used to call the country, until I became an I.C.C. referee. Ironically my first refereeing appointment was to Sri Lanka for the 1993 series against South Africa, and the appointment was placed in jeopardy after a query by the then secretary of the Sri Lankan Cricket Board, Neil Perera.

"I.C.C. refereeing appointments can be objected to by host countries for whatever reasons. They can't object to umpire appointments, but they can about referees. The Sri Lankan cricket authorities had a point in raising a question about me as they were under the impression that in 1993 I was still living in Johannesburg. In fact, I had been back in Taupo, New Zealand, for more than a year."

Reid was especially interested to observe cricket in Sri Lanka, after his experiences as a player in India and Pakistan. He imagined conditions and attitudes would be similar. "I had heard the horror stories brought home by some members of the 1988 New Zealand team, whose tour of that country was abandoned because of civil unrest. Even worse, New Zealand's tour of Sri Lanka in early 1993 had also been thrown into chaos by a Tamil bomb attack on a member of the Sri Lankan armed forces. Apparently a vote was taken in the New Zealand camp and coach Warren Lees and several players decided to return home, to be replaced by other players.

"The bomb had exploded very near the New Zealand team hotel. Reports at the time stated that the bomb had exploded near the breakfast/dining room of the Taj Sumundra Hotel and that various victims' body parts were hanging from trees nearby. Even so, I was surprised to hear a vote had taken place. Whatever happened to management decisions?

"Having since stayed at the hotel, I question the accuracy of the reports we received. I had to travel quite a distance to the attack site, out to the end of the hotel drive, then turn right onto the main highway, and then go to the end of the hotel's boundary to a side road/turning area. It was certainly nowhere near the hotel dining room. Another point: if the experience was so frightening, how was it that on that same night a team member was stopped by security after a late-night liaison? The Tamils shortly afterwards made a statement, reaffirmed during the 1996 World Cup, that there would not be any disruption to cricket matches as, like all Sri Lankans, they loved their cricket.

"On the three occasions I have refereed in Sri Lanka, security has been very tight. The I.C.C. panel umpires and myself have been well looked after. I had a chief inspector of police in the room next to me and he accompanied me everywhere. If I had a private dinner engagement (and there were several, as Sri Lanka is a very hospitable country), the chief inspector and my driver checked it first, delivered me, asked how long I was likely to be, and were there waiting to escort me home. It was great to take them on shopping excursions with their floppy shirts and only partially concealed guns guaranteeing them quick access to most places and great bargaining powers."

In the early 1990s, Colombo had five grounds on which test cricket could be played. "The authorities have since reduced the number to three, but have added matches in Kandy in the hill country – a great tea area – and at Galle, on the southern tip of the country.

"The cricket is confined to what is basically club cricket, as opposed to state, provincial or county, and is played mainly in and around Colombo and Kandy. The standard is high, as can be seen by the high-quality players Sri Lanka regularly produces. There is a problem with administration, as all team selections are referred to the Sports Minister for clearance and more often than not there is a politician on the large selection panel.

"I have enjoyed my trips to Sri Lanka, where the history, the scenery and the friendliness of the people make for an enjoyable stay. However, I have not ventured further north than Kandy because the country is at war – such a pity."

~

JOHN REID'S VIEW INDIAN SUB-CONTINENT – THE PLAYERS

INDIA

Subhash Gupte: An interesting leg-spin and googly bowler. On wickets that helped him, or when he was on top, he was as good a leg-spin bowler as has been around. He had deception, variety and the ability to really turn the ball. But he wasn't a good fighter, and once he got hit, he would fall to pieces. Bert Sutcliffe and I eventually got on top of him at New Delhi in 1955 when we added 222 and took New Zealand's total to 450-2, and he virtually gave up. At times like that he would bowl very wide and negatively. During the Calcutta test, he repeatedly bowled so wide that to show my disapproval, I never moved a muscle to play one ball. I simply retained my stance and stared at Gupte as if he had not bowled. His response was dramatic – some loud cursing and oaths, followed by the next ball delivered with less than a straight arm and straight at my head.

Vijay Mandrekar: A classic strokemaker – his son, Sanjay, had a similar style – who was dropped too soon by the Indian selectors for no good reason I could see. I suspect he was on the wrong end of some cricket politics. He scored a lovely 102 not out against us in the first test at Madras in 1965, and was then dropped, never to play test cricket again. At the time, he'd have made most test sides in the world, especially as, unlike some Indian batsmen of his era, he was very sound against pace bowling.

Vinoo Mankad: Patient and sound. He was more of an accumulator than a dominator. He reminded me of Ken Barrington in that he didn't beat you up, but would grind away. Mankad had some memorable performances in test cricket. He scored two centuries against Australia in 1947-48 and against

England at Headingley in 1952 scored 72 and 184 and, bowling left-arm spin, took 5-231 off 91 overs. I recall him chiefly for the soul-destroying eight-hour partnership he and Pankaj Roy put together against us at Madras in 1955. Mankad made 231 and Roy 173 and they set a world test record for the first wicket. As Mankad had already scored 223 against us at Bombay, I got to know his batting pretty well!

The Nawab of Pataudi: I didn't class Pataudi as a world great, but he was a free-scoring, uninhibited batsman who made some big scores in test cricket and not just against New Zealand. Considering the sight in his right eye was nearly totally lost in a road accident, Pataudi's batting was remarkable. I found him an approachable person and enjoyed my captaincy battles against him. Pataudi's title was later taken from him and he played under the name of Mansur Ali Khan, losing the test captaincy for a while. He was an I.C.C. referee for a short period.

Srinivas Venkataraghavan: Venkat, or Rent-A-Caravan, as he was known, was an excellent off-spinner who turned the ball and had good control. Despite bowling in an era when India had several outstanding spinners, he played 57 tests and took 156 wickets. He was good enough to captain India. I put him just below Laker and Tayfield as an off-spinner. Venkat is one of the world's leading test umpires these days, a capable, unruffled official who shows the benefit of his experience as a player.

Sunil Gavaskar: Sonny played 125 tests and in them scored more than 10,000 runs and hit a record of 34 centuries. It is remarkable, therefore, to think that during his long career I never really saw him strike the sort of form that earned him a test average of 51. He toured New Zealand in 1976, when I was helping select the New Zealand team, but did not do his talents justice. He made one test century, 116 in Auckland, but it took him more than six hours. I was left with the impression of a composed, balanced player with shots all around the wicket and time to spare when playing shots. For me, an indication of Gavaskar's quality was his play against the West Indies. In his first test series, he toured the West Indies in 1971 and produced scores of 116 (on debut), 117 not out, 124 and 220 (the last two in the same match). He scored a further nine centuries against the West Indies, even though their fearsome array of quick bowlers was not designed to make life easy for an opening batsman. These days I see Sonny regularly out in the middle, not with bat and ball, but discussing for the benefit of television viewers hidden gremlins lurking in the pitch.

Kapil Dev: Kapil will probably be first recalled by New Zealand cricket followers as the man who broke Richard Hadlee's world test record of 431 wickets. Yet despite Kapil's wonderful wicket tally, I did not regard him as a bowler of the class of a Hadlee or a Malcolm Marshall. He was a lively pace bowler who performed marvels on the often unhelpful (to pace bowlers) pitches of his home country. For me, Kapil fitted better the description of a bowling all-rounder. In his 131 tests, he scored 5248 runs at an average of 31 and made eight centuries. He generally scored his runs quickly and was often dynamic in one-day matches.

Kapil is still heavily involved in the active side of cricket, as a coach and commentator, and offers good, sensible advice to anyone who wants to listen. During 1999 he became the Indian test team coach, though with the turnover rate of that job Kapil would be best advised not to abandon his television links. We also served together on the I.C.C.'s advisory panel for illegal deliveries until Kapil resigned on being appointed Indian coach.

Mohammad Azharuddin: Life is never easy as captain of India. Like Sunil Gavaskar, Sachin Tendulkar and others, Azharuddin has suffered from the whims of Indian selectors, having won, lost, regained and lost again the Indian captaincy. After India's disappointing showing at the 1999 World Cup, he was again demoted. Politics aside, I've found Azza to be a very fine cricketer, a batsman who can handle the various styles of bowling, being especially effective against spin, an excellent fieldsman and a captain who, from my observations, did a very good job.

Azharuddin also had a fine degree of respect for the way the game is played and one time when called upon to try to cool a riotous crowd at Bangalore, his home ground, he ventured out among the missiles, hands held high in a conciliatory manner, and in fact did manage to quieten the crowd so the game could continue. Azza himself was the unwitting cause of the unrest because, with India losing three quick wickets, he was given out (harshly), which left India 29-4, with a bad beating on the cards, and the crowd reacted.

Anil Kumble: Wrist-spinners are still relatively rare in world cricket these days. Shane Warne and Stuart McGill (Australia), Mushtaq Ahmed (Pakistan), Paul Strang (Zimbabwe) and Kumble make up the extent of real international talent available. Most of these bowlers turn the ball considerably, but Kumble is more of a top-spinner, making the ball come in from the off, so if a batsman plays him as a leg-spinner, he is in big trouble. Kumble presents other difficulties. He is a tall man, so he gets the ball to bounce, and he pushes it through at a good pace. With these attributes, plus his accuracy, he is a handy man to have in your side – just ask the Pakistanis. He took 10-74 off 26 overs against them early in 1999, to become only the second bowler (after Jim Laker) to take all 10 in an innings.

Sachin Tendulkar: Bradman has described Tendulkar as the batsman most like him of anyone he's seen, and that's praise of the highest order. Tendulkar is a very complete player, equally at home off the front foot or the back. He uses the full face of the bat, and is technically very sound, though he can be inventive. He's of double value to his team because he is as effective in one-day cricket, where he can rip an attack to shreds, as in test cricket, where he is a consistently heavy scorer, reaching the milestone of his 20th test century at the age of just 26. Already he deserves to be placed among the game's best. If he continues scoring heavily for another few years, that rating will only rise.

Rahul Dravid: Rahul has probably the most correct batting technique on show in world cricket today. He doesn't hit the ball as hard as some, or delve into flamboyant stroke-making, but his consistent run-scoring is a pleasure to watch. He flows through an innings without apparent difficulty, his success based on a model technique. Rahul is also a pleasant, approachable fellow with a respect for the traditions of the game he plays so well.

PAKISTAN

Fazal Mahmood: You don't read a lot about Fazal now, but he was a terrific bowler, the more so when playing at home on matting wickets. He took 13-114 against Australia in 1956 at Karachi on matting. Fazal wasn't just good on the matting, though. He'd caused England a lot of problems earlier in 1954 and his 12-99 at the Oval steered Pakistan to their first win over England. He was tall and bowled fast-medium off-cutters – quicker than Bob Appleyard – and got a lot of bounce. He had a certain authority about his bowling, so perhaps it's not surprising he went on to become a police superintendent.

Hanif Mohammad: A grafter who scored a lot of his runs with pushes and glances. Hanif had buckets of patience – his 337 against the West Indies in 1958 took him 16 hours 10 minutes, and until November 1999 was the longest innings (by three hours) ever played. He once scored 499, which was the world record for many years, and was then run out. All I can say is that he must have been halfway down the pitch to be given out at home at that stage! You can't deny his figures – 12 test centuries – but away from Pakistan he was not especially formidable. We got right on top of him when he toured New Zealand in 1965 and Richard Collinge dismissed him five times in six innings.

Saeed Ahmed: Unlike some of his team-mates, Saeed was a dashing strokemaker. He didn't have the happiest of times during the test series in New Zealand in 1965, but hit a punishing 172 against us in the last test, at Karachi, a few months later. He is now a holy man with a beard that stretches down to his knees, and the game of cricket is no longer a factor in his life.

Javed Miandad: Deserves to be placed very high on any list. You don't play 124 tests and average 52.5 with 23 centuries unless you've got yourself fairly organised. He began his test career at the age of 19 against New Zealand in 1976 by scoring 163, 25 not out, 25, 206 and 85, having forced his way into the team with an unbeaten century for the Chief Minister's XI. Thereafter for the next two decades, he always seemed in charge, and could control the tempo of his innings. This was never better illustrated than during 1992 World Cup semifinal at Auckland when his clever, measured batting allowed Inzamam ul-Haq to blast Pakistan to victory. Miandad, who was given and then sacked from the Pakistani test captaincy more times than he'd care to remember, gained a reputation as a needler and a niggler, but he was able to back up the talk with runs, and that's the test.

Wasim Akram and Waqar Younis: They formed the best attack in world cricket in the early 1990s. In his prime, Waqar had lethal pace, was accurate and, of course, was famous for his reverse swing. He was an aggressive, attacking bowler, but I liked him because he didn't resort to merely bowling short and at the batsman. Waqar's strike rate of a wicket every 44 balls bears ample testimony to his brilliance as a wicket-taker. Wasim was just 18 when he toured New Zealand in 1985, and he didn't take long to show his class. In just his second test he claimed 5-56 and 5-72. They were good wickets he took, too, including Geoff Howarth (twice), John F. Reid (twice), Martin Crowe and Jeff Crowe (twice). Akram is a magnificent left-arm bowler who has everything – pace, movement, aggression. He is a very awkward customer, a bowler you have to watch the whole time. I place him alongside Alan Davidson as the best left-arm paceman I've seen. He ran into trouble with the authorities over match-fixing allegations, though he strenuously proclaimed his innocence and was eventually exonerated. In the swirling world of Pakistani cricket politics it is sometimes difficult to know exactly what is fact.

SRI LANKA
Aravinda de Silva: Entering the 21st century, he ranks in the top five batsmen in the world. He is as at home against pace as spin, and has shots all around the wicket, though it is the wristiness of his strokeplay that I find most attractive. Aravinda, only a whisker over 5ft 3in, always looks as if he is wielding an especially wide bat, perhaps because he uses the shortest handle of any top batsman.

Arjuna Ranatunga: A very effective player, and a smart cookie to boot, even though he has found the world of cricket politics a tough opponent. He is at his best in a battle and I've always thought of him as a good team player, able to score quickly when required. He is smart enough to annoy many of his opponents, who can't stand him. They call him "Tubby" for walking a single and abuse him, but he generally has the last say. As you'd expect, Ranatunga is a good businessman who has his own insurance company.

Arjuna was responsible for dragging Sri Lankan cricket up by its bootlaces to the extent that they won the 1996 World Cup. His batting expertise, his captaincy and his very presence were of immense value to the Sri Lankan side and I was sorry to see him relieved of the test captaincy for what seemed to be little more than political expediency.

Muttiah Muralitharan: This genial, somewhat shy Sri Lankan from Kandy has been the target of the media and headline-seekers for the last five or six years because of his unusual bowling action and because he takes stacks of wickets. I am a member of the Advisory Panel for Illegal Deliveries (A.P.I.D.), so unfortunately cannot fully comment on the panel's investigations, except to say that Murali's action has been "passed" but not cleared, and that though he has been called for throwing by three Australian umpires, his bowling has been accepted by other umpires around the world. Certainly he has an unusual action, with lots of wrist employed. As his arm is 20 per cent permanently bent, he is unable to fully straighten it at the point of delivery. This is a family trait, but it makes for an unusual delivery, and one which draws attention. Many bowlers over the years have had an unusual delivery. Sonny Ramadhin and Alf Valentine come to mind immediately – Sonny, with his black hand and long-sleeved shirt buttoned at the wrist, and Alf, with the ball screwed into his left hand with his right. But there was never any question raised about their actions.

Murali is the spearhead of the Sri Lankan attack and his control and the amount of spin he extracts from the pitch make him an exceptional problem for any batsman. He really is a prodigious spinner of the ball, making it spin more than Jim Laker and Lance Gibbs and much more than Hugh Tayfield and Ian Johnson, all world class off-spinners of my generation. For a finger spinner, it is very unusual for a bowler to obtain such spin and I am more inclined to compare his spinning capabilities with wrist-spinners like Subash Gupte and Shane Warne. Murali has also added a well-disguised top-spinner to his armoury and I'm sure he will continue to be a mystery to many test batsmen for some years.

He is a quiet, unassuming person who certainly does not deserve all the fuss and bother that has been generated by his action.

Sanath Jayasuriya: I only hope that the extra responsibility he now has, as Sri Lankan captain, does not constrict his exciting natural flair, which is so evident from the way he is willing to attack the bowling from the first over. The prospect of seeing this match-winner under way fills grounds around the world. He repeatedly got Sri Lanka off to a blazing start during the 1996 World Cup, and played a large part in helping his country cause a surprise by winning that tournament. Crowds everywhere have come to expect that sort of batting whenever Jayasuriya takes strike.

During my refereeing duties, I have been to Sri Lanka on three occasions and have witnessed Sanath in full flight. His most famous innings was probably in 1997 when his 340 helped Sri Lanka reach a world record of 952-6 in reply to India's 537. He and Roshan Mahanama (225) put on a world record partnership of 576. I was disappointed by Sanath's innings in that match because in 1994 I had been to Barbados and witnessed the terrific 375 Brian Lara scored against England. Lara's fantastic display enabled him to break Gary Sobers' world record and Sobers was on the spot to congratulate him not only on his record, but also on the manner he had batted. Jayasuriya's innings did not compare with Lara's. In fact, the contrast was so great, I became bored. He did not play in his usual style. Sri Lanka did not lose a wicket for two days and Sanath realised that he was within sight of Lara's world record. He went even further into his shell and ended up being caught at silly mid-on. Fancy being on 340 and still allowing the fielding side to post a silly mid-on! His next innings in the same series was a magnificent 177, which to me made up for his sorry world record bid.

7 | THE LONG AND WINDIES ROAD

Entering the fourth test against the West Indies at Eden Park in 1956, New Zealand's cricket stocks really had reached rock bottom.

After 46 years of test cricket, and 44 test matches, New Zealand was yet to record their first win. By comparison, Pakistan, who had been admitted to test cricket in 1954, had immediately beaten Len Hutton's England team in England and drawn the series.

What made the situation worse for New Zealand was that there was no immediate prospect of the situation changing. The glories of 1949 were but a quickly fading memory. Of the outstanding team Walter Hadlee led through England in 1949, stars like Hadlee himself, Martin Donnelly, Merv Wallace, Verdun Scott, Jack Cowie and Tom Burtt had departed the international scene. They had been replaced by players nowhere near their standard.

Since 1949, New Zealand's results had been uninspiring, to say the least. There were home series losses in official tests against England (twice), South Africa and the West Indies, plus an embarrassing capitulation against an Australia B team in 1950. The New Zealanders, under Geoff Rabone, had been hammered in South Africa in 1953-54. Perhaps the ultimate humiliation came in 1955 when New Zealand was bowled out for a world test record low of 26.

Optimists hoped for better in the 1955-56 season. An ambitious eight-test tour of Pakistan and India had been planned, followed by a four-test series at home against the West Indies. Who could tell? Perhaps Harry Cave's team would find their feet in India and Pakistan and put some test wins on the board. Heartened by those results, the West Indies might then be rolled back home.

Such were the dreams. In fact, the New Zealanders faced an horrific schedule in Pakistan and India. They had to play test after test with no time to find their form. Accommodation, food, sanitary conditions were all appalling and the team suffered a run of heavy defeats.

No sooner had the players returned than they were thrown into a series against a West Indies team boasting Everton Weekes, Alf Valentine and Sonny Ramadhin, Dennis Atkinson, Collie Smith (to die tragically in a road accident in 1959) and a young Garfield Sobers. Worse, the New

Zealanders were still suffering from ill-health.

The first three tests against the West Indies were sorry affairs from a New Zealand point of view, resulting in defeats by an innings and 71, an innings and 64, and then nine wickets. After the first test, in Dunedin, a New Zealand cricket official informed the team that if performances didn't improve, the planned 1958 tour of England would be cancelled. The five-man New Zealand selection committee had shuffled players around in desperation. Cave had been forced to drop out after the first test because of ill-health, to be replaced as captain by Reid. When Cave returned for the third test, Reid kept the captaincy. Sutcliffe was simply too ill to play and after two tests, he withdrew from the series. One positive was the introduction of Merv Wallace as coach after the second test.

But midway through the series, New Zealand sports followers could be excused for forgetting the cricket and casting their minds ahead to the All Black-Springbok rugby series – the battle for the world rugby crown – that loomed later in the year.

It was in this atmosphere of frenetic change, desperation and heavy defeats that Reid assumed the captaincy. "It wasn't an easy time," he says. "But I knew we weren't that bad. We didn't have tremendous depth, but we had some pretty good players. We just had to get the most out of ourselves."

Reid says one of the problems New Zealand faced at that time was an inconsistent selection policy. "This was still the dark ages of New Zealand selecting. Instead of picking players and giving them a reasonable chance to come right at test level, the selectors were looking for miracle players and would chop and change match by match." During the series, New Zealand used 20 players and only Reid, John Beck and Noel McGregor played all four tests.

"I took over the captaincy of the team for the second test, so I had a say in the selection for the final three matches. Merv Wallace, once he became team coach, and I were advisors. With Merv and I, plus the five selectors, it was a case of selection by compromise. It took hours and hours to pick that fourth test team, not because we had too many good players, but because the selectors did not agree with Merv's and my ideas.

"We got the panel back to three selectors soon after, though there were still some very poor selections made, and it was only in 1961, when we toured South Africa, that we began to adopt consistent selection policies.

"If you looked at our team in 1956, we had some reasonably tight pacemen in Tony MacGibbon, Harry Cave, Don Beard and me. That was what we would base our attack around, with Jack Alabaster to provide the spin. It so happened that MacGibbon was batting at No 3 in that series. He was a tall, front foot, driving batsman, who proved quite solid. But overall our batting wasn't strong and I wanted the team to bat down to No 8, since two of the batsmen were bowlers.

"Trevor Barber, a middle-order batsman from Wellington, had looked quite reasonable in the third test. The trouble was that he'd come in at No 7 in that match and the selectors were horrified that a specialist batsman should come in so low. So Barber wasn't picked for the fourth test. Instead, the selectors replaced Barber with Murray Chapple, and Canterbury spinner Ian Sinclair with Alabaster. My own view was that Alabaster should come in for Sinclair and Barber be retained. The selectors felt Chapple's left-arm spin would be useful. I told them we would be basing our attack around pace and that Chapple wouldn't be bowled. I didn't think it was fair on Barber or Chapple. Murray hadn't played a first class match for six weeks before the fourth test. It was probably as unfair on Murray to bring him in in those circumstances as it was on Barber to leave him out. As it was, Alabaster bowled only eight overs in that fourth test, and Murray didn't bowl at all – predictable in view of our pre-match strategy.

"I was also very keen to have Sam Guillen in the side. He'd kept wickets for the West Indies on their previous tour to New Zealand in the 1951-52 season and was now available to us. He was a useful batsmen and had plenty of experience, which was in short supply in our team that year. So Sam played the last three tests and actually played a major part in our win. He scored a vital 41 in the second innings and stumped Valentine to finish the match.

"In looking at the background to the match, you can't stress too strongly the effect of the gruelling tour of Pakistan and India. It was the sort of tour you have nightmares about for the rest of your life. No one who went on that tour was really fit to play in the series against the West Indies. Bert missed the win in Auckland, which was a real injustice. He was never part of a winning test side, and no one deserved to be so more than him. Others in the test side was not really in good health."

Wallace says he enjoyed particularly working with Reid. "It was really a continuation of 1949 for us. As a captain he would always listen to me. We worked together, thinking through the batting order, the bowling options, the tactics. People ask what sort of a captain John was. I thought he was pretty good, but having said that, it's always a lot easier to be a good captain when you have a team of top players. John never enjoyed that luxury.

"Looking at the West Indies, Weekes was obviously the key. He had made a lot of hundreds. But I'd seen him a few times and I thought we could get him. We were a bit unlucky in the Wellington test when he was dropped early. We felt if we kept the ball up to him and ran it away, he would try to push a single. In Wellington he did just that and snicked it to Beard, who dropped it!

"John and I had a look at their team, and we felt they all had areas we could exploit. For instance, young Roberts opened up when the ball was on the off, so we wanted to get Harry Cave to bring the ball back from the leg to him. The West Indians all gave you a chance. They had a crack at the ball."

There are some images about the fourth test which will remain forever in the memories of those who saw it... Reid, playing in his 100th first class match, clipping his wicket with his boot after playing a routine defensive stroke with his score on 84 (the only New Zealand half-century of the game), Atkinson's superb bowling in the second innings (7-53 from 40 overs) as he attempted to prevent defeat, Guillen's invaluable innings of 41, the tight New Zealand bowling, especially from Cave, the scramble for souvenir stumps and bails after Guillen had stumped Valentine just after tea on the last day.

But there is one special piece of action – Weekes' dismissal by Alabaster – which was the decisive point of the match. It is the moment everyone recalls first. It came when the West Indies, needing 268 to win on the last afternoon, were 68-6. They had collapsed, losing six wickets for 22 runs in what Reid calls "the most incredible 40 minutes of my career". But slowly Weekes, the danger man, and Alfred Binns had begun to turn the game around. During their partnership, Eden Park's numbers swelled to 9000. Office workers, following proceedings by radio, packed up and headed for Eden Park. Mothers wrapped up their young ones and rushed to Eden Park. Up in the stands, Merv Wallace, usually so calm and under-stated, chain smoked, waiting for the breakthrough that would seal the match.

Weekes was rightly feared by all New Zealand cricket followers. His scores in the first three tests were 123, 103, 156. He'd scored three other centuries in provincial matches and was capable of slaughtering any attack in the world. Now he had reached 31 and was threatening to wrest the initiative off New Zealand. The tea interval loomed and Reid decided to add some variety to the attack. He brought on Alabaster.

"Weekes was the key to everything," says Reid. "He was the guy we had to get out. He was susceptible early on, but in the first three tests we'd dropped him in the slips and he'd gone on to score a century. In Auckland he was caught behind for only five in the first innings. In the second innings he'd got a start and was looking good. It was the time to introduce some variation. I didn't want to leave it until the last minute."

At that point, Alabaster didn't have the sort of credentials to strike fear into a world class player like Weekes. He'd never played a first class match before being chosen for the tour of Pakistan and India. On that tour he emerged with test figures of two wickets for 329 runs, average 164.5.

"Jack immediately bowled a long hop," recalls Reid. "You could almost see Weekes licking his lips. He hooked it, but didn't hit it properly. He got it too high up the bat. The ball went very high and we all held our breath. Then I looked and saw little Noel McGregor moving around from square leg to mid-wicket to get under it and I remember thinking, 'That's good. You need some luck sometimes.' Noel was a very safe catcher and I had no qualms about him catching it."

Sure enough, McGregor took the catch gratefully and sank to the ground in relief. But while Reid might have had no qualms about McGregor accepting the vital chance, the man under the ball wasn't quite so confident.

"I'll never forget how I felt," says McGregor. "I was the poor little fellow out on the boundary. Everton mis-hit it, otherwise it would probably have gone into Queen Street. I waited an awfully long time for that ball to come down. I was used to fielding at square leg – I'd been there for a number of years. But that was a real pressure catch. If I'd dropped it, I'd have climbed over the fence and run into town. I don't remember many details about the match, but I'll never forget circling under that ball."

Another with special reason to remember the occasion was Guillen. "It was a really bad ball," says Guillen. "In fact, it almost bounced twice before it got to Everton, a real half-tracker. After Noel took the catch, everyone rushed up the pitch to congratulate Jack on his bowling. That was the ironic part. They should have been going over to pat Noel on the back. I looked over to Noel on the boundary and gave him a wave."

McGregor: "In those days, we didn't all slap each other on the back and gather round between wickets. After I'd taken the catch, I stayed on the boundary. It was nice to get that wave of congratulations and thanks from Sam."

There's always a bit of intrigue about leg-spinners. They tend to smile knowingly and do things most cricketers can't contemplate... the mystery of the googly and all that. When they get hit for four, they will nod as if it's all part of the grand plan. Alabaster won't quite concede he bowled a long hop at Eden Park. It was, he says, "on the shortish side, but hurried on to Weekes".

Reid smiles when he hears this. "I made three major tours with Jack, and he was a great bowler. Not only did he have the penetration of a leg-spinner, but he had unusual accuracy. He was superb in South Africa in 1961-62. I saw Jack bowl thousands of fine deliveries. That one to Weekes wasn't one of them. But then that's cricket. The luck has to go with you sometimes."

Weekes remarked later that he had charged forward, too eager for the kill: "Ah got the ball in the middle of the bat, man, but ah got it maybe three-four inches too high up the blade."

At tea the West Indies were 77-9. Dark clouds rolled towards Eden Park. It was not a time to mess about and eight balls after the resumption Guillen stumped Valentine off Cave. As Cave was about the pace of Ewen Chatfield or Dion Nash, it was not the sort of dismissal you would expect to see today when wicketkeepers opt far more often to stand back.

The match was tightly fought from the outset. New Zealand, batting first, struggled to 255. Fast bowler Tom Dewdney got plenty of life from the damp pitch and Collie Smith wheeled down 12 consecutive overs of maidens with his off-breaks. Only Reid and John Beck, who put on 101 for the fifth wicket, batted with any assurance. Reid's innings, which ended so unluckily, proved to be pivotal.

When the West Indies batted, Beard, MacGibbon and Reid bowled frugally, but Cave was the star of the show. MacGibbon, producing his best form of the summer, got rid of Weekes, the prize wicket, and also sent packing Sobers, Alfonso Roberts and Binns. Cave carried on the good work and the West Indies were bowled out for just 145, a startling turnaround in fortunes after the first three tests. It was the second lowest test score then made against New Zealand.

New Zealand began their second innings 100 minutes before stumps on the third day, with rain about. West Indian captain Atkinson began a superb spell of 40 overs which brought him 7-53. New Zealand plunged to 109-7 on the fifth morning and defeat loomed. Enter chirpy Sam Guillen.

"I was joined by Don Beard," Guillen recalls. "He came over and told me that the captain's instructions were to not get out. I had a good laugh about that. If I just stayed there, who was going to bat with me? I decided if the ball was within reach, I'd throw my bat. My first big scoring stroke was a 6 off Atkinson and I hit Valentine for a 6 over the scoreboard... "

Finally, Reid was able to declare at 157-9 and leave the West Indies four hours to score 268. Cave took command, bowling Bruce Pairaudeau, then MacGibbon took a brilliant slips catch that sent Furlonge on his way. The West Indies slumped to 22-6 and it was panic stations. Only Weekes stood between New Zealand victory. Enter the Alabaster/McGregor double act...

At the end of the game, there was a mad scramble for souvenirs. Guillen grabbed all three wickets and held onto the ball. "I gave one of the stumps to Murray Chapple, another to someone else and threw the ball to John Reid. That left me with one stump. Then Giff Vivian, one of the selectors, told me he had nothing to remember the game by. I gave him the one remaining stump and told him to keep it because the memory of the game would always be with me."

Before the match, New Zealand's test record was: played 44, drew 22, lost 22. Now it was: played 45, won 1, drew 22, lost 22. It may not seem such a notable change on paper, but the fact that a column was now required for wins meant everything to New Zealand cricket followers.

Afterwards the spectators massed below the stand. The New Zealanders emerged to cheers. Reid and Atkinson spoke. Reid, typically optimistic, said how proud he was and that he hoped it would be the first of many such victories now that New Zealand had finally broken their test duck. "We now have a team which should serve us well. It has team spirit and that is a great thing."

Atkinson, a wonderful sportsman in the truest sense of the word, said the New Zealand team was "the finest bunch of fellows we have ever played against".

Reid, a tee totaller, tasted his first champagne that afternoon. There were several highlights in his long career. He was a member of the famous Forty-Niners. He led New Zealand to South Africa in 1961-62 when the series was squared 2-2 and batted as well as anyone in the world. He smashed a world record of 15 6s in an innings one crazy day at the Basin Reserve. He captained a genuine World XI in 1965. As a batsman, his form in South Africa stands above anything else he did.

THE STAR, Friday, April 19, 1985

REPRODUCED COURTESY OF N.Z. HERALD. MARCH 14, 1956

FIRST TEST VICTORY IN N.Z. CRICKET

Excited Ovation for Reid's Team

By CANTAB

In a day of thrills, excitement and sensations, New Zealand gained the first victory in its test cricket history at Eden Park yesterday by defeating the West Indies by 190 runs.

It was a glorious day for New Zealand cricket, one which put the team back on the test map and one which will be of inestimable value to the game throughout the Dominion. There were rounds of cheers for the captain, J. R. Reid, and the New Zealand team as the crowd surged on the field at the end of play.

The victory was most popular and the first to offer their hearty congratulations were the West Indies players. There was little doubt that New Zealand thoroughly deserved to win and it was most refreshing that the side, after rather disappointing performances in the previous three tests, should come through with such honours on this occasion.

Neither the pitch nor the weather could be blamed for West Indies' failure. The pitch yesterday played well, the outfield was fast and generally there was bright sunshine. Actually the test proved probably the most popular and sporting yet played in New Zealand.

D. Atkinson, captain of the visiting team, over the loudspeaker at the ground in response to demands from the crowd, said that the West Indies never wished to play against a better sporting team or in front of a more sporting public than the New Zealanders.

Forcing the Pace

It was expected when play was resumed yesterday morning that the New Zealand batsmen would attempt to force the pace. In their efforts they were not too successful and at one stage six wickets were down for 101 and the side was far from out of the wood. All six wickets had been taken by Atkinson at a cost of 39 runs.

Incidentally, Atkinson bowled unchanged throughout New Zealand's second innings and in all sent down 40 overs, 21 maidens, for 53 runs and seven wickets. Always maintaining a good length, he varied his deliveries with A. Roberts in the Auckland match, when these batsmen were run out. Surprisingly for him, he mis-hit the leg-spinner J. C. Alabaster, and was caught on the mid-wicket boundary by S. N. McGregor. The fieldsman judged a high catch perfectly.

There was no doubt that the West Indies had the intentions of going for the runs. This was indicated when Atkinson went in first wicket down, but like others he fell to accurate bowling and closely set attacking field.

Again, too much praise cannot be bestowed on the New Zealand bowlers and fieldsmen who throughout the match did a remarkable job. Some splendid catches were taken which made all the difference.

The palm can be handed to Cave, who has always been most reliable and has done so much for the game in the Dominion. Like Atkinson, for West Indies, he was a great leader of the attack.

Splendid Bowling

In his first spell Cave bowled 11 overs, 8 maidens, for 17 runs and three wickets. His lifting and moving deliveries kept the batsmen on the alert and in the end his four wickets for 21 runs were a most pleasing reward for his great efforts.

Cave had excellent support. Beard, three for 22, MacGibbon and Alabaster. The last-named leg-spinners, although inclined a little short in length at times with two wickets in five overs, runs and also had the taking the wicket of Weekes.

So the story within an sac in its 40 tests land has Detail

The scramble for stumps.—Happy players making off with their mementoes of the match. From left are Reid, Chapple, Guillen, Beard, Taylor and Valentine.

SPECTATORS INVADE THE PITCH

When New Zealand cricket, shortly after 4 yesterday afternoon ended 26 years of striving by victory in a test match, thousands of Auckland thrilled as the players. Hundreds ... raced for the pitch. Hundreds ... New Zealand captain, J. R. ... warriors and joyfully wr... chanted. "Three ch...

"We want Reid," part

New Zealand Herald coverage of the first test win over the West Indies, in 1956, reproduced 29 years later as part of an advertisement.

NEW ZEALAND

First innings

SN McGregor c Smith b Dewdney	2
LSM Miller c Weekes b Valentine	47
AR MacGibbon b Smith	9
DD Taylor lbw Valentine	11
JR Reid hit wicket b Dewdney	84
JEF Beck c Sobers b Ramadhin	38
SC Guillen run out	6
ME Chapple c Atkinson b Dewdney	3
DD Beard c Binns b Dewdney	31
HB Cave c Smith b Dewdney	11
JC Alabaster not out	1
Extras: byes 7, leg byes 5	12
Total	255

Fall of wickets: 9, 45, 66, 87, 191, 203,205, 210, 250, 255.

Bowling	O	M	R	W
Dewdney	19.5	11	21	5
Atkinson	32	14	45	0
Valentine	41	20	46	2
Ramadhin	23	8	41	1
Smith	31	19	55	1
Sobers	20	7	35	0

Second innings

c Binns v Atkinson	5
c Weekes b Atkinson	25
c Weekes b Atkinson	35
c Valentine b Atkinson	16
c Binns b Atkinson	12
lbw Atkinson	2
st Binns b Valentine	41
lbw Ramadhin	1
not out	6
(11) not out	0
(10) b Atkinson	5
Extras: byes 4, leg byes 5	9
Total for 9 wickets dec	157

Fall of wickets: 14, 61, 66, 91, 100, 101, 109, 146, 155.

O	M	R	W
12	5	22	0
40	21	53	7
6	0	29	1
18	6	26	1
4	0	18	0

WEST INDIES

First innings

HA Furlonge c Guillen b Cave	64
BH Pairaudeau c MacGibbon b Cave	9
GS Sobers c Guillen b MacGibbon	1
ED Weekes c Guillen b MacGibbon	5
OG Smith b Beard	2
DS Atkinson b Reid	28
AT Roberts b MacGibbon	28
AP Binns lbw MacGibbon	0
S Ramadhin b Cave	3
AL Valentine c Taylor b Cave	0
DT Dewdney not out	0
Extras: byes 1, leg byes 3, no balls 1	5
Total	145

Fall of wickets: 25, 32, 46, 59, 94, 139, 140, 145, 145, 145.

Bowling	O	M	R	W
MacGibbon	21	5	44	4
Cave	27.3	17	22	4
Reid	18	5	48	1
Beard	9	4	20	1
Alabaster	3	1	6	0

Second innings

c MacGibbon b Beard	3
b Cave	3
(6) run out	1
c McGregor b Alabaster	31
b Cave	0
(3) c Chapple b Cave	10
b Beard	0
b Alabaster	20
c Miller b Beard	0
st Guillen b Cave	5
not out	4
Extras:	0
Total	77

Fall of wickets: 4, 16, 16, 16, 18, 22, 68, 68, 68, 77.

O	M	R	W
6	1	16	0
13.1	9	21	4
6	2	14	0
15	7	22	3
5	4	4	2

New Zealand won by 190 runs

But of his 246 first class matches, he nominates that victory at Eden Park as the most memorable, and March 13, 1956, as the greatest single day. "It was our first test win, and only my third test as captain. It was a truly magic moment."

They didn't go overboard in those days, not like they do now with wraparound newspaper supplements, victory parades and the rest. But, considering those restrained times, the media reaction was positively euphoric. Wellington's *Evening Post* called it "the greatest boilover in New Zealand's sporting history". Cantab (Charles Guiney) of the *New Zealand Herald* described the fifth day as one of "thrills, excitement and sensations". The boost to the New Zealand team's spirits with Reid's arrival as captain was likened to what Winston Churchill did for Britain when he became Prime Minister in 1940, and General Montgomery's effect on the 8th Army.

There were many heroes for New Zealand. The planning Reid and Wallace put into the game paid off. "For once," says Reid, "it wasn't us who bowled the one loose ball each over, or who dropped the vital catch. We were tighter than them." After some appalling fielding in the preceding three tests, not a catch was dropped in either West Indian innings. Wallace did a marvellous job with the inexperienced team. He offered some technical assistance (for instance, advising Reid to get off his heels and back onto the balls of his feet as he waited at the crease) and helped the team understand that if they played up to their ability they could compete with the West Indians.

Lawrie Miller scored 47 and 25 in a low-scoring match. MacGibbon took four wickets and scored 35 in the second innings. Beck's first innings 38 was invaluable. So was Don Beard's 31, plus match figures of 4-42 off 24 overs. Guillen kept well and contributed his crashing even-time 41. Alabaster grabbed 2-4 at the end to mop up the West Indies second innings. Cave was brilliant, moving the ball in late to the West Indians seeking to play attacking strokes. His match figures of 8-43 off 40.4 overs spoke volumes for his character. How many players, having lost the test captaincy, would offer their successor such whole-hearted support? But despite these performances, New Zealand's man of the match was Reid. He captained confidently and attacked when he could, he produced the top score of the match with his 84, including 11 boundaries, he bowled 24 tight overs and picked up the useful wicket of Atkinson. His 84 was his highest score in a home test to that point.

It was a team triumph, but it was the powerful young skipper who epitomised the new hope that the victory brought to New Zealand cricket.

As Reid walked off Eden Park that day, he had etched his name indelibly in the story of New Zealand cricket. All true sports followers know Roger Bannister was the first person to run a mile in under four minutes. How many can say who was second? Mt Everest is the highest mountain. What's the next highest? Barrie Devenport was the first person to swim Cook Strait. Who was the second? So it was that day at Eden Park.

A lot of fine New Zealand cricketers had preceded Reid. Players like Ernie Upham, Alex Downes, Daniel Reese and Syd Hiddleston never got the chance to even play test cricket. Others, such as Stewie Dempster, Roger Blunt, Tom Lowry, Jack Cowie and Martin Donnelly had retired before New Zealand ever got off the mark.

So, in a case of "Cometh the hour, cometh the man", it fell to 27-year-old John Reid to lead New Zealand into a new era. He was to captain New Zealand for the next decade. How the memory of that performance at Eden Park must have sustained him during some of the forgettable moments that were to follow.

~

JOHN REID'S VIEW
WEST INDIES – THE PLAYERS

Sir Frank Worrell: One of the three famous Ws of West Indian cricket, Worrell was a complete batsman, and very cultured, more of an artist than someone who bludgeoned the bowling. Rahul Dravid of modern players reminds me a little of Frank, though Frank had more flair. He was also a fine left-arm bowler – either pace or spin – and a good fieldsman.

Frank was an absolute gentleman. He once bailed me out of an awkward situation during my Central Lancashire league days in England. I needed to catch a boat to return home at a certain date and it meant I would have to miss the last league match I was committed to. I would either have to refund the club quite a substantial amount, or find an adequate replacement. Frank heard about my predicament and offered to fill in for me. I said that I could not afford to pay him the level he would expect, but he just laughed. He was happy to play for nothing except petrol money, as a favour to me. It was a marvellous gesture. Needless to say, the club was overjoyed to have Frank Worrell playing for it – he was the best pro in the league. Frank's death through leukaemia at the age of 42 was a tragedy for cricket, but he had made a contribution that lasted decades. He was the first black West Indian to captain the test team regularly, and the way he welded his team and kept them calm in times of crisis was inspiring. Frank led the West Indies in two memorable test series, against Australia in 1960-61 and against England in 1963. The exciting cricket in those series did much to revive a game that was struggling at the time.

Sir Everton Weekes: It is difficult to imagine any batsman able to murder bowling more brutally than Weekes, not even Vivian Richards in full flight. Everton had a fantastic array of great shots, but the thing that stood out was how hard he hit. Perhaps he was at his best smashing through the covers, but I can picture him punishing bowlers all around the wicket. Weekes had some incredible runs of scores. From 1947-49 he scored five successive test centuries and was run out for 90 in his next test innings. In New Zealand in 1956, he scored 940 runs at an average of 104. He tended to give an early chance, but if you didn't accept it, you were often made to pay heavily. Weekes, who was predominantly a back foot player, averaged 58.6 in his 81 test innings. For a batsman of his style, that is remarkable. Incidentally, Weekes was also a national representative bridge player, not something you'd expect when you watched him bat!

Sir Clyde Walcott: The third of the three Ws. He was the biggest of the three physically, and was the hardest driver of the ball. He loved to get onto the back foot and crash the ball through the covers. All three of the Ws were in the top bracket, right up there alongside a player like Peter May. Walcott was initially a wicketkeeper as well, then gave that up and bowled useful medium pace. But his batting was what set him apart. He averaged 56.6 in tests and against Australia in 1955 he scored five centuries in the series. I remember his brilliant batting in the Lancashire league while I was in England. One time, I played in a match against a West Indies XI at Colwyn Bay. I was on the extra cover boundary and Walcott kept driving the ball so hard off the back foot that if it was wide of me by more than about four metres, I couldn't get to it.

Clyde has also contributed greatly to West Indies cricket as an administrator over the years and is now carrying on after his chairmanship of the I.C.C. as chairman of the I.C.C. Cricket Committee, to which he brings a fund of cricket knowlege and wise and cooling counsel.

Sonny Ramadhin: For a long time he was a mystery to me. When he came to New Zealand in 1953, he gave me all sorts of problems. I was in the middle of a bad trot, and just couldn't pick him. I used to misread him regularly. I'd play for leg-spin and find out it was his offie. Sonny was a puzzle not only to me, but to many of the world's top batsmen of the time. He had a very wristy action, not unlike Sri Lankan spin wizard Muttiah Muralitharan, spun the ball a lot each way and was very difficult to pick.

He finally met his masters in England in 1957 when Peter May and Colin Cowdrey wore him down during a marathon partnership during the first test at Edgbaston. Ramadhin took 7-49 in the England first innings, and when he took two quick wickets in the second innings, it appeared he was about to bowl the West Indies to victory. Then during a 495-minute stand of 411, May and Cowdrey used their heads and, I expect, their pads, to such good effect that May scored 285 not out and Crowdrey 154. Ramadhin bowled 98 overs in that second innings, the most ever bowled in one innings of a test, and took 2-179. He was never quite the same force again. I was interested, when discussing the innings with May much later, to learn that they had played Sonny as an off-spinner, reasoning that the undetected leg-spinner would pass safely outside the edge of the bat to the wicketkeeper.

Independently I had also decided to play Sonny as an off-spinner. I came to be able to pick his leg-spinner, which was floated more. But he was difficult to read. He bowled with his sleeves down and with a dark ball, and his black hand and the arm coming over in a flurry, it was not easy for a batsman to feel comfortable. It wasn't until I played Ramadhin in league cricket in England that I really felt I'd got on top of him. Even then, I respected him as one of the great bowlers of world cricket.

Alf Valentine: Sonny Ramadhin's spin bowling partner. He was a prodigious left-arm spinner. He used to really uncoil. In this respect, his run-up was reminiscent of South African left-arm spinner Paul Adams, though his actual delivery was much more orthodox. Considering how much work Valentine put on the ball, he was fairly accurate and was a good foil for Ramadhin. It would be interesting to see them operating today. I have a feeling they would still cause batsmen a lot of problems.

Sir Garfield Sobers: New Zealanders didn't see the best of him. He was still a youngster when he toured in 1956, and was a shade past his best when he returned in 1969. However he did make 142 against New Zealand at Barbados in 1972 to help save his team from defeat, and he made a blazing 75 for Arthur Gilligan's XI against us at Hastings in 1958. They were glimpses of what we knew he could do. Gary must rate as the finest cricketer of his generation and I place him among my five best this century. How could I not? Not only did he average 57.7 with the bat, but he was a three-in-one bowler – whippy, medium-fast, orthodox left-arm finger spin and back-of-the-hand Chinaman and googly bowling. He was also a brilliant fieldsman anywhere. The amazing thing was that he always seemed as keen on his next round of golf or on finding out the result of the latest big horse race as he was on the cricket.

Wes Hall: One of the great figures of world cricket in the 1960s. Hall was a frightening sight. He came in off a run that seemed to begin just inside the boundary and, with the gold chain around his neck swinging ominously, had a fearsome delivery leap. He was probably the fastest bowler in the world in his prime, and had the ability to bowl for long periods. He adored Frank Worrell and really put in the work for him. In tandem, Hall and Charlie Griffith were a menacing duo, as quick and fierce as any pair in cricket history. I would rate Wes in the Glenn McGrath class for sheer pace, but with a much more frightening effect on the batsman. Though he was so intimidating on the field, Hall had a wonderful personality. He was always smiling, and was great fun in the dressing room, as I discovered in 1965 when I captained a Rest of the World XI that included him. He had a passion for horse racing and always seemed to be on to a sure winner.

Rohan Kanhai: I liked the way he played. Sobers was the great batsman in the West Indies sides of the 1960s, but Kanhai was barely his inferior. He was short in stature, played attractive shots all around the wicket and was always ready to chance his arm. No bowler dominated Kanhai for long. It would be hard to compare Rohan to any present-day New Zealand batsman, though Stewie Dempster, whom I saw only at the end of his career, had a touch of the same style about him. The closest to Rohan these days is Aravinda de Silva, another brilliant and consistent run-getter.

Rohan had a stint as West Indies test coach in the mid-1990s, but went the way of many test coaches these days. They tend to rise and fall, often very quickly, depending on their teams' results. Even when the failures cannot fairly be blamed on the coach, it is often the coach who is given his marching orders.

Clive Lloyd: Clive is these days the manager of the West Indies team for which he played 110 tests and 87 one-day internationals. He was their captain during the most successful period of their cricket history. Clive was also one of the early I.C.C. referees and carried out his duties with a commendable sense of responsibility.

Cricket followers will easily recall Lloyd as a tall, rangy, bespectacled hitter with an enviable record as a player (7515 test runs at 46.7, with 19 centuries). With 35 wins from his 74 tests as captain, he is the second most successful test skipper ever, after Allan Border. That's the story on paper. But what statistics don't tell you is that the M.C.C. was forced to bring in a new over-rate law – a minimum of 15 overs an hour – to speed up the game which had been brought almost to a standstill by Lloyd's deliberate policy of using his five fast bowlers at a rate of as few as eight overs an hour. This obviously restricted the opposition to a vastly reduced number of balls faced in a day's play, not much more than half the normal amount. The speedsters he had at his disposal (Roberts, Holding, Garner, Croft, Marshall and others) were devastating. Each bowler needed to bowl not much more than 12 or 13 overs in a day, so remained fresh and available all day. By comparison, opposing fast bowlers were getting through about 19 or 20 overs a day.

As I have said, Clive proved to be a good, effective referee, so I wonder how as a referee he would have handled the barging of New Zealand umpire Fred Goodall by Colin Croft merely because Croft didn't like a not out decision to a caught behind appeal against Richard Hadlee in Christchurch in 1980. He certainly didn't handle it well as a captain, remaining in his fielding position at first slip. This was clearly a Code 4 violation (intimidation and/or assault). And similarly, I wonder how Clive would have handled the situation where Michael Holding kicked over the stumps after an appeal for caught behind had been rejected in the test at Carisbrook. This action would have qualified for a Code 1 or 2 violation, where the captain is responsible for his team's on-field behaviour or any action that brings the game into disrepute. And how would Lloyd the referee have regarded the 20-minute extension of one tea break that the West Indies took while they considered whether they would abandon their tour and go home? This would have qualified for Code 1, 2 or possibly even 8 – captains responsible for the spirit in which the game is played, bringing the game into disrepute, no public detrimental comment about the game, tour, boards or competing teams.

I feel that Clive Lloyd the referee would, looking back, feel very embarrassed indeed. He would know that his captaincy merited a suspension and a big fine for each of the offences mentioned.

The other side of Clive Lloyd the referee was seen when he abandoned the semifinal match between India and Sri Lanka at the Calcutta Stadium in 1996 because of the unruly behaviour of the crowd, awarding the match to Sri Lanka by default. India at that point were eight wickets down and had virtually no chance of victory. Clive's was the correct decision, but was a brave one because at the time it was, strictly speaking, outside the authority of the referee.

Incidentally, I met Colin Croft in Barbados in 1994 when he was a part-time television commentator and a fulltime airline pilot based in Miami. We met in the middle while inspecting the pitch and he offered me an apology for his actions in that charging incident, which I'd watched from the sidelines.

Gordon Greenidge: My first meeting with this recently retired hero of the West Indies team was an awkward one. He was the coach of Bangladesh, who were playing in the I.C.C. Trophy tournament in Kuala Lumpur, and I was the only I.C.C. referee on show. This tournament was to decide which teams claimed the final three slots for the World Cup. The first nine teams were the test-playing countries and the other three places went to the top three finishers at the I.C.C. Trophy tournament.

Bangladesh had played five matches before I was appointed to one of their games. Like all the other teams, they seemed to have little knowledge of, or concern for, the I.C.C. Code of Conduct. As it happened, the Bangladesh opening bowler shouted for an lbw decision and continued his follow-through until he was face-to-face with the batsman, all the time dispensing his own version of words of wisdom. This is intimidation and sledging is certainly something I don't stand for, so I found the Bangladesh manager and asked him to send a drink out and get the bowler to calm down. It was just a warning. Then another Bangladesh official (I knew full well who it was) came up to me and asked me what the bowler had said. I replied that the body language told a story, that he wasn't saying "Well played", and that, by the way, "Who are you?" I informed him I talk only to the manager and captain. Well, I wasn't on Gordon's Christmas card list for a while, but we were speaking again during the 1999 World Cup, so all is well.

Perhaps my inquiry about Greenidge's identity was a little cheeky. After all, the man did play 108 test matches, score more than 7500 runs and hit 19 centuries. That's quite apart from 128 one-day internationals! I knew full well that Greenidge and Desmond Haynes had formed one of the great opening partnerships, but felt that his slightly impertinent inquiry into my understanding of foreign languages deserved a reply in kind.

Sir Vivian Richards: Richards was obviously one of the great batsmen of his time. He was powerful, athletic and confident and like Everton Weekes in that he could murder an attack. He really carved up the bowling and brought a hint of arrogance to his batting. For instance, he always disdained the use of a helmet. Richards would have stood out in any era.

Malcolm Marshall: When I was asked by the editor of *Wisden* to name my five Cricketers of the Century, I thought deeply about the great fast bowlers in history and eventually included Malcolm Marshall. I loved the way he really tore into his work. Chris Cairns once related some advice Marshall had given him, when he stressed the necessity of "attacking the bowling crease". I liked that phrase. It encapsulates what a good fast bowler must do. Marshall was always looking to make something happen. He was extremely fast – perhaps the quickest bowler in the world of his time – and always looked to take his wickets with skill. He pitched the ball up and employed lethal late in-swing. Marshall played 81 tests and took 376 wickets at under 21 apiece. I consider that to be an outstanding effort. He was part of a four or five-pronged West Indian pace attack which must have assisted him in one way – relentless pressure on the batsmen – but also meant that he got only so many opportunities to bowl. His strike rate of 46.7 balls per wicket is as good as virtually anything in test history and speaks volumes for his consistency and venom.

Like all cricket followers, I was shocked by his death at the age of 41, in 1999, after a short battle with cancer. For such a ferocious fast bowler on the field, Marshall was a genuinely lovely person off it, always eager to talk cricket and to help.

Courtney Walsh: You don't take more than 400 test wickets unless you know a thing or two about bowling. Walsh has been a very good bowler for the West Indies for 10 years. He can be quick, though probably not quite as quick as McGrath. He moves the ball away and his height gives him plenty of bounce. I'm sure he has been helped by the fact that for so long the West Indies fast bowlers have hunted in packs, and in his case his "pack partner" has been Curtly Ambrose. Walsh's longevity has impressed me. Most people would have expected his departure from the test scene in the mid-1990s, but he has managed to not only prolong his career, but remain as effective as ever.

Curtly Ambrose: As a fast bowler, he is a nasty customer. He has imposing height and uses it well to gain awkward lift. He tends to move the ball into the batsman, which only increases the batsman's discomfiture. It's no fun fending off delivery after delivery as it rockets towards the body. Cricket purists would have preferred to see Ambrose pitch the ball up more often, incorporating swing and seam, but it wasn't really his style, a pity as he owns a devastating yorker. In his prime, Ambrose was genuinely fast, certainly faster than Walsh. Though both were fine bowlers, I wouldn't place either in an all-time-best West Indies team – the competition is just too hot.

Brian Lara: He has to prove himself further. We all know he's brilliant, but he has to keep going if he is to end up ranked on the very top rung. I'm somewhat sceptical of his 501 against Durham in 1994. It was county cricket, and the standard can be pretty ordinary. But I saw his test 375 against England a couple of months earlier and that was a superb innings. He has a unique shot, taking a ball that is short of a length outside the off and sending it through square leg. Lara began his test career with a flourish, then faltered. I don't think he has handled the fame and the fortune particularly well. However, there were signs in 1999 that he had reapplied himself. His batting against Australia when his captaincy was under extreme pressure was brilliant. He was winning tests off his own bat. Lara is like Gary Sobers in that he has a high backlift and really goes for his shots. But Sobers maintained his standard over a very long career. That's the challenge for Lara.

8 | POST-WAR BLUES & BAGGY GREENS

In the first test match played after the Second World War, Australia thrashed New Zealand at the Basin Reserve by an innings and 103 runs. It was a most unfortunate result that was to have lasting repercussions for New Zealand cricket.

Australia's team included Bill Brown, Ken Meuleman, Sid Barnes, Keith Miller, Lindsay Hassett, Colin McCool, Ian Johnson, Don Tallon, Ray Lindwall, Ernie Toshack and Bill O'Reilly. All were fine cricketers and at least five of them would be serious contenders in any all-time Australian XI. Against them, New Zealand's team was missing two of their greatest batsmen, Martin Donnelly and Bert Sutcliffe, both of whom were still overseas in the forces. Six players made their test debut in the match and four of them – Len Butterfield, Don McRae, Gordon Rowe and Mac Anderson – never played another test. Don Cleverley was making his first test appearance in 14 years.

It shaped as an uneven battle. The condition of the pitch made it even more so. There had been heavy rain in the days beforehand and when the captains, Walter Hadlee and Bill Brown, inspected the wicket, they sensed a problem. "The pitch was unplayable," says Hadlee. "But Bill and I stood out in the middle and had a look around the ground at the big crowd that had gathered at the Basin. There had been no international cricket in New Zealand for seven years and we hadn't played a test for nine years. There was a thirst for cricket. We decided to have a strip cut alongside the original wicket, and use that."

The next problem was deciding what to do on winning the toss. Hadlee, who did not have a great record as a tosser, won one that he would have preferred to have lost and chose to bat, sensing that, bad as the wicket was, it was bound to deteriorate further.

What followed was a debacle. Only Verdun Scott (14) and Merv Wallace (10) reached double figures and New Zealand was bowled out for 42. O'Reilly, playing his final test, took 5-14 and Toshack, who bowled throughout, 4-12 from 19 overs. The Australians struggled, too, but by stumps were 146-3.

The match finished on the second day in front of 20,000 spectators, including 17-year-old John Reid. Australia progressed to 199-8 before declaring. Jack Cowie confirmed his world class status by finishing the Australian innings with 6-40. Cricket followers wondered how the Australian batsmen would have enjoyed facing Lindwall, Toshack, Miller, O'Reilly and company.

New Zealand, in their second innings, were bowled out for 54, with Wallace again (14) and Eric Tindill (13) the only batsmen to reach double figures. The match was all over in well under nine hours.

While there was no doubt the Australians were a very powerful combination, to be supplemented the following season by the return of Don Bradman and the emergence of Arthur Morris, New Zealand was not as weak as the result made them appear. Within three years, with Donnelly, Sutcliffe and John Reid in the team, the batting was world class, and Tom Burtt's left-arm spin greatly enhanced the attack. But this didn't matter. That result was to hang over New Zealand cricket for decades.

"During the 1950s and '60s," says Reid, "the Australian Cricket Board seemed to decide their trans-Tasman cousins were not good enough to warrant playing test matches. They were able to point to that one lop-sided result from 1946. During the whole of my career of 58 test matches, I did not play one official test against Australia. Not one test in 17 years – pathetic! We were certainly capable of meeting them on competitive terms as we showed several times when they sent over various 'B' team combinations. In hindsight, the Australian attitude must be categorised as patronising. Their teams might have been labelled 'B' teams, but the players wore Australian Cricket Board blazers!

"What's interesting is that they were not backward in sending over their top players, plus a smattering of youngsters, to get experience in conditions that would be very similar to what would be encountered in England."

The first "unofficial" Australian team after the war toured New Zealand in 1950 and played 14 matches, including one "test". The Australians clearly regarded it as an opportunity to groom some of their promising players by having their tour with a group of experienced veterans. So Bill Brown captained a team which included Doug Ring and Don Tallon, all three of whom had toured England under Don Bradman in 1948. In addition, players such as Alan Davidson, Jack Iverson and Jim Burke, who were to play important roles in coming Ashes campaigns, were included.

Reid encountered the Australians three times and batted well twice. For Hutt Valley, he smashed 61 at a run a minute, and for Wellington he contributed a first innings 74 when the next highest score was 14. In the "test", New Zealand, 231 and 76-9, just held out for a draw against Australia's 299. Reid's scores were 8 and 1, though he did take 2-39 from his 28 overs.

This match seemed to cement Australian feelings towards New Zealand cricket and though in the first decade after the war, Australia played test series against India, England, South Africa, the West Indies and Pakistan, New Zealand was not put back on the test schedule.

An Australian "B" side, captained by Ian Craig, next visited New Zealand in 1957. With players of the stature of Neil Harvey, Peter Burge, Bobby Simpson, Richie Benaud, Les Favell, Barry Jarman, Norman O'Neill, Johnny Martin, Ian Meckiff and Lindsay Kline, it was farcical to call it an unofficial Australian team. "A real slap in the face," says Reid.

The *New Zealand Cricket Almanack*, normally very under-stated on such issues, noted: "Eager to prove that their new-found success in the test arena was no flash in the pan, New Zealanders were greatly disappointed when it was announced that Australia's three fixtures against New Zealand was to be labelled merely as 'unofficial' tests, and much advance interest in a team from overseas evaporated. New Zealanders felt that Australian cricket must be at a very low ebb indeed if its assessment of its strength feared to risk a trial of strength with New Zealand at official test level. Interest livened somewhat when the composition of the team was published and it was seen that Australia was in fact sending practically its strongest available selection."

The pity of the Australian snub was that New Zealand was fielding a competent side just then. With Merv Wallace still coaching the team, and Reid establishing himself as a forceful captain, and buoyed by the test win over the West Indies the season before, New Zealand took on the strong Australian team with some conviction.

Three matches were played in the series. The first two were drawn with honours even, and the third was won handsomely by Australia. In hindsight, the results were about on a par with those achieved by Peter May's much-vaunted England side in Australia in 1958-59, against much the same group of Australians.

In the first test, at Christchurch, Harry Cave bowled superbly in the first innings and Australia was tumbled out for just 216. In reply all the New Zealand batsmen made a start, though only Reid (58) managed a half-century. New Zealand finished with a lead of 52. Ian Craig and Neil Harvey batted well for Australia in the second innings, but the match petered out on the last afternoon.

"I was disappointed with the Australian attitude in that match," says Reid. "Craig delayed the declaration on the last afternoon for so long that we were left to score 233 in 138 minutes. In today's conditions, that would be an asking rate of just about seven runs an over – very generous! But back then, when there was no daily minimum for overs bowled, they could have slowed it down as much as they wanted. They were happy to play for a draw."

The second test, at Wellington, followed similar lines, with Blair and Cave bowling out Australia for 215 and New Zealand, courtesy of a Bert Sutcliffe century, reaching 249, a lead of 34. "That was a lovely innings by Bert. With Neil Harvey in the opposition, there was interest in comparing the two famous left-handed batsmen. Harvey had sparkling footwork, but he did not have Bert's graceful style. It was an indication that Bert belonged in the top rung of world batsmen." Unfortunately poor weather cut into the three days allotted for the match. By stumps, Cave had taken five wickets and Australia were 146-6. It was a moral victory for New Zealand.

Only in the third test did Australia get on top. The New Zealanders were caught on a lively wicket in their first innings and never got back into the match, with Reid providing the only half-century by a New Zealander. It was interesting that in an interview at the end of the tour, Craig said New Zealand was "handicapped by an inferiority complex". In fact, Reid and his team-mates had shown they could compete with Australia, but the Australian Cricket Board would not acknowledge the fact.

It wasn't just New Zealanders who felt the situation was unfair. Richie Benaud, in *On Reflection*, describes the Australian attitude as "baffling".

"New Zealand, just over the water, was not only ignored for many years," wrote Benaud, "it were insulted by not being offered the chance to play test cricket with Australia. It was a travesty that we were not prepared, because of the thought of losing money on a tour, to have a New Zealand team in Australia for a test series until 1973.

"The first time I properly watched a New Zealand test cricketer in action was in 1957 when Ian Craig's team played three representative matches and other games against Plunket Shield sides. No tests! That was eight years after I had made my debut in first class cricket in Australia. These days there is a cry that there is too much test cricket played between countries. You could certainly never use that as an excuse in those days when tours came along just often enough for the amateur administrators and players to cope. Australia was never allowed to see cricketers such as Sutcliffe, Reid, Donnelly and Richard Hadlee's father, Walter, in action on a full-scale tour. Our administrators gave them the occasional crumb, with a New Zealand team returning from another tour being permitted to play some matches against the Australian southern states, but it was poor fare for everyone."

Benaud pointed out it took New Zealand 27 years after that test in 1946 before Australia would grant another official test. "Can you believe it? New Zealand's administrators were far from blameless in allowing Australia to get away with it for so long. Their reaction was their players were not good enough and they should wait their time. My reaction then, and it is now, is that this 'wet' approach held back New Zealand cricket to a ridiculous degree. Had their cricket officials stood up for their players as they should have done, the upsurge in New Zealand cricket could have come in 1960, not 1980."

Another "crumb", as Benaud termed it, came New Zealand's way in 1960 when Ian Craig again led an unofficial Australian team on tour in New Zealand. "The team was again filled with test players and tour prospects," says Reid. "Besides Craig, there was Bobby Simpson, Brian Booth, Grahame Thomas, Len Maddocks, Johnny Martin, Ron Gaunt, Frank Misson and Keith Slater – a lot of players the Australians were keen to see tested in our conditions with a tour of England to take place a few months later. Bobby Simpson was the batting star in that team. He came to

New Zealand with a fantastic average from the Australian season – 902 runs at 300.66! We lowered the average a little, but he still averaged nearly 70 for the four internationals."

The big news of this four-match series was the emergence of 19-year-old Blenheim fast bowler Gary Bartlett, who remains the fastest bowler produced by New Zealand. In the first test, Bartlett upset the Australians' equilibrium, taking six wickets, and he remained a menace throughout the series. For once, it was New Zealand that held the big gun. Bartlett gave Craig, in particular, a terrible time, dismissing him the first five times he batted in the "tests". "Bartlett's bowling was a great morale-booster for a New Zealand captain," says Reid. "Yet more than that, the effect of Gary's bowling on the New Zealand team as a whole was noticeable. Invariably it had been our batsmen ducking and diving at bowling from overseas speedsters. Now things had turned around."

Reid smiles when he recalls the Australians' reaction to Bartlett's hostility. "None of them was comfortable. He had Ian Craig weaving away and ducking uncomfortably. Even Simpson, their best player, didn't always look settled. At Wellington, in the first international, Len Maddocks, batting at No 7, was distinctly unhappy. After hurrying one off his nose for a single, he ran straight up to Bartlett to deliver his 'message'. 'Be careful, sonny. Don't start something you can't finish,' he said. I was close by and told Maddocks that he was batting at No 7 and that that was a batsman's spot and one which certainly did not warrant protection under the gentlemen's no-bouncer agreement for lower-order batsmen.

"Ian Craig used different tactics. Craig, suave and cool, showed vast concern for Bartlett's welfare. He suggested the teenager was in danger of being over-bowled and what a tragedy this would be for such a promising prospect. Why not leave him out of the third 'test'?, Craig suggested. We did not act on Craig's advice!"

It was just after the end of this tour that word reached New Zealand that Gary Bartlett was a "chucker" – that he threw. "I've heard this suggestion repeated over the years, often from Australians of that period," says Reid. "They should know, I suppose, because their teams included players like Jim Burke and Ian Meckiff, with dubious actions. I noticed that the Australian Cricket Board had no problem including such bowlers in their teams.

"I was on the receiving end of various chuckers over the years, including Geoff Griffin of Rhodesia and South Africa, and Meckiff. It is reasonably easy to pick a chucker when you are batting as you find yourself looking at the wrong area to pick up the ball. The batsman is looking at the arm's full extended height at the moment of delivery. If the ball is thrown, the batsman struggles to pick it up because such balls are delivered from ear height. I faced Gary Bartlett and he certainly surprised me with his pace as he whistled the ball past my nose. I did not have a problem picking up the ball, though."

As in 1957, New Zealand again acquitted itself well. In the first match, at

Wellington, Reid hit an unbeaten 73 to lift New Zealand to 229 and then Bartlett's 5-51 rocked the Australians, who were dismissed for 201. New Zealand made 193 in their second innings, leaving the Australians requiring 222 runs at a run a minute. They were in trouble at the close – 201-7.

The Australians were even closer to defeat in the second match, at Christchurch. Sutcliffe (108), Reid (57) and John Sparling (54) all batted well and New Zealand reached 374. In reply, Australia crumbled in the face of good bowling by Bartlett, Dick Motz and Reid and were all out for 256, a deficit of 118. New Zealand chased quick runs in their second innings and Reid left them 262 to make in even time. By the close they were in panic stations – 211-8. Incidentally, when Simpson was dismissed for 17 in the first innings, it ended a run of nine consecutive scores over 50. The world record at the time was 10.

It is interesting comparing Reid's declaration with Craig's on the previous tour. Reid left Australia needing to score at just under four runs an over for victory, which typified the attacking way he liked to play his cricket. Even on the international stage, he tended to seek victory rather than try to avoid defeat. The same could not be said for many other test captains.

Australia came back in the final two tests, winning the third by eight wickets and having the better of a draw in the fourth. But overall, it could not be said that Australia was the dominant side.

Australian journalist Phil Tressider wrote: "The New Zealand test team surprised the touring Australians by its high standard. It is a sad thought that such fine players as John Reid and Bert Sutcliffe have not appeared in a test at the Sydney Cricket Ground, just three and a half hours' flying time from Auckland. A New Zealand visit should be a must for Australian cricket legislators."

Reid's view: "In the two series, we were by no means disgraced against what were virtually the full Australian test teams. I think we proved our point. When New Zealand finally resumed playing official tests against Australia in 1973, it was very satisfying for me to see New Zealand quickly match Australia. We would have won in Sydney that season, but for losing two days to bad weather, and on the return tour a couple of months later beat them in Christchurch. It was a victory which put a smile on the faces of a generation of cricketers who felt a wrong had finally been righted."

~

JOHN REID'S VIEW
AUSTRALIA – THE PLAYERS

Neil Harvey: I put him in the same bracket as Bert Sutcliffe. As a stylist, he fell between Bert and Martin Donnelly. He is way up near the top of Australia's best batsmen, on the same level as Greg Chappell. By the age of 21, he had scored five test centuries and was averaging 120, and Aussie cricket lovers were labelling him the next Bradman, which is a tough tag to live up to. Yet throughout his long career, Neil was consistently successful and batted attractively. His footwork to spinners was his trademark. Neil was extremely fast between the wickets and was a superb fieldsman anywhere.

Richie Benaud: The complete cricketer. He was a great fieldsman and a handy, aggressive batsman, but it was his bowling which lifted him. He was an excellent bowler who developed the flipper and the wrong 'un. He had excellent variety and, even though he didn't turn the ball a lot, was difficult to play. Richie bowled at about Anil Kumble's pace, but used more variety. He was an outstanding captain who always had his players under control. Richie was captain of the Ron Roberts Cavaliers in Southern Africa in 1963. The team included three international captains at the time – Ted Dexter, Richie and me – and other world-famous players such as Graham McKenzie, Arthur Morris, Bill Alley, Norman O'Neill, Bill Edrich and Micky Stewart. We had a fairly easy five-week tour and, cricket being cricket, each of the so-called stars happened to perform well on different days. At the end of the tour, we were returned to our various homes around the world. My flight was to leave at the unearthly hour of 5am. But there in the hotel foyer was our captain, with a bottle of champagne on hand to wish me bon voyage. It just wouldn't happen today!

I always got the impression Richie thought a lot about his cricket. He did his preparation as a captain, and that same trait has shone through in his commentaries. As a referee, I see quite a bit of Richie and find him to be the pick of television commentators. He doesn't state the obvious, when it is on the television for all to see, and expands on his fund of knowledge and experience for the viewers' benefit.

Alan Davidson: I have particularly fond memories of Alan because I got some runs for Hutt Valley against him in 1950. I remember putting Jack Iverson onto the top of the pavilion that day. Jack was the Australian mystery bowler who used his middle finger to flick and turn the ball either way. At the age of 21, I didn't know that so just played him as an off-spinner who should end up in "cow shot corner" – long on. Davidson took all 10 in an innings against Wairarapa on that tour, and made a century on the same day, and that takes some doing in any grade of cricket. He was a classic left-armer who moved the ball dramatically. He was pretty nippy, perhaps the same pace as Richard Collinge, but did a lot more with the ball. Added to that he was an explosive batsman and, like so many Australians, a great fieldsman.

Bobby Simpson: A very good player of all sorts of bowling. He made a couple of trips to New Zealand in the late 1950s. On one occasion he tried to con me about Gary Bartlett throwing, but I took that as an indication that Bartlett had the Aussies worried with his extreme pace. Bobby introduced the technique of swaying away to the leg when facing a bouncer. It is not to be recommended, though it suited him. Besides his batting, Simpson was a useful leg-spinner and a great slip, as good at least as Mark Taylor. As a batsman he was better than Taylor and perhaps just below Hutton. He was certainly one of Australia's best. He made a huge difference when he took over as coach of the Australian side, turning them from a group of strugglers into the best team in the world.

I have had a lot of contact with Bobby in recent years, and not just when he was Australian coach. He was an I.C.C. referee briefly, before stepping down when he began helping to coach the Indian team, and is a fellow member of the I.C.C.'s advisory panel on illegal deliveries. We also share an interest in the outcome of replacement knee operations, but on that subject I lead him 2-1 at present!

Ian Chappell: I suppose he was a captain of his times. I admired his fighting qualities and the way he was always ready to take the battle to the opposition. He always sought to dominate at the crease, and hooked and cut bravely and effectively. I was not a fan of many of his actions as a skipper and believe he had a detrimental effect on the standard of behaviour at top-level cricket. I was there when he abused Glenn Turner while captaining Australia at Lancaster Park in 1974, and it was not the sort of thing I feel enhances cricket. However, as I say, perhaps he was typical of his era. He arrived at a time of rebellion, when people were becoming much more questioning of authority, and he fitted that mould.

Dennis Lillee: This legendary Australian fast bowler came into my cricket sphere when he toured New Zealand in 1977 and I was a test selector. As he always did, Lillee bowled magnificently in that series – he was hostile, strong and a constant menace to the batsman. He certainly gave our best batsman of that time, Glenn Turner, a good working over. I recall Glenn trying not to look upset by the frequency of the short-pitched deliveries. Australia won that series 1-0, and Lillee was undoubtedly the Australian trump card. Lillee had genuine pace, but was more than just a tearaway bowler. He was in the mould of Ray Lindwall and Fred Trueman – all fast bowlers who were master craftsmen.

It is a pity, therefore, that my outstanding memory of him is of his contretemps with Javed Miandad at Perth in 1982, when Lillee kicked at Miandad and Miandad went after Lillee with his bat. Lillee played a large part in ensuring that I.C.C. referees were appointed. It is a fine thing being a macho fast bowler, but a semblance of self-control is essential. Perhaps I can sum up my feelings by saying I admired his bowling more than his behaviour.

Greg Chappell: One of the finest batsmen Australia has produced. Like all class players, he always seemed to have time to play his strokes. He stood tall at the crease, making good use of his height and had an array of shots all around the wicket, with his driving being outstanding. Chappell is notorious, particularly in New Zealand, for the underarm incident, and it is something he will have to live with for the rest of his life. A lot has been said about the incident, and will be in the future, as it was one of the most glaring examples of poor sportsmanship that has taken place in cricket. Even the respective countries' Prime Ministers got into the act, Rob Muldoon famously stating that it was appropriate the Australians were wearing yellow.

I have read that Chappell regrets instructing his brother Trevor to bowl that ball, but it wasn't a heat of the moment act. It was more calculating and cold-blooded than that. He even took no notice of his wicketkeeper and long-time colleague Rod Marsh, who could see what was about to happen and was waving his arms about to indicate his disagreement with the plan. I hope I never see such an act again anywhere in the sports arena.

I said in an interview with an Indian journalist some years ago when asked about sledging and my obligations as an I.C.C. referee under the Code of Conduct that the Chappell brothers had a lot to answer for in that regard. Both Ian and Greg declined to stop – and even seemed to encourage – some of the players they captained to sledge, terming it "gamesmanship". In these cases, under the Code of Conduct, the captain is at all times responsible for his team's actions. Both the Chappells have since tackled me about that interview. They felt my comments were unnecessary and critical, but I was on the sideline and saw the Chappells in action. It was unsavoury stuff.

Steve Rixon: I include Rixon here not because of the record he built in a 13-test career for Australia, but because he is of particular interest to New Zealanders. From 1996-99 he was the New Zealand team coach. During one of our infrequent chats, Rixon reminded me that contrary to what I had thought, we had previously met. He was the wicketkeeper for Kim Hughes' rebel Australians who visited South Africa during the mid-1980s. I was coach/manager of Northern Transvaal and later manager of the South African team for one "test" against the Australians at Johannesburg in 1985-86.

I was somewhat sceptical of a former Australian keeper being appointed to coach the New Zealand side, even though I was aware of his solid reputation as a coach of the New South Wales Sheffield Shield side. It must be remembered that New South Wales probably has a lot more talent available than the whole of New Zealand. Rixon had a difficult task when he took on the New Zealand job. Former coach Glenn Turner and manager Gren Alabaster had left their jobs under a cloud, the team lacked discipline on and off the field (which Turner had tried to correct) and there was a new broom in action cleaning up the mess that was New Zealand Cricket. The chairman, Peter McDermott, and the Chief Executive Officer, Graham

Dowling, had departed rather suddenly, and Rod Fulton, another New Zealand Cricket official, was pushed out. So that meant five people in top management had gone.

Rixon's three-year stint ended on a high note after New Zealand made the World Cup semifinals in 1999 and followed that by beating England 2-1 in a test series in England. I was thrilled for Rixon and the team, but do feel Rixon was a little fortunate. I have taken a close interest in the progress of the New Zealand team since returning from South Africa in 1992, and frankly have found very little improvement in players' techniques, despite the assortment of coaches and technical coaches employed by New Zealand Cricket.

I see the players making the same mistakes year after year. Surely we should be able to see some improvement. In fact, we should demand it. If it's not apparent, the coaches should be sacked. Rixon worried me when he was making his demands and criticism of players in the media. I can only hope that he was repeating those views to the players in the dressing room, where they should have stayed.

Allan Border: Two hours after my youngest grandchild, Angus John Reid (son of Richard and Debbie), was born in Wellington in 1993, he had a bat – of appropriate size! – tucked into his cot and autographed by Allan. We had been celebrating Gus' birth nearby during a brief visit to Wellington by the Australian captain and thought the autograph on that bat would be something the little fellow could look up to.

I did not see terribly much of Border's career because I was living in South Africa at the time, but I followed his fortunes on television. In conjunction with Bobby Simpson, Allan rejuvenated the Australian team and transformed them from a bunch of struggling individuals into the outstanding unit we see today. Border must get a lot of credit for that, the more so as for the first few years he did not seem especially keen to captain the side.

Border was a very astute left-handed batsman and captain. To score 11,174 runs and to average a tick over 50 an innings through 156 test matches is an indication of a sound technique and a good temperament. But I had a slight caveat next to his batting. To bat so often down at No 5 or 6 in the order and arrive at the wicket after the heat had passed meant that to me he did not rate in the same bracket as some of his predecessors, including Hassett, Harvey and Greg Chappell, quite apart from Bradman.

As a captain, he had an enviable record, and you cannot quibble with the results. He would possibly run into trouble with today's new era of refereeing as he was not backward in expressing his likes and dislikes in true Aussie style about umpiring decisions, opponents' heritage and officials in general.

Allan has now moved into the coaching area, temporarily succeeding Geoff Marsh as Australian team coach in 1999. If he continues in the coaching arena, I'm sure he will be aware of the presence these days of the I.C.C. referee, and of the need to exercise his best diplomatic skills, which were rather rusty during his later playing days.

Ian Healy: In my time as an I.C.C. referee, I have had occasion to talk to many of the world's leading wicketkeepers – Moin Kahn of Pakistan ("Just supporting the bowler, sir"), Nayan Mongia of India for standing permanently outside leg stump and for intimidation, Romesh Kaluwitharana of Sri Lanka for charging the umpire for a decision, and Ian Healy of Australia for intimidation, sledging and dissent. It is probably just as well that I do not referee any New Zealand matches as Adam Parore could be another wicketkeeper I might have occasion to chat to.

Healy was an excellent keeper and he and Shane Warne formed a formidable combination. But Healy did lose his rag too easily on some occasions, which I believe led to his demotion from the Australian vice-captaincy after he incurred a two-match suspension from referee Raman Subba Row. I have trouble understanding the purpose behind players losing their on-field discipline, especially over umpires' decisions, because I have never known an umpire to change his mind just because of player abuse. A class player like Healy, who holds the world test record for dismissals by a wicketkeeper, should have been looking to set an example with his good behaviour, not incur officials' wrath because he could not control himself.

Glenn McGrath: I rate him very highly as a fast bowler. He moves the ball both ways, which is unsettling for a batsman, and has genuine pace. Like many of the leading bowlers these days, he has a good change of pace. He should become a worthy member of test cricket's 300-wicket club. It's a pity he sometimes gets lippy out in the middle. He doesn't need to try to portray that macho image. A fast bowler can be aggressive without that and off the field, Glenn is a fine team man and an agreeable companion.

Shane Warne: In 1999, I was asked by the editor of *Wisden* to nominate my five Players of the Century. He had sought the opinions of 100 cricket followers around the world and wanted to then be able to publish *Wisden*'s five Cricketers of the Century. It was a very difficult task. I included Bradman, Sobers and Hobbs, as most people would, and then had to find two more from my short list of about 15. Eventually I went for Malcolm Marshall, a magnificent fast bowler, and Shane Warne. There is no doubt that Warne has been one of the most influential figures in cricket history. He has virtually single-handedly re-introduced the art of leg-spin bowling at test level. You can see his influence everywhere, especially in the number of children now able to bowl leg-spin. In that respect he has been very positive for cricket. Before his shoulder injury I felt he had the potential to be the best leg-spinner in history. After his operation he struggled more, though he still turned in two terrific performances when it counted at the 1999 World Cup.

Warne has incredible variety in his bowling. He has the quick top-spinner, the big leg-spinner, the wrong 'un, and he really spins the ball viciously. On top of that, he is amazingly accurate. Unfortunately, I am not a fan of his attitude. Because of his fame, he has become a role model for a generation of youngsters and I am unhappy with the example he sets. He is too brash and brazen for my liking. This may become a problem for him. Because of his many sponsorships, he will have to be careful not to tarnish his image.

Steve Waugh: One of the most solid batsmen in the world. What I like about his batting is that he scores so many of his runs in critical situations. He has all the shots and bats well under pressure. He has a belligerent attitude to bowlers and can play some magnificent strokes. He gets his body in position and hits the ball off the back foot. I don't regard him as the most natural of players, but he has worked hard at his game and has a fine temperament. We saw that in 1999 when he became Australian captain. He batted gallantly in the West Indies and then it was his batting which did so much to rescue a seemingly lost cause for Australia at the World Cup. He is now one of the best team captains that a referee has to deal with.

Mark Waugh: Though Mark and Steve Waugh are twins, they are entirely different guys. Mark is a magnificent strokeplayer, but is not as consistent as his brother. He seems to have oodles of time to play his shots and is a beautiful player off his pads. He is a natural who opens the batting in one-day internationals and can win a game by himself. In addition, he is an excellent fieldsman, especially in the slips.

9 | BUTCHER OF THE BASIN

When John Reid was a fresh-faced youngster, just out of Hutt Valley High School, he was practising with the Wellington Plunket Shield squad in the Basin Reserve nets. Reid, still a boy in age but a man in physical stature, was having a great old time of it, picking up the Wellington bowlers and smashing them over square leg and into the playground beside the grandstand.

Stewie Dempster, one of the great figures of New Zealand cricket, was overseeing the practice. Dempster was at that time the best batsman ever produced by New Zealand. Some say Dempster, with his test batting average of 65.7, still deserves that honour. By 1947, he was well past his prime as a batsman. But he had returned from more than a decade of living in England and was involved again in Wellington cricket.

"Hey," said Dempster to the young Reid. "Don't think that's a good shot. It's out. Every time you hit the ball in the air like that, you'd be dismissed if it was a match." It was the same sort of advice that coaches all over the world give to youngsters in the nets. Keep the ball on the ground.

However, though Dempster didn't realise it at the time, Reid was an exception. He had the strength, the technique and the adventurous spirit that enabled him to be a regular smiter of 6s throughout his career. As a schoolboy he had inspired awe among his team-mates and young opponents by lifting the ball clean out of the park and into the faraway trees. It was power that was virtually unheard of at college level. Reid retained his interest in 6-hitting right through until his retirement from the first class game in 1965.

During his last overseas tour as a player, he smashed four 6s in 10 balls on the first morning of the test match at Calcutta. In South Africa in 1962, Reid was 96 not out overnight against Natal. The next morning, South African speedster Neil Adcock opened the bowling. His first ball was a half-volley on leg stick. Reid drop-kicked it over the mid-wicket boundary to raise his century. It typified Reid's attitude to batting. If the shot is on: go for it.

Nineteen times during his career he hit three or more 6s in an innings. With Reid, even mis-hits sometimes carried the boundary. He hit the ball as hard as Lance Cairns of a later generation, but whereas Cairns was a lower-order batsman whose hit and hope tactics came off occasionally, Reid was a cultured, stylish player who was regarded as among the best straight-out batsmen in the world in his era.

Of all the big-hitting displays Reid turned on, nothing came close to his innings of 296 – his highest score in first class cricket – against Northern Districts at the Basin Reserve on January 15, 1963. Reid hit a world record of 15 6s that day, quite apart from the matter of 35 4s. For 220 minutes he electrified the crowd with the most glorious display of power hitting imaginable.

In discussing the innings, a couple of factors must be mentioned immediately. This was not a case of a batsman striking form on a postage stamp of a ground and lifting the ball just over the ropes. The Basin Reserve was one of the biggest specialist cricket grounds in New Zealand, with much longer boundaries than on provincial grounds like Cook's Gardens in Wanganui and Pukekura Park in New Plymouth. And Reid's 6s didn't just clear the boundary. Some of them ended up along Adelaide Road, or down Cambridge Terrace.

The second point is that the Northern Districts attack, while not possessing the firepower of Tyson, Trueman, Lock and Laker, was not a bad one. Northern Districts were led that season led by former West Indian test player Bruce Pairaudeau and their squad included past or future New Zealand representatives Bert Sutcliffe, Don Beard, Gren Alabaster, Wynne Bradburn, Brian Dunning, Eric Petrie and Tom Puna. They went on to win the Plunket Shield in 1963, their reverse against Wellington in this match being their only defeat of the season. They had big Don Clarke, a good lively fast-medium bowler, opening the attack. Clarke won sports fame as a great rugby fullback, but he was a good cricketer who weeks earlier had taken 8-37 in the second innings against Central Districts. Two off-spin bowlers, Puna and Alabaster, both of whom were later to represent New Zealand, were meant to provide the bulk of the Northern Districts overs. Peter Barton was the promising swing bowler while Peter McGregor and Terry Shaw were there to fill in where required. It was a solid provincial attack, and Reid butchered it.

On the first day, there was no hint of the pyrotechnics to follow. ND were bowled out for 226 and Wellington limped to 49-2 by stumps. Just before the close Reid arrived at the crease, and when stumps were drawn he had not opened his account.

By lunchtime the following day, Reid had turned the game into a one-man exhibition. Paul Barton was the next highest scorer for Wellington, and he contributed just 24. But no one noticed Barton, or Bruce Murray, Grahame Bilby, Barry Sinclair and Artie Dick, the other test batsmen in the Wellington lineup. In the 140 minutes to lunch, Wellington added 227, of which Reid smashed 174. It was suggested later that this was the record score by a batsman before lunch. The ND bowlers seemed to be shuffling about, trying not to make eye contact with Pairaudeau.

At lunchtime, Pairaudeau looked shell-shocked. As a former West Indian vice-captain, he was a fine forcing player. During the West Indies' 1957 tour of England, he had watched the famous three Ws – Everton Weekes, Frank Worrell and Clyde Walcott – at their devastating best. "I watched the three Ws murder attacks all over the world. Nothing they did ever approached what Reid is doing," said Pairaudeau. "This is the greatest display of hitting I've ever seen. No one has ever torn an attack apart like this."

One of the delighted spectators that day was Don Neely, who soon after was to succeed Reid as Wellington Plunket Shield captain and who later became a long-serving national selector. "It was carnage," Neely recalls. "Wellington hadn't had a great season, and Northern Districts was leading the Plunket Shield table. The innings was a shock in that respect, though with Reid that sort of hitting was always a possibility."

The *Evening Post* the next day reported the case of the elderly (at least, it's presumed he was elderly) gentleman arriving at the ground in mid-afternoon, just in time to watch Reid being caught on the boundary. "Typical Reid. Bull at a gate and out he goes!" was the irritated spectator's reaction. Hopefully he was soon made to realise what a fabulous display of strokeplay he had missed.

In modern parlance, the ND bowlers certainly took some stick. Clarke conceded 82 runs off 27 overs, Barton 69 off 13, McGregor 74 off 17, Puna 82 off 21, Alabaster 55 off 15 and Shaw 49 off 8. They are the sorts of runs per over rates one-day bowlers today might record on an off-day.

Reid and Bruce Morrison added 50 for the last wicket, of which Reid contributed 48, Morrison one and extras one. That was the sort of dominance Reid displayed throughout his run blitz.

Clarke retains vivid memories of the hammering. "It was the most fabulous display of hitting I've ever seen. It was impossible to bowl to him because he was equally punishing all around the wicket. That innings has stayed in my mind ever since. In my long career of playing and watching sport, I've never seen anything more spectacular."

Alabaster recalls bowling to Reid the previous evening. "He came in with a couple of overs remaining and was content just to keep his wicket intact. In the last over I bowled him a gem of an arm ball. It was getting dark, and he was intent on defence. He played and missed and it brushed past his off stump. I didn't know it then, but that was my last chance. The next day he pulverised us. He made the Basin Reserve seem like a small suburban park, such was his power and accuracy."

Bowling to Reid was always difficult for Alabaster. "My problem was that he played off-spin bowlers particularly well. He was the only top player in New Zealand of my time I never got out. He had his technique sorted out. He had that little back and across movement, and also he wasn't afraid to withdraw outside the leg so he could smash the ball through the off-side. No matter how tight a line I bowled, he was able to give himself room to attack. It's important when recalling that innings of 296 not just to consider the 6s. He hit 35 4s that day and played some beautiful shots through the off-side."

Pairaudeau tried everything. "At one point," says Alabaster, "Bruce suggested we set a trap for Reid. He asked me to bowl the first couple of balls fairly flat, and then to float one up. In the meantime he would signal Peter Barton to quietly drop back to long on. So I duly floated one up and Reid lifted it right towards Barton. I thought, 'Got you.' The one problem was that it cleared Barton by 30 metres! I was misguided enough to think I could do it next time, but he belted me for another 6."

Reid's innings ended when he got an inside edge in attempting to drive McGregor and was caught by Alabaster on the mid-wicket boundary, in front of the clock on the old stand. "I was right back on the boundary," says Alabaster. "If I hadn't caught it, it would probably have gone for 6."

These days Reid is philosophical. "Fancy being caught on the boundary on 296! All their fieldsmen were right back on the fence. If I'd wanted I could have pushed a couple and reached 300 that way, but it never occurred to me. I didn't play by the scoreboard. I never knew it was a world record for 6s until I read it in *The Dominion* the next morning.

"It was one of the rare times in New Zealand when my batting recaptured my form in South Africa in 1961-62. Over there, I found myself able to start hitting the ball hard as soon as I got to the crease, and that's what it was like that day at the Basin Reserve."

Neely says the ND bowlers never gave up. "They were helpless, but they tried everything. They bowled wide of the leg, wide of the off, short and just before lunch Clarke even bowled a beamer, from the Caledonian Hotel end. Reid pivoted and hooked it off his nose for 6. The ball hit the metal light pole and reverberated like a tuning fork. It was mayhem. Northern Districts were annihilated by a cyclone."

Peter Barton is a little-known figure in New Zealand cricket, but Neely recalls that he was a very promising schoolboy bowler who made a big impression at Wanganui Collegiate. He was in his first season of first class cricket, and bowling at brisk fast-medium, had been progressing nicely until he struck Reid. "John seemed to take a liking to Barton's bowling," says Neely. "He didn't just hit him for 6s, but he hit him out of the ground and onto the bottom field at St Pat's. That was a colossal hit. The next over he repeated the shot.

"It became a carnival atmosphere. People were laughing. They couldn't believe it. Back then, there wasn't the same awareness of statistics that there is now. These days there is a flood of stats. I told the people I was with that Reid was approaching the world record for 6s, but it wasn't a factor, really."

It transpired Reid had blasted his way into *Wisden*. The previous world record for 6s in an innings was 11, held jointly by Cottari (C.K.) Nayudu

John Reid with the New Zealand Sportsman of the Year Trophy, and other associated silverware, 1955.

The New Zealanders watch proceedings during the test at Peshawar in 1955. From left: Iain Galloway (radio broadcaster), Trevor McMahon, Noel Harford, Matt Poore, Bert Sutcliffe, Tony MacGibbon, Alex Moir and Noel McGregor.

Gordon Leggat's bathing discomfort sums up the difficulties the New Zealanders faced during their tour of Pakistan and India in 1955-56. This photo was taken at Peshawar.

Reid (right) and Bert Sutcliffe during the tour of Pakistan in 1955.

Reid (left) and Bert Sutcliffe leave the field after their record unbroken partnership of 222 at New Delhi in 1955. Reid made 119 not out and Sutcliffe 230 not out.

The New Zealand team that beat the West Indies in 1956. Back row, from left: Gordon Burgess (manager), Jack Alabaster, Harry Cave, Tony MacGibbon, Don Beard, Sam Guillen, Lawrie Miller, Merv Wallace (coach). Front row: Ian Sinclair (12th man), Murray Chapple, Don Taylor, John Reid (captain), John Beck, Noel McGregor.

INTERNATIONAL CRICKET

Fourth Test

West Indies

V

New Zealand

EDEN PARK AUCKLAND

Friday, Saturday, Monday, Tuesday

MARCH 9, 10, 12, 13, 1956

Souvenir Programme 1/-

Programme from New Zealand's historic first test win at Eden Park in 1956.

The scene at Eden Park after New Zealand's famous win over the West Indies.

Reid (ready to bat) and England great Denis Compton, pictured during New Zealand's tour of England in 1958.

Zin Harris rides an ostrich during a Sunday outing in South Africa in 1962.

The design for John Reid's Squash Centre, which was to become a Wellington landmark.

The start of a bike race – an unusual diversion for the 1965 New Zealand team in Bermuda. From left: Vic Pollard, Graham Vivian, Richard Collinge, Ross Morgan, John Reid, Artie Dick and Bevan Congdon (making repairs to his bike).

Reid coaching at a clinic in South Africa in 1989.

Reid the fisherman. Another successful day on Lake Taupo.

Four famous cricket identities gather at the National Cricket Museum at the Basin Reserve. From left, Sir Richard Hadlee, Alan Davidson, Eric Tindill, John Reid. That's Don Bradman looking down on them.

Plenty to talk about for Reid and Sir Donald Bradman as they watch the Ashes test in Adelaide in 1995.

Norli and John Reid, pictured in front of the Taj Mahal in 1996.

Four New Zealand sports greats pictured during a Halberg Trust function in Auckland. From left: Sir Wilson Whineray, John Reid, Sean Fitzpatrick, and Grant Fox.

Shane Warne... one of the most influential figures in cricket history.

Darren Gough... on a par with Brian Statham and Bob Willis.

Shaun Pollock... possibly the finest bowling all-rounder of his time.

Sachin Tendulkar... already he deserves to be placed among the game's greats.

Wasim Akram... a magnificent left-arm bowler who has everything.

Brian Lara... capable of greatness.

(Hindus v M.C.C., 1926), Charles Barnett (Gloucester v Somerset, 1934) and Richie Benaud (Australia v Tom Pearce's XI, 1953). Reid's record endured until 1995 when Andrew Symonds of Gloucestershire hit 16 6s on his way to scoring 254 against Glamorgan. The following day, Symonds hit another four in his second innings of 76 to take his total of 6s for the match to 20, thereby breaking Jim Stewart's total of 17, set in 1959. Previous to Reid, the New Zealand record for 6s in an innings belonged to Ces Dacre, who smashed eight for New Zealand against Derbyshire in 1927.

For all its ferocity, Reid's innings built up steam in a logical manner. His first 50 was made in 67 minutes (including the few minutes the previous evening) and contained eleven 4s and no 6s. Then Reid began to really go after the bowling. His second 50 took him just 32 minutes, with five 4s and three 6s. The third 50 was almost a replica – 35 minutes, six 4s and three 6s. Reid moved from 150 to 200 in 33 minutes. There were no 6s, but eight 4s. After that it was chaos. He raced from 200 to 250 in 28 minutes, with four 4s and four 6s. His final 46 runs, with the fieldsmen dotted all around the boundary, came in a mere 25 minutes, with one 4 and five 6s.

Reid was even-handed about his 6-hitting. His 6s came from Puna (two), Alabaster, Clarke and Barton (three each) and Shaw (four).

Experienced cricketers who watched Reid's virtuoso effort couldn't praise it enough. Bert Sutcliffe said, "His bat was a sword and he gave the most magnificent exhibition of controlled hitting I have ever seen. Someone suffers from Reid every season. This time it was us. I will remember those superb shots which went for 6 between square and fine leg and over long-on."

Gordon Leggat said Reid's batting was on a par with his two most spectacular innings in South Africa, 165 against South African Colts and 203 against Western Province: "He probably hits the ball more consistently hard than any other batsman in the world."

Frank Mooney recalled another innings Reid played in South Africa, on his first tour a decade earlier. "I saw him make 116 in 120 minutes at Cape Town in 1954 against bowlers like Adcock, Tayfield, Ironside and van Ryneveld. This innings was comparable. I class him as the finest player of off-spin bowling in the world."

There was an interesting postscript to one of the great days in New Zealand cricket, as Neely recalls. "Things were just settling down again after Reid's fireworks. Northern Districts were going along comfortably at 67-2 when Bob Blair did the hat-trick. It was a good hat-trick, too, with Pairaudeau, Sutcliffe and McGregor. So it turned out to be a remarkable day – a world record for 6s and then a hat-trick."

10 | ON TOP OF THE WORLD XI

John Reid's selection as captain of a Rest of the World team to play England in 1965 was as big a compliment as has been paid any New Zealand cricketer. These days "World XIs" are commonplace and seldom merit the tag. They are often a selection of cricketers pulled together from nearby to help celebrate a benefit match. There is no attempt to choose the world's best; more often it is a case of availability and finances.

But it was different back in 1965. Reid was named as captain of the first genuine collection of world stars. It was billed as the greatest gathering of cricketers ever assembled. The team was picked by a British television audience and the whole event was organised by a panel headed by Trevor Bailey and underwritten by Rothmans.

To be even selected in such a side was a rare tribute. If we think back to New Zealand's entry into test cricket, in 1930, how many of our players have truly merited selection in a world side? Dempster, Cowie, Donnelly, Sutcliffe, Richard Hadlee, Martin Crowe. Some may add Burtt, Turner and Ian Smith. That's not many. Reid not only belonged in that elevated company, but he was the obvious choice to captain the team.

Here was the team he led: John Reid (NZ, captain), Nawab of Pataudi (India), Hanif Mohammad (Pakistan), Garfield Sobers (West Indies), Conrad Hunte (West Indies), Wes Hall (West Indies), Rohan Kanhai (West Indies), Lance Gibbs (West Indies), Charlie Griffith (West Indies), Wally Grout (Australia), Colin Bland (South Africa), Eddie Barlow (South Africa).

It is arguably still the finest collection of cricketers to be found in one team. Reid's side between them scored 82 test centuries and took 961 test wickets. Five of them – Reid, Sobers, Pataudi, Hanif and Kanhai – were or became long-serving test captains. There were two notable absentees. Australians Bobby Simpson and Norman O'Neill, though selected, declined to take part. Simpson at the time worked for a rival cigarette company, and O'Neill had publicly announced he would not play with or against speed bowler Griffith, whom he believed was a "chucker".

"I was tremendously honoured to be chosen to lead such a team," says Reid. "In fact, I can still recall opening the letter from Trevor Bailey inviting me to captain the Rest of World XI. I was sitting in my office at the squash centre in Kelburn, and for a while I went into a bit of a dream, thinking back to my days as a young boy when I'd played knock-up games of cricket with my mates along our makeshift pitch. I always wanted to be Bradman, and we always picked the best players in the world. To be invited to lead such a team thrilled me."

There were problems. "The timing was tricky for me. The squash centre was going very well, and we were planning a three-court extension. As it was, I was going to be away for several months on tour in India, Pakistan and England. To return home in August, then return to England a month later was asking a lot of the centre's other directors, but they strongly encouraged me to go. Another worry was that I would be returning to England in the middle of our winter and wouldn't have had any cricket for several weeks. But over-riding any concerns was the chance to be part of such an occasion."

These days, of course, test cricket is a continual merry-go-round. Teams play 15 or more tests a year, so within the space of just three or four seasons, established players would have met each other often, either in the test arena or at a World Cup. It wasn't like that in 1965, when there was far less international cricket, and travel was a more major undertaking.

Reid had played one series against Pataudi, three against Hanif, two against Barlow and Bland, one against Sobers (a decade earlier) and had never played in tests against Grout, Hall, Griffith, Gibbs, Kanhai or Hunte, some of whom he had never even met.

"I can't say I was overawed at the prospect of captaining a team full of these great players, but I did wonder how everyone would fit in. At that time India and Pakistan were at war, so having Hanif and Pataudi in the same team was an issue. There were two South Africans, plus all the West Indians. In view of South Africa's apartheid policies, this could have been an awkward situation.

"Besides the political issues, there were cricket questions. Would there be any trouble over the allegations that Griffith threw? After all, by then such respected figures as Richie Benaud and Ken Barrington, besides O'Neill, had made that accusation. Who would field at silly mid-on? What would the batting order be? What would I say in a team talk? All these questions were running through my head as I headed back to England."

Though the weather did its best to ruin the cricket, it still turned out to be a magnificent experience. "Having so many West Indians in the side meant we couldn't help but have fun. Wes Hall came up to me and said he knew I was from New Zealand, but that all he knew about New Zealand was that it produced Canterbury lamb and good horses. The West Indians were very keen followers of horse racing, and some of them bet quite heavily. They seemed to walk around with a transistor radio attached to their ears. The West Indians made the dressing room a fun place, with their continual banter and relaxed attitude. The subject of horse racing and betting was never far away and often they'd be chipping away at someone or another after some unfortunate losses the previous day. It became one of the duties of the 12th man to keep his team-mates out on the field appraised with up-to-the-minute results from the big races around the country.

"I'd heard a lot about big Charlie Griffith, who had a rather fierce reputation. Apparently his bowling had been frightening in England in 1963. I found him easy to get along with. My first conversation with him was in his room at the Waldorf Hotel in London. I sat on his bed and he told me what he felt I should say to him and the rest of the players. Some of the West Indians were very extroverted, but Conrad Hunte was much quieter. These days he is a lay preacher in South Africa. Even back in the 1960s he was deeply religious. One day Wes Hall asked him about his recent engagement to a West Indian woman – Conrad had said he had had a "message" to get engaged.

"'Are you married yet, Con?' asked Hall.

"'No. I got another message,' said Hunte.

"Hall: 'What! Even God makin' mistakes these days?'"

Obviously such a collection of stars meant rich pickings for the British media. Hanif and Pataudi were asked to pose together, and were pictured next to each other in the changing room and signing the hotel register together. "Cricketers tend to get on well and don't dwell on the political. I assigned Hanif and Pataudi to room together without even thinking about the ramifications. It was never a problem.

"However, it was hard to ignore the political situation – the Indians were bombing Karachi, and that's where Hanif's family were. So our team got together and discussed the matter. We decided to send a telegram to Indian Prime Minister Shastri and Pakistani President Ayub Khan.

"It read: 'WE WORLD CRICKET TEAM WISH EXPRESS DEEP REGRET AT DECLARED WAR BETWEEN INDIA PAKISTAN STOP COMING FROM DIFFERENT COUNTRIES BACKGROUNDS RELIGIONS WE FIND UNITY ON CRICKET FIELD BY REACHING FOR COMMON OBJECTIVE STOP FERVENTLY HOPE BOTH COUNTRIES CAN MEET AND FIND AMICABLE SOLUTION.'

"It was signed by our entire team and by Mike Smith, the England captain."

Reid retains lasting impressions of the players in the world team. "Sobers, my vice-captain, was the best all-rounder of my era, maybe of any era, a brilliant batsman, versatile bowler, top class fieldsman and a great guy to have around. Kanhai was a very smooth batsman, as good as I've seen, with all the shots. Gibbs I didn't see much of. Obviously he was a class bowler – he did go on to hold the world record for most test wickets – but he didn't get much opportunity with us in England because the wet wickets didn't really suit him.

"Hall was a big personality. He was in his prime as a pace bowler, but in the dressing room he always had a huge smile on his face. Griffith was as quick as Hall, but not nearly as outgoing a person. I had a net against Hall and Griffith before the first match. They were really only rolling over their arms, but they were still very quick. In the match, it was quite something watching them in action and I was more than happy to be in the gully.

"I didn't put Bland right in the top level of batsmen, though his final test average is nearly 50. However, as a fieldsman he was as good as I've seen. He fielded at either cover or mid-wicket, quite deep. His pick-up and release were like lightning and it was incredible the way he could throw down the stumps. He'd be as good as the best you see now. Barlow was an annoying batsman to play against. He had the ability to score runs by hitting over the slips, which was very frustrating. He nearly drove Gary Bartlett to distraction doing that in 1961-62. Later in his career he became a good bowler.

"Hunte was a very classy opening batsman. He isn't spoken of a great deal now, but in his time he was as good as any opener in the world. He had that West Indian flair, plus a very sound basic technique. Grout was a great character. He was a superb wicketkeeper who went about his job very professionally, and he was a pleasure to have around.

"Pataudi was a rather unconventional player, but he fitted in well in this team. He had captained India against us a few months earlier and I always felt he benefited at home from some generous umpiring decisions. Despite losing much of the sight in one eye after a car accident quite early in his career, he still played 46 tests and overcame the handicap without too much noticeable difficulty. Hanif was not as open or easy to get to know as Pataudi, and I felt that when New Zealand played Pakistan, our pace bowlers were able to intimidate him. He was an especially good player in his own country, a glancer with a good defence, rather than a big hitter.

Two World v England matches were arranged, at Scarborough and Lord's. Unfortunately both were spoiled by rain, although they still drew big crowds.

At Scarborough, the world team struggled to reach 215, of which Bland stroked an elegant 62. One of Reid's memories of the game is of the warm and genuine way Sobers congratulated Bland on his fine innings. It required an eighth-wicket stand of 57 between Bland and Griffith to lift the world past 200. Reid was bowled by leg-spinner Bob Barber for nine. It didn't seem too significant at the time, as there was still the second innings and the Lord's match to follow but, as it transpired, this was to be the last of his 418 first class innings. England, endeavouring to make up for time lost through rain, reached 160-2, then declared. The World, in their second innings, raced to 153-4, with Hunte and Barlow cracking 100 for the first wicket. The match was poised nicely, with England needing 209 in 160 minutes, but then the rain came again.

Rain interfered even more drastically with the Lord's game. Because no play was possible until midway through the second day, it was decided to change it from a first class to a limited-over fixture and each side was allocated 70 overs. Reid sent in England and Cowdrey, Smith, Barber, Edrich, Parfitt, Barrington and company struggled to counter Sobers' bowling. Eventually Sobers picked up five cheap wickets and England could muster just 175. Hunte was again in slashing form and he made 88 and helped Hanif put on 106 for the first wicket. The World won by nine wickets.

For Reid, it was his final appearance at Lord's, which isn't known as "The Home of Cricket" for nothing. "I read about the ground and felt very honoured when I played there in 1949. Over the years I didn't enjoy a lot of success at the ground, but anyone who follows cricket will understand what I mean when I say how proud I was to lead the world team at Lord's."

In view of the organisation and expense that went into gathering so fine a team, it was a pity there were not more matches scheduled. Nevertheless, Reid retains many warm memories of the 10 days the team spent together.

"The West Indians were amazingly laid-back. They never seemed to want to practise, and I had to really twist Lance Gibbs' arm to get him to bowl me a few in the nets one day. They seemed to make an art of arriving at the dressing room at the last possible moment before play began. I was used to captaining New Zealand and expecting my players at the ground an hour or 90 minutes before play. But at Lord's, 20 minutes before play was to begin, I looked around our dressing room and there were only three of us there. We had to go out to field and I was starting to get a little twitchy. Wes Hall was the last to arrive, about four minutes before play began. He burst into the dressing room, shirt unbuttoned, a big grin on his face. I could never be sure, but I felt their delayed arrival must have had something to do with a big horse race somewhere."

Reid speaks very highly of Grout, who died soon after his test career ended. "Wally was a great personality, just what you want in a wicketkeeper. He did his job well, but had a sense of humour which could lift a team. He used to chip away at Pataudi and Hanif, suggesting that if there had to be a war, then a good idea would be to send all their umpires to the front immediately."

11 | PADDING UP DEEP DOWN UNDER

The most unusual place cricket has been played? W.G. Grace might have cocked an interested eye and scratched his ample beard if he'd been told that a century after his test career closed, the world's best players would be in the habit of descending on the desert location of Sharjah to play an annual tournament. These days international cricketers willing to pack their boots and travel can end up playing at all sorts of venues in traditionally non-cricket countries.

But John Reid can justifiably claim to have gone where few cricketers have gone before... or since – Antarctica. In 1970, Reid was invited to travel to Antarctica with a group of 150 people as part of the United States Deep Freeze operation in the area. "The invitation came out of the blue, but it was a bit different and I was very keen to take part. There were politicians and leaders from various sections of the community," he says.

"We were well looked after. We were given all the woollen gear required for such sub-freezing temperatures, including air boots. We lived in the army barracks at the US base, and spent some time at Scott Base. We ate with the crew and, typically American, had flapjacks and ice cream for breakfast.

"At about eight in the morning we would be taken by helicopter to one of the bases. There were five bases, including the South Pole, where they have an underground facility. We had a look at Shackleton's Hut, and went out on an ice-breaker to watch killer whales. We saw nature at work. Some whales tipped over an ice float and got hold of some penguins for lunch. There was a flight over ice glaciers with huge crevasses. The area is vast. We flew by helicopter over Mt Erebus, an active volcano that a few years later was the site of the air tragedy. It was incredibly cold – 54 degrees below – and we had to keep an eye on each others' noses in case they went white. One of the officers had a flask of water in his parka. He sprayed it and by the time the water reached the ground, it had frozen."

Like any keen cricketer, Reid took a bat and ball with him, though the sun-baked fields of Newlands and New Delhi seemed far away. "The admiral bowled the first ball to me. I hit it straight at the South Pole and as far as I know, it's still there. It was a shot that went around the world. The admiral would probably be 'called' as he pitched the ball at me, baseball style."

New Zealand never toured the West Indies during Reid's career, but he did play in Bermuda on the return journey of the 1965 team. "It was in Bermuda that Dick Motz, our fast bowler, let his frustrations at the local umpiring override his good sense. He quickly found that no matter how well he bowled, he was never going to win an lbw appeal if it was shouted with a New Zealand accent. After Dick had had a succession of appeals turned down or simply ignored, he let rip with a shoulder-high bouncer that caught the edge of the bat. The appeal for caught behind was also declined, with the batsman making a great show of rubbing his shoulder. It was too much for Dick, who fired out a few choice oaths and some pointed comments which would have got him into trouble with today's I.C.C. referees. The upshot was that the New Zealand manager and captain had to attend a meeting and offer an apology to the umpire in question, but not without a reminder from the captain for the umpire to be more vigilant in future, or words to that effect!"

The 1965 side then travelled to Los Angeles – a city at boiling point at the time because of the Bilko race riots – and they played a southern California team on a matting wicket on the Sir Aubrey Smith ground. Smith, known as "Round the Corner Smith" because of his sharply angled run-up, was a Sussex cricketer who captained the first England team to visit South Africa in 1888-89. He was one of many English immigrants who moved to Hollywood to work in the film industry and helped take cricket to southern California. Smith's enthusiasm led to the formation of the Hollywood Cricket Club. Many English and Australian teams stopped in Los Angeles and played games organised by Smith. Famous Hollywood actors, such as Boris Karloff, Charlie Chaplin and Douglas Fairbanks, often took part.

Earlier on that 1965 team's journey of more than five months, the cricketers had travelled overland through Europe on their way to England after completing the India/Pakistan segment of the tour. The team visited cities such as Venice, Interlaken, Lucerne and Cologne. After completing their matches in England, Ireland and Scotland, they played a fixture against the Netherlands at The Hague on a matting pitch laid over crushed gravel and sand.

Cricket took Reid to a many other places not normally associated with cricket. In 1949, the New Zealand team played a match against the Combined Services at Bad Oyenhausen in Germany, and then travelled to Berlin, where they ran around the Olympic track a good deal slower than their compatriot Jack Lovelock had done 13 years earlier. After Berlin, they wound up their trip with a night in Paris.

In 1963, Reid travelled through Africa with Ron Roberts' Commonwealth team. He recalls playing one match in oppressive heat at Nairobi, the capital of Kenya, when Kenya was much more of a cricket minnow than it is now.

The cricket world is changing. When Reid played, Sri Lanka was Ceylon, and he played in Rhodesia, now Zimbabwe, and East Pakistan, now Bangladesh. As a test referee, Reid has officiated in Malaysia during the 1998 Commonwealth Games, and at Guwhati, India, near the Burma border.

12 | A (SQUASH) CENTRE OF ATTENTION

Though it was sold and renamed in 1978, John Reid's Squash Centre is still a landmark in Wellington. Even two decades later, people giving directions are likely to say, "You go up the Terrace, past John Reid's and the university... " For 16 years, John Reid's Squash Centre was one of Wellington's biggest attractions.

Local businessmen would troop up towards Kelburn in their lunch hours for a game. Victoria University students spent hours there. The squash centre hosted Wellington interclub, junior tournaments and "midweek ladies". In 1966 the North Island squash champs were held there, with Charlie and Megan Waugh cleaning up the men's and women's open.

Until 1963, when Reid opened his squash centre, the sport was almost like a secret society in New Zealand. There were pockets of interest, notably in Timaru and Palmerston North. Occasionally overseas stars like Hashim and Roshan Khan, or Ken Hiscoe, would tour New Zealand. But few people, even dedicated sports followers, knew about squash.

After John Reid's Squash Centre opened in Wellington, the popularity of the sport rocketed. Within a few years, Wellington had a dozen private clubs dotted around its suburbs and every New Zealand town of decent size had its own squash club. But though all these clubs were private, it was Reid's commercial centre which remained a central point for the sport.

Wellingtonians joined the club that was based in the centre and club nights were extremely popular. Visitors to Wellington often made a point of popping into the centre for a bit of exercise and because it was an ideal meeting place.

Reid's timing was perfect. He had the centre built just in time to create and then ride the sport's popularity. Overseas stars like Heather McKay and Geoff Hunt played there and the charming and immensely personable Egyptian coach Dardir often ran clinics there.

Before the centre opened, the few Wellingtonians wanting to play squash had three choices. There was a court at Government House, another in the Wellington Club on the Terrace, and a third in a private residence in the Hutt Valley. That was it. Understandably the sport stagnated.

But while squash was a mystery to most New Zealanders in the early 1960s, Reid himself had been playing for years. In 1949, while in England, he played some squash early in the tour as a means of keeping fit. When he was based in Oamaru from 1955 to 1958, he played at the local courts, especially during the winter, using squash, and a couple of seasons of rugby refereeing, as the basis of his off-season training.

After returning to live in Wellington, the idea of opening a commercial squash centre gradually increased in appeal. "I first got serious about it in 1961," he says. "I had been with B.P. for seven years by then and was ready for a change. I was keen to work for myself. For the next year or so, I continued to be employed at B.P., but gradually began to put in place plans to build the squash centre.

"I took holidays in Sydney and spent a lot of time at a commercial squash complex at Rushcutters Bay. The owner was very helpful, giving me pointers on what a successful centre needed and what the pitfalls were.

"I came home and starting to look for land to build the centre on. Eventually some land off Salamanca Road came under consideration. I needed a zoning dispensation from the council before I could begin building because the land we required was part of the city's designated Green Belt. I suppose it didn't hurt at that point that I was the New Zealand cricket captain, and knew some of the leading civic officials fairly well."

As the building was a major undertaking, Reid also required financial backers. His first port of call was his good friend John Oakley, who was a prominent Wellington lawyer and had played cricket with and against Reid. "John was very enthusiastic and supportive, as he has been of all my ventures. Through my cricket, I also knew the Norwood family well and I approached Sir Walter Norwood, who was equally enthusiastic. I was put onto Jack Francis, the chairman of the stock exchange, and made a presentation to him. He hardly even hesitated to consider it. He could see immediately that it was a viable business venture and threw in his weight. It was agreed that Jack Francis, John Oakley and Walter Norwood would be directors and that we also needed an accountant. Malcolm McCaw, an accountant whom I knew through school, also agreed to come on board as a director.

"So that was the board. It was to meet once a month. I was to be the managing director. There were some questions asked about my ability to run the business, but while I had never run a business, I was not totally naive in this area. I was used to organising myself, through my work with B.P., especially when I was responsible for a large part of the South Island.

"And courtesy of B.P., which was looking to promote me, I had done some study at Victoria University. I'd taken commercial and company law. There was a good incentive scheme working: if I passed, they paid for me! So I passed my exams, and that knowledge gave me a good basis for what was ahead."

Work on the squash centre, which was designed by Ming Nightingale, one of Reid's best friends at Hutt Valley High School, began in 1962 and it opened the following year. Opening day was a big occasion, with splash newspaper coverage. Back in the early '60s, the squash centre was a significant addition to the Wellington scene and therefore a major local story.

Reid recalls opening day ruefully. The carpark had not been tarsealed at that stage, so was very dusty at the best of times. On the day of the opening, there was torrential rain, but the crowds flocked to have a look at the centre and at this new-fangled game called squash. They were able to have a go at playing at no charge and all equipment – balls, rackets and shoes – were supplied free of charge. The new carpets inside the complex took a terrible battering, being caked in mud well before proceedings were over.

Nevertheless, the opening was a spectacular success, mainly because the product was so good. Squash was an enjoyable sport that could be played competitively, or merely as a form of exercise. And the five-court centre was ideally situated and very appealing.

Two courts had windows built into the back wall, an innovation at the time, and a precursor of today's glass courts. The windows provided interested spectators with the opportunity to watch the game from court level. The fifth court was curtained off. This might seem a quaint custom now, but back in 1963, some people preferred to take their exercise in private, especially when attired in squash clothes, and the huge curtain afforded that privacy.

The courts were booked out almost immediately and use remained virtually at capacity, especially during peak hours, until Reid sold the centre to the New Zealand Squash Rackets Association in 1978. The centre was so successful in 1963 that within three years three further courts downstairs had been built, and Reid was looking at other ways to capitalise on the immense appeal of the centre.

A restaurant was built on the top floor, and there was a snack bar and a shop next to reception. Then Reid hit upon the idea of installing a golf driving range. These days, of course, driving ranges are hugely popular, but Reid was probably a decade ahead of his time. The range was duly built. It comprised a huge netted area 30m long and 21m wide. The driving range was three storeys high and the net was specially made and imported from overseas. Leading Australian golfer Kel Nagle opened it.

But there were hitches. It was not easy designing a system for retrieving the balls, and the nets the balls were driven into tended to develop holes. The net strength gradually deteriorated because of the reaction of ultra-violet sun rays. "Residents nearby got fed up with balls which had gone through the netting rolling down the Terrace, and even occasionally going through a house window, and we were served with various injunctions. Eventually we had to build a protective wire netting cage to cover the whole area to try to contain the balls. Also, we had a problems with golf balls being stolen. Not just the odd one or two, either. Some of the kids must have made quite a business out of it, and we'd have balls missing by the sackful. The next thing I knew, I'd see our golf balls being driven down the fairway at the local golf clubs!"

Reid himself was a good squash player, a solid B grader, but he did not enter many tournaments, though in the early years he spent hours on court coaching.

Even when squash's popularity surged and private clubs sprang up all over the place, the appeal of the commercial centre never seemed to diminish.

Strangely, in view of the kick-start that the centre gave New Zealand squash, Reid quickly found himself at loggerheads with the New Zealand Squash Rackets Association. "Far from being welcomed, I was perceived as a threat to their comfortable little world and the squash association did all it could to make things difficult for me. I had particular trouble with Roy Haddon, a leading squash official, who resented an outsider coming into squash and becoming involved in the commercial side. It was silly, really. They tried to have every person who played at the centre branded a professional, and put as many obstacles in my way as they could."

Reid set about organising an association for commercial centre operators, though there were very few such complexes – just a couple in Auckland and then one in Rotorua. When Colin Brownlee of Rotorua was considering building his commercial complex, he stayed a week in Wellington and Reid gave him as much advice and assistance as he could. He reasoned that Brownlee's centre would not affect his business and could only foster the sport. In due course, Brownlee's centre was to be the breeding ground of many outstanding players, including his son Bruce Brownlee and future world champion Dame Susan Devoy.

As in any business, there were problems, though many seem humorous in hindsight. "We used to have squash shoes and rackets for hire. We would write the size on the back of each shoe in heavy felt pen, but even so a large number of them walked out of the club and were later seen heading across the road to lectures at the university. Our cakes of soap and toilet rolls bolstered the supplies of many student bathrooms in flats around the Upland Road area. But generally I got on well with the university. It behoved me to. The last thing I wanted was the university building its own courts and taking away all that potential custom, so we offered students very good rates."

By the mid-1970s, with the squash centre humming, Reid was looking to diversify. He was a good golfer himself, with a handicap that got as low as eight, and eventually decided to buy a golf complex at Whiteman's Valley in the Hutt Valley. A nine-hole course was expanded to 18 holes, and hot pools, saunas, tennis courts, restaurant and chalet accommodation was planned. The complex, known as Blue Mountains Golf and Country Club, opened in 1973, but was not as successful as hoped.

Once again, Reid was ahead of his time. Such complexes are immensely popular these days, and many far less attractive than Blue Mountains run successfully all over the world. But Reid's involvement preceded the golf boom. After sticking with it for a while, he eventually sold his interest in Blue Mountains. In 1978, after Reid sold the squash centre, he, his wife, Norli, and their youngest daughter, Ann, shifted to Taupo where new challenges lay ahead.

13 | HIGHS AND LOWS ON THE VELD

The New Zealand Sports Hall of Fame was launched with a lavish ceremony in Wellington in December 1990. Many of the all-time greats of New Zealand sport were there – Edmund Hillary, Bob Charles, Colin Meads, Wilson Whineray, Bert Sutcliffe, Ivan Mauger, Peter Snell, Murray Halberg and Yvette Williams among them. Taking his place in this elite group, as by right, was John Reid. Yet he nearly wasn't invited.

It wasn't lack of finance. Organisers of the function received a grant of several hundred thousand dollars from the then Labour Government to help fund the function. Rather, one of the organisers, the person charged with contacting the many New Zealand stars then based overseas, was reluctant to contact John Reid in South Africa. "I'll bet he's got a Black servant working for him," was this person's explanation when I asked why Reid wasn't on the list of those invited. Eventually sanity prevailed and Reid was contacted.

He flew into Wellington and spent a happy few days with many sports stars who had been his contemporaries, including two of his fellow Forty-Niners, Sutcliffe and Martin Donnelly, who were also honoured guests at the Sports Hall of Fame ceremony. (Since then, two other members of the side, Walter Hadlee and Jack Cowie, have also been inducted.)

There is no question that Reid, like other New Zealand sportsmen, including rugby players Don Clarke, Kevin Eveleigh and Lawrie Knight, made himself unpopular in some quarters by electing to live in South Africa through the 1980s. The issue of contact with South Africa was a sensitive one for New Zealanders at that time. There was much increased awareness of the reality of apartheid and the calls for boycotts of sports contact with South Africa became overwhelming.

The South African issue had gradually built up. All Black rugby teams that visited South Africa in 1928, 1949 and 1960 were not permitted to include dark-skinned players, but this was not a major issue for the New Zealand Rugby Union, which bowed to the wishes of its hosts. By the late 1960s, the mood had changed. A planned visit to South Africa in 1967 was called off when Maori and Polynesian players were not allowed to be included in the side. In 1970, when New Zealand next toured, four dark-skinned players, Sid Going, Blair Furlong, Bryan Williams and Buff Milner, were included. But by then the forces were gathering against South Africa.

Springbok teams met huge protests when they toured Britain and Australia and the 1973 tour of New Zealand was cancelled. The All Black tour of South Africa in 1976 provoked a Black African boycott of the Montreal Olympic Games that year. The 1981 Springbok tour of New Zealand tore the country asunder, pitting family members against each other. Some people claimed that to continue to play sport with South Africa was tacit support of apartheid; others said they wished to keep sport and politics separate.

Rugby, as South Africa's national sport, received the most attention, but the gathering sports boycott impacted on other sports, especially cricket. New Zealand had toured South Africa twice, in 1953-54 and 1961-62, and South African teams had visited New Zealand in 1953 and 1964. Because cricket was not played to a high level by many Maoris and Polynesians, the question of including dark-skinned players in touring sides to South Africa did not arise. It would have been interesting had Adam Parore been New Zealand's wicketkeeper in the 1950s, rather than the 1990s. Gradually South Africa became isolated by the international sports community. After their home series against Bill Lawry's Australians in 1970, South Africa had to wait more than 20 years to play another official test match, not returning to the fold until after the apartheid laws had been abolished.

In looking at this history now, especially as it pertains to John Reid, it is important to keep things in historical perspective. The world had not overly concerned itself in the problems of the apartheid laws in the 1950s and early '60s. You can read Dick Brittenden's *Silver Fern on the Veld* or Dick Whitington's *John Reid's Kiwis*, or the various rugby tour books by Winston McCarthy, Terry McLean and others and see hardly a mention of the whole issue.

Perhaps the writers were ignorant of it, or maybe it was merely a case of ignorance being bliss. The sportsmen of the times reflected that thinking.

"During my first tour there in 1953-54, we were basically oblivious of the apartheid regime that held Black Africans down in a vice-like grip," says Reid. "Our attitude was that we were in South Africa to play cricket. We had very little contact with the local Black African or Coloured populations. I do remember being appalled at how some of the South African officials and guests at official functions treated the staff. We noted the Nie Blanks (No Whites) notices around the cities, the separate Black and White toilet facilities, buses for Whites only and the tremendous support the New Zealand team received from the barbed wire corner of the cricket grounds, where the Africans and Coloureds were permitted to watch from. But our attitude was that it was their country, we were guests and we really kept our heads down and played cricket. We were naive politically.

"Things had not changed much by 1961 when I led the next New

Zealand team to South Africa, though on reflection the situation by then was starting to get a little more volatile – I remember a couple of bombs went off while we were touring, though they were not near us. The only Africans we met were the staff at hotels and the servants at the private houses, where we were royally entertained. We were somewhat aware that the mines around Johannesburg and the other centres had compounds that housed the workers who had travelled from their homes to find work that was apparently not available in their homelands. But again, we were there as cricketers, and were not looking to either judge the political situation or make political statements."

That was the last time Reid visited South Africa until 1981, when he and his wife, Norli, decided to move there for what turned out to be an 11-year stint. "We had been living in Taupo since selling the squash centre in 1978. I had been running John Reid Sports Ltd in Taupo, but it wasn't going particularly well – there were too many shops in Taupo selling fishing gear. I found I wasn't busy enough, so I sat my real estate exams and began selling real estate, as well as managing the sports shop.

"A friend from South Africa, Joe Pamensky, stopped off to see us in Taupo and we got to talking about our plans. I mentioned I was thinking of moving to Auckland to sell real estate. I was missing the buzz of living in a bigger city and I needed a job. Joe suggested I think about living in South Africa. At first, it seemed like too big a step. At the age of 50, to move all the way to South Africa seemed a very big step. But Joe investigated the job scene and within a month or so had lined up several possible jobs for me. Norli and I thought about it, and decided to give it a go. I got a tourist visa and off we went. I had never contemplated emigrating at that stage of my life. What do you put in five suitcases?

"We weren't alone over there. Joe had organised a basic flat for our temporary accommodation near the Wanderers club and, of course, we caught up with our son Richard, who had gone on ahead of us and was a Transvaal cricket coach, working at schools and clubs around Johannesburg. We stayed with Richard for a short time until we found our own accommodation. I took up employment at the Nissan Motor Company. It was a good job, well reimbursed, and it didn't hurt that a lot of clients and people I was dealing with recalled my playing cricket over there."

Reid was a dealer promotions manager for Nissan, which involved a good deal of travel about South Africa. Norli sat her real estate exams and sold property in and around Halfway House, so named because it was halfway between Johannesburg and Pretoria, two major cities 50km apart.

The image held by some people in New Zealand was that the Reids lived in a palace with ornate ballrooms, games rooms, swimming pools and several Black servants to attend to their every whim.

"It wasn't like that at all," says Reid. "At first we rented a small flat in Hillbrow, which was not the best area to be living in, even in 1981. So as soon as we could we went to live in Halfway House, which was nearer where I was working. But for most of our stay we rented a small cottage on a doctor's property in Morningside, close to the Sandton business complex, about 20km north of the Johannesburg city centre. At the Nissan factory in Pretoria, and later, when I had a change of job, to Nissan truck rental, I had a lot of contact with the Black African staff. At one point I had 120 Black drivers working with me. I had a Black foreman. This association with Blacks came very naturally to a New Zealander who went to Waiwhetu school in Lower Hutt, where I had plenty of Maori sports mates. I got on well with the Black Africans, but by then I could understand how badly some Black Africans were being treated. Even back in the early 1980s, you could sense a mood of change was rising."

At home, the Reids soon became used to having Black African servants about. "There were three servants employed at the doctor's house," says Reid, "so we used 'Joburg', an African from Zimbabwe, as required and contributed to his wages. Later, when we were living at Halfway House, we employed our own help as we were both working long hours. I coached cricket in the evenings and Norli was a real estate agent. Having a servant was a new experience for us. As New Zealanders, we were used to working and playing sport with Maoris, and Leah, our African maid, was treated no differently. However, because of the way she had lived in other households, she couldn't understand our rather casual attitude. Although she was welcome to have the same meals as us, she preferred her own food with little variety from a mixture of corn meal, a little meat, onions and tomatoes. She cooked in our kitchen, but not when she was concocting her special green tripe recipe, which had a most frightful smell. For this, we supplied her with a burner to use outside!

"I felt the criticism of White South Africans having servants – sometimes three per household with a cook, a gardener and a driver/handyman – was unwarranted. These duties provided employment for thousands of native peoples who would otherwise have been unable to feed their families. There was a constant stream of illegal – now legal – immigrants into South Africa from countries like Mozambique and Zimbabwe, because the conditions and work availability were so much better. A high percentage of them had no educational qualifications, yet were able to earn money, much of which they sent to their families, and to have their own accommodation. Generally, the servants would be treated well, and their accommodation would often include televisions, etc, but as in all walks of life, there are people who let the side down and treated their servants badly."

Reid lived in South Africa during the times of maximum civil unrest. He arrived only a few years after the Soweto and Sharpsville riots. "During our years there, there was plenty of unrest inside the homelands and townships, in places like Soweto, Tembisa and Alexandria. There was terrible over-crowding and poverty, and violence was commonplace. The various tribes and sub-tribes were crowded together in these places and were still fighting tribal wars that had gone on for decades or more. For instance, the Zulus from Natal had been fighting the Xhosa people from Port Elizabeth for centuries. The problem for the people was that they needed to be near where work was available, but the living conditions were often horrific, though the Indian townships seemed to be of a better standard.

"Having said that, there were areas, especially south of Johannesburg, where the more affluent Africans lived in quite superb homes and drove Mercedes and BMWs and not as chauffeurs, as many people seemed to think."

Reid arrived in South Africa at a turbulent time. The Springboks had just finished their tumultuous rugby tour of New Zealand and for the first time, through the images broadcast on television, South Africans could gauge the true depth of feeling in other countries about apartheid. South Africa's exclusion from world sport was increasing, especially in cricket. The South African cricket authorities decided the only way they could foster their sport was by providing some international opposition for their players. As normal cricket relations had been abandoned, a series of rebel tours was undertaken. These teams generally contained high-profile players, often past their best, who were looking for a lucrative way to close out their careers.

There were tours by the West Indies, captained by Lawrence Rowe, in 1981-82 and 1983-84 – the West Indians received life bans. A Sri Lankan rebel team captained by Bandula Warnapura arrived in 1982 (the players were banned for 25 years by Sri Lankan cricket authorities), and there were two England teams, one in 1982 led by Graham Gooch, who replaced Geoff Boycott as captain (each touring player received a three-year ban) and another led by Mike Gatting seven years later (his players also received three-years bans). Australia toured twice, led each time by Kim Hughes, in 1985-86 and 1986-87 (the Australians were banned for five years). "My previous knowledge of Hughes was limited, but intriguing. He came to New Zealand as a junior batsman in Greg Chappell's 1977 Australian side. Then in 1984, I saw him in tears during a television interview in which he resigned the Australian captaincy and spoke about the team looking for a psychologist to help them stand up to the fearsome West Indies pace attack. I remember thinking at the time that perhaps a batting coach would have been a better bet.

"The cloak and dagger antics over several years were like an on-going serial from a best-selling novel, because initially the tours were very popular. They filled a gap for the starved cricket public and obviously put some money in the pockets of players who had mostly missed out on the Kerry Packer World Series bonanza a few years earlier. It didn't last, though, and when Mike Gatting captained an England selection to South Africa in 1989-90, the demonstrations by the A.N.C-led protesters convinced Dr Ali

Bacher, the South African Cricket Board chief to take a unilateral decision to go out with Gatting among the protesters during a rally in Johannesburg and call off the tour. It was a very brave act by both of them. Ali was not the flavour of the month with his bosses after that, but it was a decision of common-sense and earned the support of Steve Tswete, who was to become A.N.C. Minister of Sport."

During the 1980s, Reid was opposed to sports boycotts. He didn't like to see sport used as a political tool, and felt more good could be achieved by maintaining contact. Now, he concedes he might have been wrong. "The various countries and international sports bodies who, because of the apartheid policy, boycotted South Africa, often denying their representatives entry visas, were probably correct. The sports boycott really hurt the White South African population – the Afrikaaners for rugby and the English-speaking South Africans for cricket. The boycotts hastened political change in South Africa, and the abolition of apartheid. What remains to be seen, though, is how well the new regime can control its millions who have suddenly got freedom from apartheid, but found that few election promises have been fulfilled."

Though he had a full-time job involving a senior managerial position, it was not surprising that Reid was soon deeply involved in South African cricket, initially as coach/manager of the Northern Transvaal team. At the end of the 1982-83 season, he was asked to present the Northern Transvaal provincial winners' trophies and the next season he was the team's coach-manager, a job he kept for seven years, a spell broken only by the short time he and Norli spent back in New Zealand when they relocated his ageing parents.

"Northern Transvaal had just been promoted from the B section of the South African domestic competitions and were struggling. But they had a very shrewd president, Dr Willie Basson, who was to oversee the rise to unprecedented heights of Northern Transvaal cricket. One of his most impressive feats was to use his influence and business acumen to have the Centurion Park cricket complex in Pretoria designed and built on friendly financial terms with the city council. Together we had a successful period of eight years in which the Northern Transvaal team performed well, reaching the finals of some competitions for the first time.

"The bulk of the Northern Transvaal players were Afrikaaners. English was not their first language and, in fact, they spoke English only with a heavy accent. It's not generally realised by New Zealanders that Afrikaaners struggle with English. Allan Donald, for instance, never learned English until he started playing county cricket. I had some difficulty pronouncing some of the names of the Afrikaans players and ended up giving them all nicknames, which as a spin-off helped bring us closer together as a team.

"It was during this time I was asked to help the designers of Centurion Park with some tips about 'wet' areas in the dressing room. Because of my experience in running John Reid's Squash Centre, with its eight courts, I had no lack of experience in the matter of wet areas." Reid's commitments with Northern Transvaal cricket dovetailed well with his job at Nissan. "I'd work from 7am to 3.30pm at Nissan, then go off to work with the cricketers. When required I was able to get Fridays and/or Mondays off if our team was travelling."

Reid was fortunate in one respect in his timing as Northern Transvaal coach. "All through the 1980s, South Africa was basically at war with Angola. Pretoria, the biggest city in the province, was the main military base, with conscripts being drafted there for their two years of military service. Among those called up were many current and future South African players, including Fanie de Villiers, Dave Richardson, Brian McMillan and Pat Symcox. All had home base duties and so spent a season or two with Northern Transvaal. On the flip side of this, though, was the fact that because the players knew they were going to be at Pretoria for only a short time, not all of them were especially committed to the team."

From the South African viewpoint, Reid's work with Northern Transvaal cricket was a revelation. "You have to understand," says Dr Basson, "that when John arrived, Northern Transvaal was not really a cricket force. It was a struggling cricket area with no finances and no traditions. When I took over as president, I was part of a group that identified several issues that needed to be addressed if things were to change. One was the building of a good cricket stadium, and John Reid assisted us with some design ideas there. But the big necessity was to get a good captain and coach for the Northern Transvaal side. We picked Lee Barnard as our captain and as soon as we realised John was available to coach, we grabbed him.

"At the time it was unusual thinking for South Africa. John was the only non-South African to coach a leading team. Other teams used foreign players, but kept to home-grown coaches. We had a policy of selecting only South African players, but went further afield for our coach. John proved to be a massive success. He has the reputation of being a stern character, a tough disciplinarian, but he tempered those traits when working with the Northern Transvaal players. He knew that while he had some hard workers in the team, there was not a vast amount of talent, and he demanded only what he knew they were capable of delivering. It was an impressive performance from him as a coach.

"Initially there were a lot of sceptics when we appointed him, and I suppose it was a risk, but he did more than we could ever have wanted. Very soon he was our convener of selectors and we left the entire running of the team to John and Lee, while we got on with administrative matters. John was well-known to the older generation in South Africa as a great player, but that was not really a factor with the players of the 1980s. He had to win them over with his performance as a coach, and he very quickly did that. He came to be looked upon as a father-figure by many of them.

"Northern Transvaal improved quickly and not long after John became coach, we made the final of all the major domestic competitions, one-day and first class. John's organisational ability was outstanding. He was structured and methodical, a deep thinker on the game. His ability came to be recognised outside Northern Transvaal and he was later appointed manager of the South African team, which was a real tribute to him."

Dr Basson makes another point worth noting. "John also contributed through his camera. Everywhere he went, he took that camera and he captured all the important cricket moments over that decade – play, prize-givings, off-the-field activities, important figures in Northern Transvaal cricket. Now we have a complete photographic record of an important era in our cricket, all through that camera of John Reid."

Besides his work with the Northern Transvaal team, Reid was involved in helping run various coaching clinics. "In 1988, Ali Bacher and the South African Cricket Board held their first Plascon Cricket (Krieket) Academy for the coaching of 42 mixed race budding cricketers. There were 12 coaches with Frank Tyson the head coach. Robin Jackman, Vince van der Bijl, Peter Pollock, Peter Kirsten and I were among the specialist coaches. Some of our pupils went on to become leading cricketers. Among them were Brian McMillan, Fanie de Villiers, Jonty Rhodes, Richard Snell and Hanse Cronje.

"In 1991, there was a follow-up of the cricket academy with West Indian Clive Lloyd as chief coach and Bob Woolmer and I included among another list of high-profile coaches. It was interesting to note that the percentage of Coloured and Black African pupils had been increased."

Perhaps the biggest compliment Reid received during his time in South Africa came in 1985 when he managed a South African team captained by Clive Rice against the rebel Australian side led by Kim Hughes. When the South Africans gathered for the international in Johannesburg, Reid reflected that the last times he had had any contact with a South African national team was back in 1961-62 and in 1964 when he captained New Zealand against them.

Reid left Northern Transvaal in 1989, his departure coinciding with the retirement of Dr Basson. But within two days, he had been invited by the Transvaal Cricket Association to manage their team under Clive Rice. "The assignment was not nearly as enjoyable as my time with Northern Transvaal. The chairman of selectors, former test wicketkeeper Lee Irvine, wanted me to report any dressing room gossip that management might find useful. He asked the wrong guy. On another occasion, Clive Rice saw me talking to Jimmy Cook, who, after a great English county season, could hardly score a run for Transvaal. Clive wanted to know what I'd been talking to Jimmy about. I told him Jimmy was being lazy after his run bonanza in England and wasn't getting his front foot to the line of the ball. Clive was satisfied, but I could feel that there was some question as to whether I knew what I was about. One season at Transvaal was enough.

"Travelling with the Northern Transvaal and Transvaal teams around this beautiful, sophisticated country (at that stage) was a joy. I was also able to observe the top South African players and to get an insight into the depth of cricket talent in the country, which I assessed during the 1980s as being quite shallow. It wasn't as meagre as New Zealand, but with such a significant proportion of the population being Africans, there were vast areas where virtually no cricket was being played. Their schools insist that the first term of the new year is devoted to their main summer sport, athletics. So cricket at school is confined to the third term – October-December. Soccer, of course, is the main game for Black Africans and they play it all year. The South African national team is comprised entirely of Black Africans, who are very skilled players. When you think about it, soccer's popularity is not so surprising. In the very poor homelands, townships or compounds, a game of soccer is played on an area of ground and requires a couple of jerseys for goals and a ball. Cricket, by contrast, requires a flattish pitch, a bat, pads, gloves, a decent ball and so on.

"Dr Ali Bacher has had high hopes of encouraging the Africans to play cricket. Up to 120 English professionals have been contracted to coach in southern Africa, and Ali has had some success in attracting a small proportion of Africans to play the game. But basically the cricketers are recruited from among the relatively small English-speaking percentage of the population, some Afrikaaners and an even smaller contribution from the Coloured and Indian sections. Some of these players have gone on to represent South Africa. Now there is a movement by the A.N.C. Government to insist that up to three Blacks must be included in provincial teams, regardless of merit. This Government edict is likely to be upgraded to other sports at national level. It has already caused problems in rugby, where Springbok coach Nick Mallett fought hard to be able to select the players he wanted, regardless of skin colour."

During Reid's time in South Africa the national team captain for some years was the rather controversial Afrikaaner from Bloemfontein, Kepler Wessels, who had an intriguing cricket history. He had left South Africa to join Kerry Packer's World Series, and had then gone on to play for Australia for several seasons. He returned to South Africa eventually and captained them against some of the visiting rebel teams. "Kepler was a reasonably good player in the dour and somewhat selfish mode," says Reid. "He wasn't blessed with the classic left-handed technique of a Bert Sutcliffe.

"Clive Rice took over from him as South African captain, and was a complete contrast in his approach to the game. I saw him only towards the end of his career, but he was still a very good all-rounder, a fastish bowler about the pace of Danny Morrison, and a hard-hitting batsman. I had the opportunity to see other great South African players. Garth le Roux was a genuine fast bowler from Cape Town. He also had a successful spell for Sussex in English county cricket. He was similar in action and about the same pace as the Australian opening bowler of the same time, Craig McDermott. Vincent van der Bijl was a very tall fast-medium bowler from Natal. He was about the pace of Harry Cave and had similar control of line, length and swing. Vince was another who had a successful, if short, career in English county cricket, helping Middlesex win the county championship in 1980.

"Peter Kirsten, the older brother of the current South African opener Gary, was perhaps the best South African batsman of the 1980s, a man of small stature, but one who was unafraid and had all the shots. He scored heavily for Derbyshire and Western Province. Barry Richards, one of the greatest batsmen in cricket history, was still playing for Natal during the early part of my tenure as Northern Transvaal manager-coach and his casual, effortless batting technique was there for all to see."

Despite the enjoyment he was getting from his involvement with cricket, Reid says he was never tempted to remain permanently in South Africa. "We went there for a set period and always intended returning home. Then things began to change in South Africa and there was even less reason to stay." Eventually the Reids returned to New Zealand in early 1992. "During my time away, Richard [his son] had been selected to play one-day cricket for New Zealand, and had done fairly well by all accounts. I was very sorry I missed that. I led a supporters' tour group of 24 people back to New Zealand for the 1992 World Cup, and was initially hopeful of seeing Richard represent his country during that tournament. But by then he was putting his job with Nike first and had to make himself unavailable for the New Zealand side. After the World Cup, I travelled with my group as far as Melbourne, where we parted. I headed home to Taupo and they went back to South Africa."

Reid says he and his wife were in South Africa to see the effects of the contrasting messages of Nelson Mandela and his former wife, Winnie. "We witnessed the rallies of Winnie Mandela with the cry of 'By necklacing we will win.' If you don't know what necklacing is, it's a car tyre filled with petrol being put around the victim's neck and then set alight. Before the abolition of apartheid, there was a lot of unrest in the townships, particularly if you were not A.N.C.-orientated. I had a number of Africans say they wished things were as they had been, as they had lost friends in the fighting, and political promises had not been fulfilled.

"We were also around for the release after nearly 30 years in prison of Nelson Mandela, who proved to be a very remarkable man. For a person aged over 70, his stamina and energy were remarkable. He showed tolerance and understanding as he travelled the world gathering support for his A.N.C. 'abolish apartheid' message. But despite the message of restraint preached by Nelson Mandela, things did not go smoothly in the new order. Violence escalated alarmingly. The last straw for us was the shooting of the accountant where I worked. I had passed the gunmen leaving the building as I came in, which was a bit close for comfort. Also, the firm where Norli worked had been held up at gunpoint on three occasions. On two of these she had arrived at the door as the robbers were dashing out."

The Reids were back in New Zealand when Mandela's A.N.C. party won the election and took over the running of the country from the ruling National Party. Naturally, though, they have kept in touch with friends in South Africa and been rather disturbed to hear of some of the happenings.

"I returned to South Africa in 1998 to referee the South Africa-Pakistan test series and the one-day tournament which also involved Sri Lanka. In the 10 weeks I was there I visited friends and former clients and caught up with past Northern Transvaal players I had got to know through my eight-year association with the team. To say I was disenchanted with the decline in many spheres of South African life would be to put it mildly.

"South Africa is now the most violent country in the world, with an average of 63 murders a day, not to mention vast numbers of rapes, hijacks, robberies, assaults, car thefts and home invasions. It adds up to a huge decline in security and a rise in graft and corruption, which points to the sad fact that South Africa is about to join the other 27 countries in Africa that are either run by dictators or are one-party states.

"I was certainly lucky that I lived in South Africa in a more tranquil atmosphere with the magnificent scenery of mountains and beaches, the fascinating game parks and when there was not the worry of security whenever leaving the hotel. It must be awful to spend life looking over one's shoulder."

14 | OH, BROTHER!

For 58 years John Reid believed he was an only child. Then, in 1986, came a bolt from nowhere. He discovered he had a half-sister, Maureen Rowlands, of Kirwee, near Christchurch.

"I had been living in South Africa, but returned briefly in 1986 to re-settle my ageing parents. While I was back in New Zealand, I received a most unexpected phone call, from the Adult Adoption Agency in Christchurch. I was told that I had a half-sister who would like to contact our mother, if she was still alive.

"Now this was staggering news to someone who had lived so long believing himself an only child. Then, within a few minutes of the call from the Adult Adoption Agency, my new half-sister rang. It was a strange situation. On the one hand, we were closely related; on the other we were absolute strangers. We made arrangements to meet in Wellington.

"I had the difficult task of approaching my mother, who was nearly 80 years of age and was in the early stages of dementia. There were all sorts of questions swirling around in my head. The most glaring was: did dad know of the situation? It was a very emotional and awkward time, and it took quite a lengthy conversation before mum finally felt at ease enough to explain to me the full story. I'm sure it was typical of many in the 1920s. She was just a teenager when she had had her daughter. It must have been extremely difficult for her to cope with that situation and after some months, she felt she needed to give the baby girl up for adoption.

"This was apparently done in a way which would be totally unacceptable today. She was told to visit a certain house, open the front door and leave her baby inside. She was then to leave and put the incident far from her mind. This she did to the best of her ability, though I am certain that the knowledge that she had had a baby girl and the hopes that the child would have been well cared for must have been with her for the rest of her life. As with many adoption situations, it is a terribly poignant story."

Happily, this is one story with a good ending. Arrangements were made for Maureen to meet her birth mother. Understandably it was an emotional occasion, which clearly meant equally as much to the mother and the daughter. Maureen went on to meet her birth mother on several occasions before Mrs Reid died.

Since then John has maintained regular contact with Maureen and her family. "We keep in touch as best we can," says John. "If I'm down in Christchurch, we try to have dinner together, and Maureen has been to Taupo to visit Norli and me. There can be no doubt that Maureen is my mother's daughter – she is the living image of her, and has inherited her musical talent. Strangely enough, Maureen also has many of my mother's mannerisms."

It must be a strange thing, to be an only child for nearly 60 years and then discover a sister. It cannot be the same as growing up from infancy in the same household. But in John's case he has been fortunate. "Maureen was very eager to track down her birth mother and relatives, and I am pleased she did. Finding I have a sister has added a dimension to my life. She is my strongest supporter, even keeping a scrapbook on me!"

Reid found himself in a similar situation to many other children from broken or adopted families. It was estimated that in 1986 there were 50,000 New Zealand-born adults who had been adopted by strangers. A law change in September 1986 gave birth parents and adopted persons the right to officially seek contact with each other, once the adopted person reached the age of 20. In the first six months after the Adult Adoption Information Act came into force, 5843 adult adopted persons – including Maureen – received their original birth certificates, and 1128 birth parents requested the Social Welfare Department trace their son or daughter.

While the law was changed with every good intention, it created some extremely difficult situations for people who had lived to middle age or older and were then confronted with news they might have wished had remained secret.

Though things worked out well in this case, Reid says things could have gone wrong. He is not overly impressed with the way the Social Welfare Department interpreted the Adult Adoption Information Act. "The initial phone call happened to come to me. But what would have happened had the department contacted my mother instead? My father would have taken the call, and that would have led to a vast amount of unnecessary anguish. As it was, he died without knowing anything of this episode of mum's life. It seems to be that very little thought went into that phone call and no consideration was given to the fact that the mother must have been nearing 80, with a child of 60.

"In my case, it all turned out for the better. Mum was reunited with her daughter and I discovered I had a half-sister. But I can easily imagine that there must have been some terrible anguish suffered by birth mothers and their families during the late 1980s if the process was handled in this way in every case."

15 | NO WHISTLE, WILL TRAVEL

What does an I.C.C. referee do? Some cricket followers think that he is the person who pushes the "in-out" buttons. Or that perhaps he is the third umpire. Anyway, how can a person be a referee if he doesn't have a whistle?

The pity of it is that there needs to be a match referee at all. The referee's responsibility is to ensure players heed the I.C.C. Code of Conduct rules. It's a sign of the times that the Code of Conduct has had to be introduced. Imagine Jack Hobbs, Victor Trumper, Lindsay Hassett or Denis Compton needing to have their behaviour on the field modified by any rules! They, and their contemporaries, understood not only the laws of cricket, but the spirit in which the game was played. They were proud to be cricketers and would never have dreamed of acting in an underhand or confrontational manner.

But from the mid-1970s to the early '90s, player behaviour deteriorated so much that action clearly needed to be taken. The players were becoming abusive on the field – the modern term is sledging, which covers a multitude of sins. Not only was the players' behaviour towards their opponents unacceptable, but even the umpires were on the receiving end of an increasing amount of dissent. Where once umpires' decisions were accepted without comment, now players thought nothing of disagreeing with the umpire, and acting in an inflammatory, confrontational manner.

The world cricket hierarchy felt a serious step needed to be taken to control the players' behaviour on the field so that youngsters coming into the game did not get the wrong impression and regard this unacceptably boorish behaviour as the norm. There is nothing surer than the fact that if test players act poorly on the field, their behaviour will be repeated the next Saturday morning on parks all over the country by children who have been watching their sports heroes in action and are mirroring their behaviour.

"When I was playing," says Reid, "the term 'It isn't cricket' was used to refer to something underhand or unacceptable that had occurred in any walk of life. The expression was understood worldwide. But not nowadays. Many of the commendable, if old-fashioned, values have disappeared. Cricket is the poorer for it.

"Cricket etiquette has largely vanished. These days you do not see the clapping or acknowledgement of the captain as he arrives at the crease. It used to be accepted as normal that the fielding team would applaud a batsman who reached a fifty or a century, and sometimes even if he played a very fine stroke. These days this acknowledgement, when it is given, is usually reluctant and half-hearted. Most teams these days would not even consider socialising with the other team by having a drink in either dressing room at the end of the day's play. I have a feeling that there will not be too many team reunions taking place 20 years down the track."

So now we have a referee charged with policing the I.C.C. Code of Conduct. The important nine-point package of rules is, in summarised form:

1. Captains are responsible for ensuring that play is conducted within the spirit of the game, as well as within the laws.
2. Thou shalt not engage in conduct unbecoming to an international player.
3. Thou shalt accept the umpire's decision. (Failure to do so is known as dissent.)
4. Thou shalt not assault or intimidate anybody.
5. Thou shalt not use abusive language (sledging).
6. Thou shalt not use drugs.
7. Thou shalt not comment on an alleged breach of the Code.
8. Thou shalt not make any public statement detrimental to the match or the series.
9. Thou shalt not bet in any shape or form.

What are the referee's commitments? The day starts an hour and a half before play begins, which can be quite early. In Pakistan play often begins at 9am, so the referee will need to be at the ground by 7.30am. The referee's day finishes one hour after the close of play, or later if there is a hearing. There is a match report to be written after every match and at the end of the series, referees file a comprehensive report which covers such matters as liaison with local officials, umpiring, ground covers, sightscreens, pre and post-match ceremonies, the standard of the scorers, ticketing, travel arrangements, the media, dressing rooms, umpires' rooms, security, lighting, hotels, catering, the standard of the wickets, practice facilities, television facilities (for the third umpire) and local administration.

One of the important duties of an I.C.C. match referee is to hold a referee's meeting 24 hours before the first day's play of a test or the first match in a one-day series. This meeting involves from 12 to 14 people. Both team managements are expected to attend – including captain, vice-captain, manager and coach – plus the three (or four) umpires and the leading cricket official, usually a chief executive, of the province, state or county of wherever the match is being played. An agenda is drawn up, mainly to discuss playing conditions which, while they should be the same everywhere, are not; introduce various officials to one another; and discuss the referee's interpretation of the Code of Conduct, which should also be the same everywhere, but is not.

"There is some inconsistency in various referees' rulings," says Reid. "The rules are all to be found in the I.C.C. Code of Conduct booklet but, as in other spheres of life, there are differences of opinion on the degree of alleged breaches. It's not a life or death problem, but I know that the players would like to have a more consistent approach.

"I usually produce either a letter to the managers that I request be read out at an early team meeting, or give each person present at the referee's meeting a set of rules. Here is the letter I handed out for the series of test and one-day matches in India in October-November 1996 involving Australia, South Africa and India:

REFEREE'S POLICY STATEMENT

My recent I.C.C. Referee appointments have highlighted various consistent breaches of the I.C.C. Code of Conduct which have needed action by the referee – some are minor, some are major.

To avoid the suggestion of inconsistency with my interpretation and application of the I.C.C. Code of Conduct, I have set out some non-negotiable breaches that are not acceptable, but still arise. The breaches, which I do not want repeated on this tour, have been as follows:

* *Gesturing to a dismissed batsman.*
* *Excessive appealing or charging an umpire for a decision.*
* *Using advertising/sponsors' products on arm guards, wristlets, headbands etc. As set out in the Code.*
* *Excessive anything, bad language, intimidation or abuse.*
* *And, of course, sledging.*

I have said on other occasions that I can understand a few words in the heat of the moment, but it must not be prolonged. Remember: out in the middle you are on trial by television, with eight or more cameras being used. This list of past breaches is a long one, which I do not want added to in this series.

It is becoming increasingly obvious that the fines system for enforcing breaches of the Code in some cases is not having the desired effect in discouraging transgressions, so the sterner measures as set out in the Code of Conduct may have to be considered – suspension.

I expect the respective captains to control their players on the field and to act or react immediately the umpire asks for assistance to control the situation. The umpires are in control of this game of cricket, but if the umpire or captain cannot control the players on the field, please remember that the referee has the authority and muscle within the I.C.C. Code of Conduct to act decisively to penalise any act which brings the game of cricket into disrepute.

The referee is not here on holiday. He has a job to do. It is spelt out in the I.C.C. little book. You have a copy and I expect all players to have been made aware of what the I.C.C. Code of Conduct is all about.

This series will be watched by millions of cricket followers. You are held up as role models for all those youngsters. I would like to think you will not let them down.

John Reid O.B.E.
I.C.C. Match Referee

"The rules are fairly vast and the penalties can be severe," says Reid. "They range from a warning to a 75 per cent match fee fine and suspension from three test matches or six one-day international matches, or both. The referee can also impose a suspended sentence. This means the guilty player or official has his penalty suspended for a period and eventually waived, providing he does not offend again during his period of suspension.

"The method of procedure for a report on an alleged breach (reports can be brought by any of the three umpires, team managers, the local chief executive officer, the chief executive officer of the I.C.C. and, of course, the referee) is to hold a hearing at which the defendant is present. The referee chairs the hearing. As many witnesses as are required can be brought to the hearing. The referee must ensure that the accused has the benefit of natural justice. Usually there will be a video tape of the incident available. The referee's decision is final – there are no appeals.

"This all sounds very serious, and it is. But like all systems where the human factor is involved, it is difficult to devise a perfect system. Although the Code of Conduct and the various procedures are spelled out comprehensively in the I.C.C. handbook, inconsistencies still creep in. These can be confusing to the players.

"Throughout my playing career, I always felt it was important to maintain the best ideals of cricket. Happily, most of my opponents felt the same. Ted Dexter, Peter May, Dennis Atkinson, Jackie McGlew, the Nawab of Pataudi and other test captains I opposed played their cricket hard but fair. Sledging – what an ugly word – was pretty much non-existent.

"We had a moment in South Africa in 1961-62 when fast bowler Peter Heine had me on. I replied by suggesting he look at the scoreboard. That was the end of it. On another occasion Australian Lindsay Kline was bowling from wide of the crease, more like mid-on, towards second slip. The slips cordon of Neil Harvey, Richie Benaud and Bobby Simpson and wicketkeeper Wally Grout were congratulating him after each delivery. Their cries of 'Well bowled' became tiresome. Finally Kline dropped one short and I hooked it for 6, then turned around and said to the Aussie slips, 'What! No applause?'

"One constant source of discussion during my career was 'walking' – the batsman giving himself out caught behind without waiting for the umpire's decision. I did not walk, preferring to leave all decisions to the umpire. I believed I would sometimes be given out when I wasn't, and sometimes would gain the benefit of a lucky decision. Walking was a big issue, though. Some players did walk, and some walked when it suited them. In 1963 I chaired a seminar in the Wellington Town Hall. Several of the visiting England team – Fred Titmus, Alec Bedser, Fred Trueman, Colin Cowdrey and assistant team manager Desmond Eagar – were involved. It went very well. Then came questions from the audience, and one concerned walking. Trueman replied first, saying batsmen had to walk. Bedser agreed. Titmus said he walked, and so did Cowdrey. My experience was that many English batsmen walked only when it suited them.

"I am reminded of the attitude of another England player, Eric Russell of Middlesex. One time, I heard him asked about walking. His reply went along the lines: 'I'm a professional and it's my duty to uphold the standards and spirit of the game, so I always walk.' Well, the next day, I was fielding in the gully while Russell was batting. He got a nick and was caught behind, but remained rooted to the crease. Bearing in mind his stance of the previous evening, I told him in no uncertain terms that he should go.

"But these are isolated incidents from a career of 58 tests and nearly 250 first class matches. All would seem very mild by more recent standards and none involved abuse. Even the hot-tempered characters of my era rarely got nasty. Fred Trueman was renowned as a fiery character, but he never got personal and often his comments had a strain of humour running through them. Peter Heine and I had a beer together at the end of the day's play after our run-in."

Players of Reid's era revelled in a torrid battle, but seldom seemed to lose their enjoyment of the situation and their appreciation of the performances of their opponents. Then Reid noted how things had gradually changed.

"I grew very concerned in the years after my retirement at the deterioration in standards. During the late 1980s and early '90s when I made various speeches about the place, I used to stress the need for the umpires to have more power. I could see it was necessary because of the amount of arguing with umpires' decisions, the way some teams had developed the habit of charging umpires when appealing and the abuse of umpires and opponents that was going on. These were the days before referees. I suggested introducing something like giving the umpires the power to signal a 6 for unsportsmanlike behaviour, and to keep signalling 6 until the behaviour stopped. I felt this might put pressure on the captains to modify their teams' behaviour."

The I.C.C.'s decision to appoint referees for international matches came at the perfect time for Reid. He had returned from South Africa to live in New Zealand a year earlier and was not having much joy with New Zealand Cricket in his endeavours to become involved as a coach and/or team manager. "I had a look at the way things were running at the cricket academy in Christchurch and can't say I was overly impressed. I couldn't understand, for instance, why Mike Shrimpton was the leg-spin coach when

New Zealand's greatest leg-spinner, Jack Alabaster, was unemployed in the cricket sense just a few hours' drive away in Alexandra. I wanted to become involved in coaching, and also applied to manage various teams, but I didn't get far. My impression at the time was that some of the people running New Zealand Cricket were protecting their own patches.

"Then I heard about a series in South Africa in which Peter May was appointed referee, which was a new I.C.C. development. I rang Colin Cowdrey, who was then chairman of the I.C.C., to ask him more about the referee's role. It was a timely call as Colin felt I would be ideal for the job, and the I.C.C. was looking about for more former players who would make suitable referees. I needed to be nominated for the position by New Zealand Cricket, and that was not a problem – my feeling was that they were pleased to get me off their hands about then! My involvement as an I.C.C. match referee has suited me fine. I am a little old-fashioned and traditional and those are qualities I bring to the role of referee – it sits well with my character. I am also a bit of a stickler for discipline, on the field and off, so the role sits very well with me.

"My first appointment was for the Sri Lanka-South Africa series in Sri Lanka. There was a minor hiccup when the Sri Lankans queried my appointment. They were under the impression I was then living in South Africa, which was not the case. Early in the series I had cause to speak to Jonty Rhodes and Pat Symcox, who were fielding at cover and mid-wicket and were throwing the ball back hard dangerously near the batsmen. One batsman, Aravinda de Silva, avoided being hit only by holding up his bat in front of his face. The ball was deflected at the last moment by the bat handle. So I called in the two fieldsmen, plus Mike Procter, the South African coach, and Kepler Wessels, the captain, and spelled out what was and was not acceptable. Mike Procter was most upset as Jonty, in particular, is a very fair sportsman, but even the best can get carried away. Two dangerous throws were two too many, even if they were aberrations. I accepted their statements that the incidents were accidents and took no further action, but the message was delivered."

At about the same time as the I.C.C. decided to appoint international referees, it also drew up the Code of Conduct. "Since then," says Reid, "umpires' jobs have been made much easier because at last umpires have some support. Obviously some referees are stronger than others, but all of them offer umpires support that was missing until the early 1990s. The referees' role has been refined over the years. Initially we were tossed in the deep end without a great deal of instruction, but now we understand clearly what our responsibilities are."

Umpires certainly seem to appreciate the support they get from referees. New Zealander Brian Aldridge was one of the first to benefit. "I umpired the 1993 series between Sri Lanka and South Africa, when John Reid was the referee," says Aldridge. "It was in the very early days of referees and I felt at the time it was largely experimental. There was a teething process where we all wondered what our roles were. Umpires initially wondered if the referee would be a political appointment, whose main job was to inhabit the corporate boxes and to speak nicely with local cricket officials. But John Reid's attitude in those early days helped establish the pattern where the referee and the umpires were very much a team and helped monitor the behaviour of the players. In fact, these days the two umpires, the third umpire and the fourth umpire, plus the referee, are known officially as the Playing Control Team."

For Aldridge, the introduction of referees, and also of the Code of Conduct at about the same time, did not come a moment too soon. "We had a series in New Zealand not long before where the Pakistanis were apparently most unhappy with the New Zealand umpires. Intikhab Alam, the manager, and Imran Khan, the captain, put the two umpires, Steve Woodward and me, under unbelievable pressure, disputing our decisions, virtually calling us cheats, and calling for neutral umpires. At the time we lacked any support. Once the tour was over, the New Zealand cricket authorities supported us, but not until the final match. Maybe they were afraid if they defended us earlier, the Pakistanis would simply pack up and go home, with consequent loss of tour income. Those were the sorts of things umpires were having to put up with.

"We felt we not only lacked power, but also support. The early referees, John Reid, Peter Burge and Raman Subba Row, led the way and it was the manner in which they did their job that has made it easier for the referees who have followed."

Aldridge is in no doubt that behaviour standards have improved since the arrival of referees. "The Code of Conduct and its enforcement by referees has meant that dissent and bad sportsmanship have been toned down. There is now a set of rules that players are aware of, and that has altered players' behaviour for the better."

Leading English umpire David Shepherd echoes these views. "The referees have been a great help to umpires, a great back-up," he says. "Before the advent of referees, we had to deal with the disciplinary side of things ourselves, and it was not easy. By the end of the 1980s, the behaviour of many of the players on the field was terrible. Television was sending those images to the rest of the world. It was bad for cricket. Now we have the Code of Conduct and the referees to implement it. In addition, the referees look after the umpires. They inspect the conditions we work in, plus the transport, hotels and so on, and include it in their reports."

Shepherd says that of the referees he has dealt with, Reid would sit on the stern side. "All referees are individuals. Some are more strict than others. Different referees have different ways of applying the Code of Conduct – whether to coerce players or come down with some severity. What is required is consistency, and that's what John supplies.

"I never played with or against John, though I heard a lot about his

Reid in full cry, driving off the back foot during his whirlwind innings of 296 in 1963.

Reid the bowler.

The New Zealand team which played the M.C.C. at Wellington in 1961 takes time out from a practice at Kelburn Park. From left: Zin Harris, John Reid, Jack Alabaster, Dick Motz, Frank Cameron, Eric Petrie, Noel McGregor, Graham Dowling, Les Butler, Paul Barton, Barry Sinclair.

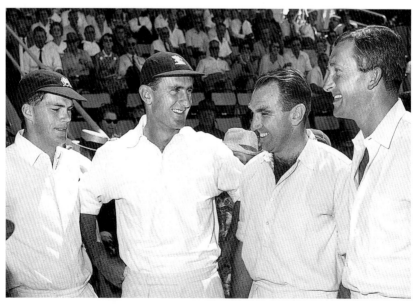

Four international captains gathered for the Ron Roberts Cavaliers match against Rhodesia in 1963. From left: Tony Pithey (Rhodesia), Ted Dexter (England), John Reid (New Zealand), Richie Benaud (Australia).

Who says batting in sunglasses is a recent innovation? Because of an eye problem, Reid batted in sunglasses during the test against Pakistan in Wellington in 1965.

Rivals and friends Colin Cowdrey (left) and John Reid prepare to toss in 1965 before New Zealand's tour opener against the Duke of Norfolk's XI at Arundel.

The Rest of the World XI that Reid captained in 1965. Back row, from left: Rohan Kanhai, Lance Gibbs, Wes Hall, Charlie Griffith, Colin Bland, Eddie Barlow, Conrad Hunte. Front row: Wally Grout, Gary Sobers, John Reid, Nawab of Pataudi, Hanif Mohammad.

Cricket – the game for any conditions? Reid batting at the South Pole during a visit to Antarctica in 1970.

Reid hits catches during a practice session with his Northern Transvaal team in 1984.

Fifteen New Zealand cricket captains gather for the launch of *Men in White* in 1986. Back row, from left: Mark Burgess, Jeremy Coney, John Parker, Geoff Rabone, Harry Cave, Graham Dowling. Middle row: Glenn Turner, Bevan Congdon, Geoff Howarth, Walter Hadlee. Front row: Merv Wallace, Barry Sinclair, Bert Sutcliffe, John Reid, Curly Page.

John and Richard Reid in front of the J.R. Reid Gate at the Basin Reserve.

reputation as a player. I must say I've enjoyed working with him. He offers umpires full support, and in the evening he is an interesting person to have a beer or a meal with."

Looking back at some of the unsavoury incidents from the 1970s and '80s, it is revealing how many of them involved Australians. Under the captaincy of Ian and Greg Chappell, sledging became very much the norm in Australian test teams, and gradually it filtered throughout the cricket world.

Incidentally the term sledging was coined in the late 1960s when Australian pace bowler Grahame Corling swore in mixed company and was admonished by a team-mate that he was "as subtle as a sledgehammer", which was subsequently abbreviated to sledging. Ian Chappell, the Australian captain through the first half of the 1970s, inspired immense loyalty in his players, but later ran into increasing problems with cricket authories, often for foul language.

It's unfair to blame the Australians entirely. W.G. Grace himself was a notable sledger. In Ranjitsinhji's *The Jubilee Book of Cricket*, published in 1897, Ranji says: "I heard the other day of another way of getting out – viz, being talked out... Batsmen are quite within their rights in requiring conversational fieldsmen to hold their tongues."

The Australians weren't the only teams doing it, but they were certainly among the most vociferous. They pushed the barriers more and more. There was abuse, racial taunts and some even less savoury incidents, such as the physical confrontation between Dennis Lillee and Javed Miandad at Perth in 1982. Ian Botham, himself no saint, says in *Beefy* that a typical Australian remark was, "Who do you think your wife was screwing last night?" West Indian opener Robert Samuels once said that each time he went in to bat against the Australians, it was like attending a sex education class.

The West Indies were also involved in some disgraceful episodes, none more so than during their 1980 tour of New Zealand. During that test series, Colin Croft shoulder-charged umpire Fred Goodall, Michael Holding kicked over the stumps in disgust, and there was a threatened mutiny of the West Indian team during the test at Christchurch.

Times have changed since the referees were appointed. "In 1994, when the West Indies were playing England," says Reid, "I fined Curtly Ambrose $US1500 at Barbados for bringing the game into disrepute. He used his bat to knock the one remaining stump out of the ground after he had been bowled, his dismissal ending the game. He initially refused to accept the jurisdiction of the hearing because the match was over. That cost him a further fine. Eventually his team manager, Rohan Kanhai, and captain, Richie Richardson, told him to keep quiet. It was interesting. I found I received a great deal of support from the West Indies board, which made me think that perhaps they were pleased that finally player power was being reined in somewhat.

"Also during that test series I fined the West Indies $US21,000 for being a total of 13 overs short of the required 15 overs per hour over-rate for the match."

Reid is emphatic that cricket standards, spirit, etiquette, behaviour and performance are linked. "I have watched the New Zealand team through the 1990s and, to be honest, since the retirement of John Wright, Richard Hadlee and Ian Smith, I haven't seen what I would term a satisfactory improvement in the new players. There were signs of an upturn in England in 1999, but overall the senior players cannot be content with their contribution over the past few years. The players have a coach, a 'technical coach', a psychologist, various support staff, videos to analyse their technique, and a vast amount of cricket exposure at international level. Why haven't they kicked on quicker? Why have they repeated their mistakes? I think at least part of the answer is in their attitude.

"Modern thinkers might scoff at me, but I get very frustrated with the discarding of blazers and ties for jeans and shorts. I like to see New Zealand teams taking pride in the silver fern and other countries' players being equally proud of their emblem. That pride will come through on the paddock. Glenn Turner, when he was coach, was starting to bring back a bit of that pride and individual responsibility. I look at the Australians. They have double-breasted blazers. The South Africans are immaculately dressed. The England team has often looked like a rag-tag bobtail team wearing 'Balmy Army' shirts on the bus, though things are improving in this respect. The Indian and Pakistani teams generally look pretty good.

"Perhaps New Zealanders only now are beginning to realise that to be a cricketer, you have to look like a cricketer. I don't like to see players being arrogant and disrespectful, and not obviously proud of the silver fern. These days when asked to attend a function or do a spot of PR work, often the first question a player asks is: 'How much?' That's bad. I know there is money around, but I prefer to see players more obviously proud to be representing their country. That's the example I like to see filtering through to the youngsters who turn up to watch their sports heroes.

"Appearance, attitude and behaviour are linked. When I look at the New Zealand team at present, several of them are sledgers and we have players who show dissent. It's disappointing.

"The dissent that has crept into world cricket since the 1980s has been terrible. You must accept the umpire's decision. You don't answer back. You don't point to your pads or your bat. You don't hang around at the crease shaking your head after you've been given out. You don't walk off swearing, shaking your head or tapping your bat.

"I recall a test in 1951 at Christchurch. Cyril Washbrook, the England opener, was given out lbw to Fen Cresswell. He dawdled from the field looking over his shoulder and tapping his pad with his bat. Wal Hadlee, our captain, got the message. He asked Fen about the decision and Fen said he had appealed out of enthusiasm and that he was now sure Washbrook had hit the ball. So Wal ran after Washbrook and recalled him. Today a referee would have fined Washbrook for dissent. On the other hand, Wal and Fen had not wanted to gain an unfair dismissal and Washbrook was recalled. Would we see that sort of sportsmanship often today?"

So what about some of the famous incidents that occurred before referees? How would Reid, in his capacity as an I.C.C. referee, have dealt with them?

1971, Sydney: England fast bowler John Snow felled Australia's No 9 Terry Jenner with a bouncer and was warned for intimidatory bowling. Shortly afterwards, when fielding on the boundary, he was the target of beer cans thrown by the crowd. Without consulting the umpires, England captain Ray Illingworth took his team from the field. The players were off the field for seven minutes. "I wouldn't have had a problem with Illingworth's actions, providing his team returned to the field as soon as conditions were suitable," says Reid. "It would, however, have been better if he'd advised the umpires of his intended course of action.

"I've been on the field a few times myself, in my capacity as a referee. At Bangalore in a South Africa-India one-dayer, India were getting beaten and the crowd reacted in a hostile manner when Azharuddin walked slowly from the field after being given out. The players were pelted with missiles, and Cronje, the fielding captain, marched his team from the field. I had a chat with the umpires and eventually Azharuddin walked over to the crowd and held up his hands, seeking some calm. I thanked him for his action and let him off a dissent charge for his show of displeasure after he was given out. It was a tempestuous time. At one point I was on the field telling the local police commissioner where to put his policemen. Far too many of them were guarding the V.I.Ps and hardly any were facing the crowd. I had them dotted around the ground, ready to pick up any spectator who threw an object onto the field."

1980, Christchurch: West Indian pace bowler Colin Croft charged umpire Fred Goodall after an umpiring decision did not go in his favour. "This was at the absolute top end of bad behaviour. He would have received the maximum penalty possible, including fines and suspensions. Clive Lloyd, the captain, would have also been in the gun, because of his failure to control his player or take action after the incident."

1980, Dunedin: Michael Holding kicked the stumps over after an umpiring decision didn't go in his favour. "Holding felt he had had John Parker caught behind. Parker did not walk and the umpire ruled not out. The merit or otherwise of the decision is irrelevant. Holding was guilty of bringing the game into disrepute and would certainly have been heavily fined and possibly suspended."

1981, Melbourne: The underarm incident. Australian captain Greg Chappell instructed his brother Trevor to deliver the final ball of a one-day international underarm so that incoming New Zealand No 11 Brian McKechnie would not be able to hit a 6 and so tie the match. "Greg Chappell would have been the major culprit. He would have been guilty of bringing the game into disrepute and of unsportsmanlike behaviour. However, nothing other than a warning could have been imposed as Greg could have answered that his action (at the time) was completely within the laws of cricket. Trevor Chappell, who delivered the underarm, would also have received a warning."

1982, Perth: Dennis Lillee and Javed Miandad, after a build-up of niggling, eventually squared up to each other. Lillee, annoyed that Miandad was hindering his follow-through, kicked at Miandad and Miandad shaped to hit Lillee with his bat. "They would have both been done for 'bringing the game into disrepute'. In addition, Lillee was guilty of assault and Miandad of abuse. Both players would have earned themselves a holiday, because if a referee had been present, they would have copped hefty suspensions."

1987, Faisalabad: England captain Mike Gatting, angry at a succession of umpiring decisions with which he disagreed, became involved in a swearing match with umpire Shakoor Rana, pointing his finger at him and speaking aggressively. "Gatting would have been suspended for dissent, and his situation would have been all the more serious because he was the captain. Poor umpiring – if indeed it was – is no excuse for dissent. A referee would have included comments on the umpiring in his report, which might have impacted on whether umpire Rana was again appointed to test cricket."

Reid says he is heartened because there has been an improvement in behaviour. "It was really bad. It's still poor, but improving. Referees could still be more aware of officiating to the letter of the law. You set your own standards. I set mine high. Players and umpires know that. The umpires know they will get support and the players know they will not get away with much.

"One thing I'm very hot on is physical contact between players. There have been various incidents. Prasad deliberately walking in front of Craig McMillan, Julian and Campbell, McGrath standing in the way of the batsmen running between wickets. The referee who sees something like that happening has to do something about it then and there. I'll go straight to the dressing room and have a message sent out with the next drinks break, or I'll write a letter to the manager of the offending team and have it delivered immediately. If the offence looks serious enough, I'll hold a hearing to get both sides of the story and then make a decision.

"In the Pakistan-Australia series in 1994, Wasim and Waqar were bowling with the second new ball against the Australians at Peshawar. They delivered 13 intimidatory balls out of 19. I wrote a message, and had it delivered immediately. It was probably a case of me exceeding my authority, but I felt action needed to be taken. Then I had a chat about it to the umpires at the next break. You have to try to do your job, but without undermining the umpires. But in this case, neither umpire had had any international cricket experience and didn't see that there was a problem.

"I have spoken to Steve Waugh for petulance. In 1996 against Sri Lanka, after he had been warned in the previous match, he went out of his way to cause a problem. He took objection to the batsman having a drink. It was silly, but if you let it go, things can mushroom. Waugh is such a class player he doesn't need to get into all that. In that match, he took three wickets, scored 60 and was Man of the Match. He did himself no favours with his behaviour and should have let the standard of his cricket speak for itself."

One of the joys for a referee, says Reid, is receiving strong and genuine support from the captains. "On one occasion I warned McGrath and Matthew Hayden, after they'd been involved in a minor skirmish during an Australia v Australia A match. It was not a big incident and I was happy just to give them a slap over the wrist. But Mark Taylor, then the Australian captain, went much further, telling them their behaviour was unacceptable. Taylor took the Code of Conduct seriously and backed up the referee."

One battle Reid has not won (yet) concerns spitting. It is difficult to imagine Don Bradman, Walter Hammond, Garfield Sobers or Reid himself spitting repeatedly during a day's play, but the habit is widespread today. "These days fans everywhere express disgust at the indiscriminate spitting by players on the field. It's worse because the television cameras beam these delightful images all over the world. In 1995 I sent a letter to the managers of the West Indies and England teams, requesting that their players refrain from expectorating on the field of play. Nothing much seems to have happened since. The habit is still around and it is still disgusting."

Another practice Reid says he makes every effort to stamp out is charging the umpire when appealing. "When I was refereeing the I.C.C. Trophy matches at Kuala Lumpur, I disciplined the Bangladesh captain. It was interesting to see that while the practice had been largely stamped out in test cricket, non-I.C.C. countries were still catching up."

Perhaps in the cool light of day, the players look at their fines philosophically. The money goes to the I.C.C. and to the coaching of children. Hopefully the players regard it as their special contribution, and a one-off at that!

"These high-profile and highly paid cricket heroes need to keep in mind their role model image," says Reid. "A sponsor is hardly likely to be pleased to be paying money to a player who has been suspended for breaches of the Code of Conduct. What's more, besides risking the loss of a valued sponsor, suspension means a player may have to work extra hard to regain his place in the team, if his replacement performs well in his absence."

16 | HOW THE RULES HAVE CHANGED

Umpires play a strangely ambiguous role in cricket. They spend more time on the field than the players, and their decisions can shape absolutely the outcome of any match. Yet they strive to be anonymous dispensers of justice. Umpires feel that the less they are noticed, the better the job they have done.

No one has had a fuller relationship with umpires than John Reid, who saw the good and the bad during his 246 first class matches, and especially during the decade he was test captain. He watched them with more than detached interest as a test selector and a coach, and since 1993 has worked closely with the best in the world in his capacity as an I.C.C. referee.

Here is Reid's assessment of umpires during his cricketing life:

'As a player, my relationship with umpires was generally very cordial. I had no real run-ins, but then people of my generation didn't. It was virtually unheard of to show the sort of dissent that is sometimes seen today. When I played, you accepted the umpires' decisions with good grace. You did not walk off the field pointing at your bat to indicate to the umpire, the television cameras and the spectators that you had hit the ball when you had just been given out lbw. You did not scowl, hands on hip, for prolonged periods when your appeal as a bowler was turned down. And you did not as a team charge towards the umpire in an intimidating manner when making an appeal.

I did not always agree with umpires' decisions, but I learned early that it was a waste of time when I was bowling to take umbrage. Umpires never change their decisions and worse, you might not get the next one. As a batsman I wasn't a walker. I left it for the umpires to rule on each appeal. However, I never showed dissent because I believed in the swings and roundabouts theory – if you give yourself out when the decision might have been not out, then the next time when you are incorrectly given out, you lose both ways!

Early in my touring days, we certainly struck the odd case of biased umpiring. In one test in Pakistan, one of the umpires was employed by the Pakistani captain, an interesting state of affairs. In India, the lbw tally when we toured there in 1955 was 15-2 against us. We had to wait until the fourth test, when India were 262-2, before we were favoured with our first leg before decision. There was a second one in the last test, when India were 537-2. In

1965 in India it was 13-1. Either our batsmen had a great propensity for getting their legs in front and our bowlers simply could not direct a ball at the stumps, or there was something funny going on. It was inhibiting because, not only did we feel we had to knock over the stumps, and make sure all three were down, to get rid of an Indian batsman, but when we were batting, we felt it unsafe to allow the ball to pass the bat. If it wasn't a leg before, it could be caught behind.

Today, as a referee, I know a lot more about umpiring than when I was playing, and during the 1990s I have seen little outright bias from umpires. Mistakes are made, but they are genuine mistakes. One factor, of course, has been the introduction of neutral umpires, which not only meets with approval from the players, but also makes life easier in countries where local umpires can get abused and threatened if they make decisions which hurt the home side.

The referee is in a unique situation to report on the umpires. He is in their company before the match, at all intervals and after stumps. He can witness the start of play nervousness, not unlike a batsman preparing to face his first ball. He will see the good days and the bad days and how umpires react to the constant television replays on huge screens now present at many major test grounds. It must be extremely difficult to know that a decision you have had to make in an instant is now being examined by 30,000 spectators who have the benefit of several slow-motion replays. That is the sort of pressure umpires from previous generations never faced.

Most of the best umpires still come from England, where all are fulltime professionals. Most have taken up first class umpiring after long and successful county careers. I say successful, because their careers wouldn't have been long if they weren't successful! The top rank of umpires would most certainly include these people:

David Shepherd (England): Played for Gloucestershire, scoring more than 10,000 first class runs, and has now been umpiring at the top level for nearly 20 years. He is probably the umpire most widely respected by test players around the world. "Shep" is fairly superstitious and as a former player gets very twitchy when Nelson's number (111, 222, 333) comes up on the scoreboard. Keep an eye on him then and you'll notice him hopping around on one foot.

Peter Willey (England): After a good career for Northants, for whom he scored more than 24,000 runs, and England, for whom he played 26 tests, Peter has risen through the ranks of umpires, having taken up the profession in the early 1990s. Peter stands for no nonsense and is respected by the players because they know he has paid his dues in test cricket. My first contact with Peter was when he was playing for Eastern Province and I was coach/manager of Northern Transvaal. We met again in India when I was the I.C.C. match referee and he was the I.C.C. panel umpire. It was there that he said: "Test umpiring is hard work. I'd rather be a househusband." I imagine that's not a remark heard often in or around test cricket. In fact, Peter is a househusband most of the time.

Srinivas Venkataraghavan (India): In our playing days we called him "Rhubarb" or "Rent-A-Caravan", but these days he is often known as "Venkat" or "Venkee". He is a long-serving contributor to cricket in many spheres. He was an off-spinner against New Zealand in 1965, and later became captain of the test side. He managed the Indian team for a time before becoming an I.C.C. referee and is now a top umpire. His total of 156 test wickets in 57 tests indicates that at least sometimes he got some positive answers to the appeals he made to the umpires of his time. Now he is able to adjudicate on the appeals of others. As an umpire he is very well thought of and stands no nonsense, which makes it easier for all concerned.

David Orchard (South Africa): "Orchie" is relatively new to the I.C.C. panel of 20 umpires. He comes from a first class cricket background and has played some years for Natal and he has gained the respect of players around the world.

Steve Bucknor (West Indies): Steve is an early appointment for any big cricket match, be it in the test or one-day arena. He has tremendous experience as an umpire, having stood in his first test in 1987, but as he was then only 41, is young enough to be able to go on for some years yet. Steve maintains good discipline on the field, perhaps helped by the fact that he is used to handling the fiery atmosphere of soccer matches. He was an international soccer referee and officiated in World Cup matches from the mid-1980s until 1992. Steve always has a smile and enjoys his umpiring appointments. His characteristic delay in lifting his finger to give the batsman out is, he says, "to give the batsman a chance to walk". There's not much chance of that these days!

Rudi Koertzen (South Africa): Rudi has been a first class umpire since the early 1980s and uses that experience well in maintaining discipline. He seeks to have cricket played in the right spirit and is a good example of how an umpire can keep control on the field. Rudi maintains communication with the players, warning them if they are getting close to no balling, and coming down hard on any backchat. Players know where they stand with him and concern themselves with getting on with the game.

Peter Manuel (Sri Lanka) and Edward Nicholls (West Indies): I have bracketed these two newcomers because I feel they have the right attitude to cricket and have started off their umpiring careers virtually together. Both are thinking people with Peter being a senior bank official and Edward an acting police superintendent. Neither is to be trifled with.

The two New Zealand umpires on the I.C.C. panel, **Steve Dunne** of Dunedin and **Doug Cowie** of Auckland, are well-respected around the world. Both were appointed to officiate in the 1999 World Cup. This was a real honour when you realise that only 12 of the 20 umpires on the I.C.C. panel were chosen.

Over the years I have obviously had a lot to do with New Zealand umpires, even to the extent of making an approach to the then New Zealand Cricket Council when I was test captain. I asked the council to alter its time-honoured but thoughtless policy of appointing the two best umpires from the province where a test was being played, without any regard as to how good the umpires were. So for a test in Dunedin, for example, two Otago umpires would be appointed, even if they were numbers 10 and 14 on the New Zealand umpires' ranking list. Invariably, the New Zealand players copped the backlash with inexperienced umpires bending over backwards to be fair. They were afraid of being accused of bias when confronted with the raucous appeals of well-known visiting bowlers like Tony Lock and Fred Trueman.

My call for the best officials for the tests did not go unheeded and for some years Trevor Martin of Wellington, our best umpire, toured the country controlling the big matches. It was a victory for common-sense. Besides Trevor Martin, other New Zealand umpires I had great respect for were Jack Cowie, my touring companion in 1949, and Eric Tindill, who was just closing his first class career for Wellington when I began. Eric, having represented New Zealand at rugby and cricket and having been a test rugby referee and a national cricket selector, had loads of experience and this showed when he umpired major cricket matches. He was calm and unruffled and players had confidence in him.

Of a more recent vintage, Brian Aldridge of Christchurch was the I.C.C. panel umpire when I officiated in my first series as a referee, in Sri Lanka. I found him to be a very good touring companion as well as an excellent umpire. The I.C.C. were disappointed to see him retire, but we all perked up when he was appointed New Zealand Umpire Manager by New Zealand Cricket.

Australian umpires have had a penchant for being in the headlines. Back in 1879 Victorian umpire George Coulthard gave New South Wales captain Billy Murdoch run out at the Sydney Cricket Ground and a riot occurred. Since then, a succession of Australian umpires have been involved in controversial incidents. George Hele, apparently one of the best umpires of his time, was a key figure as the senior umpire in the 1932-33 bodyline series and later had a book about him written, called *Bodyline Umpire*. We recall Col Egar no balling Ian Meckiff out of the game in 1963 and sparking a major controversy. In the seventh test of the 1970-71 Ashes series, at Sydney, umpire Lou Rowan angered England captain Ray Illingworth for warning his fast bowler John Snow for intimidatory bowling. After an ensuing altercation between Snow and a spectator, Illingworth took his team from the field and Rowan then told Illingworth to get back on the field or forfeit the game. Rowan wrote *The Umpire's Story* in 1972, a book which caused quite a fuss at the time. Even more than two decades after his retirement from umpiring, he was still in the news, publicly supporting Darrell Hair for no balling Sri Lankan off-spinner Muttiah Muralitharan.

Steve Randell was the top Australian umpire in 1997, when he made himself unavailable because of a pending court appearance. By then he had been umpiring at international level for 14 years and had stood in 36 test matches. In 1984, he had become the youngest Australian umpire to control a test. His two-handed drawing of an imaginary television screen when referring a decision to the third umpire – "Somebody Else's Problem" was how he described it – will be with us forever, I suspect.

During a one-day match at Brisbane in 1995, Ross Emerson and Ern McQuillan became the second and third Australian umpires, after Hair, to call Muralitharan for throwing. This brought about a close scrutiny of Muralitharan's action by the I.C.C. special advisory panel on illegal deliveries.

Perhaps this was not sufficient for Emerson. We had discussed, while he was acting as the fourth umpire during the second Ashes test in Perth in 1998, that the correct way of calling a bowler for throwing was to make a report to the referee. If there is no doubt, the umpire must call the no ball. If there is some doubt (and Emerson did not call Muralitharan until his second over), then a report is forwarded to the referee, who is responsible for further action. Perhaps Ross should have stuck to those rules.

Daryl Harper from Adelaide is a most promising Australian umpire. He hasn't found himself in the headlines yet and appears to be an unflappable and competent umpire who will improve with some more international experience.

Two other Australian umpires worth mentioning are Peter Parker of Brisbane and Simon Taufer of Sydney. I have seen Peter in action, including the Ashes series in 1994-95 and 1998-99, and have found him to be a steady, consistent umpire who in my opinion is not used enough in the international arena. Simon is, relatively speaking, a youngster. He impressed me during the 1998-99 Ashes series when as third umpire in the Sydney test, he had three close decisions to give. He handled the pressure and publicity afterwards very well. I feel he will help fill the void left by Steve Randell's departure. Simon also has charisma, not a bad attribute for an official from a cricket country like Australia.

Finally, Darrell Hair, the top Australian umpire heading into the new century. His first words when he met me in the West Indies in 1994 were, "I think you should know that I don't think much of referees." I thought, "This will be fun." The I.C.C. panel umpire, the local umpire, the third umpire and the referee are supposed to be a team, so to be greeted by those words rocked me onto the back foot. But I have learned to play well off the back foot and I think that several years on, he has come to see that having a referee around can be of immense help. However, Darrell didn't make use of Graham Dowling, the referee in 1995 when Darrell made waves (and headlines) by calling Muralitharan for throwing.

Darrell is a good umpire, but got himself into hot water by writing a book, *Decision Maker*, in which he criticised both the Australian Cricket Board and the I.C.C. for, among other things, lack of support. An I.C.C. hearing was subsequently held before a commissioner who examined four alleged breaches of the Code of Conduct arising from statements in the book. Darrell was found guilty on two of them. However a penalty could not be imposed as the word umpire did not feature in the book. Since then a whole new section pertaining to umpires has been added – more headlines!'

17 | LAND OF HOPE AND (SOME) GLORY

It can't have been easy for New Zealand cricket administrators in the early years. Compared to England and Australia, New Zealand had a weak representative team, with only a handful of players of genuine international calibre. There was little incentive for Australian and English teams to make full-length tours of New Zealand, or to host our teams.

In hindsight, it must be said that until 1930, when New Zealand gained official test status, our administrators did well. They oversaw a thriving domestic competition – the Plunket Shield – and ensured the country's best players received as much international exposure as possible, at the same time enabling New Zealand cricket followers to see some of the great names of world cricket.

From 1894, various Australian combinations (New South Wales, Queensland, Australia, Victoria, Arthur Sims' team) toured New Zealand regularly, and players of the calibre of Monty Noble, Reg Duff, Victor Trumper, Clem Hill, Syd Gregory, Warwick Armstrong, Tibby Cotter, Warren Bardsley, Charlie Kelleway, Herb Collins, Arthur Mailey, Jack Crawford, Vernon Ransford, Bert Ironmonger, Alan Kippax, Vic Richardson, Charlie Macartney, Tommy Andrews, Bert Oldfield, Hunter Hendry, Bill Woodful, Clarrie Grimmett, Bill Ponsford and Archie Jackson were seen by New Zealand spectators.

The M.C.C. teams were a more haphazard business. The first English team to meet a New Zealand team was Lord Hawke's side, which played internationals in Christchurch and Wellington in 1903. This tour was set in motion when the New Zealand Cricket Council invited Lord Hawke to form a touring team. Pelham Warner and Bernard Bosanquet (the inventor of the googly, or bosie) were the best-known players in this team. After that various relatively weak M.C.C. teams made goodwill tours and Johnny Douglas, George Simpson-Hayward (the last of the well-known lob bowlers), Percy Chapman, Tich Freeman and future New Zealand captain Tom Lowry were the better-known players who represented the M.C.C. on such ventures.

In addition, fully representative New Zealand teams were sent to Australia in 1899, 1913-14 and 1925-26. Then came the breakthrough tour of England in 1927, under the captaincy of Lowry. It was a tour which introduced talented players such as Stewie Dempster, Ces Dacre, Bill Merritt, Roger Blunt, Jack Mills, Ken James and Curly Page to English audiences and led soon after to New Zealand's admission into the test arena. The team played 38 matches (26 of them first class) and won 13. It proved an expensive undertaking and Prime Minister Gordon Coates eventually offered £1000 to help cut the financial losses.

So it can be seen that for a fledgling cricket nation, New Zealand did fairly well in the first 30 years of the century. The New Zealand Cricket Council was surprisingly adventurous. For instance, when it looked as if the proposed 1931 trip to England would fall through because of lack of finance (New Zealand was in the grip of the Depression), it offered the public 12,000 shares of £1, half of which was to be paid on subscription and the balance collected in such calls as the directors saw fit. Another source of revenue was provided by the Art Union lottery, held in conjunction with the New Zealand Football Association. Well-connected patrons of New Zealand cricket such as Arthur Sims and Daniel Reese then used their political connections to ensure the tour proceeded.

While New Zealand cricket administrators deserve credit for their work until this time, their efforts and expertise did not then keep pace with New Zealand's rise in international standing. For more than half a century after New Zealand became a test-playing country, it was a case of amateur administrators making decisions on professional matters. Some of these decisions were absurd.

For instance, where was the cricket common-sense behind the decision to send a team to Pakistan and India in 1955-56 with such a wicked itinerary? That team, coming out of a New Zealand winter played three tests in six matches in Pakistan, five tests in 10 matches in India. The team travelled with no medical staff and arrived home terribly ill, to be confronted within three weeks by four tests against the West Indies.

In 1965 John Reid led New Zealand on a six-month tour of India, Pakistan and England. In India and Pakistan the team played seven consecutive test matches and no other games. Where was the wisdom in such an impossible itinerary?

The New Zealand Cricket Council's inexperience was revealed in many other areas, from its unwillingness to appoint the best umpires to domestic tests, to its kowtowing to Australia, who played no test matches against New Zealand from 1946 to 1973. No one was in a better position to watch the New Zealand Cricket Council in action – and suffer from many of its decisions – than Reid.

"Through my years as a player [1947-65], national selector [1958-65 and 1975-78] and I.C.C. referee [1993-99]," says Reid, "I feel I've been in a unique position to compare the 'old' New Zealand Cricket Council and the new regime, now called New Zealand Cricket. In this case, new has definitely meant better.

"The New Zealand Cricket Council comprised the chairmen of the six provinces, plus six other nominations, making up a board of 12, who no doubt were excellent club cricket administrators with perhaps 20 or more years of experience. This is how one becomes a provincial chairman. But with only a few of them having first class experience, let alone cricket know-how, they were often out of their depth in the international arena.

"The board of the New Zealand Cricket Council often floundered, making some very poor decisions on some basic matters, such as touring itineraries, selectors – quite often one was appointed from each province, with more concern for geographic balance than the quality of the selectors – and incompetent team managers, both home and away. We had some good managers. Jack Phillipps was outstanding in England and Gordon Leggat's work could not have been surpassed in South Africa in 1961-62. Henry Cooper did a marvellous job in impossible circumstances in India and Pakistan in 1955-56. More recently Ian Taylor proved a fine players' manager. But for years the job of manager invariably went to a New Zealand Cricket Council board member as if of right. Many of these managers were substandard, not surprising as they had been appointed for the wrong reasons. Even relatively recently there were naive decisions, such as the appointment of team coaches who were obviously not suited to the job and allowing team members' partners to travel with the team. It was a long list of no-nos."

The New Zealand Cricket Council survived through the 1980s because the results of the national team were outstanding. Richard Hadlee repeatedly proved a match-winner and New Zealand was able to call on a dozen other players of genuine world class. Leading players like Glenn Turner, Hadlee, Geoff Howarth, John Wright and Martin Crowe had considerable experience playing county cricket and they established a platform on which the New Zealand successes were built.

New Zealand went for more than a decade without losing a series at home and scored major wins overseas, including series victories in Australia and England. But once Hadlee retired and the losses – test and one-day – mounted, the focus turned to the under-performing New Zealand Cricket Council (renamed New Zealand Cricket in the early 1990s). Eventually not only the public, but the council members themselves concluded they were not coping. A new set-up was obviously required and in 1994, the task of analysing what was happening and what was required was delegated to Auckland businessman John Hood, who was able to call on his passion for sport and his management and organisational skills.

"More than 100 interested people, myself included, were sent a comprehensive questionnaire on what was wrong with New Zealand cricket generally," says Reid. "We commented on competitions, marketing, coaching, technique, financial management, behaviour, the lot – and suggested changes. Some of the Forty-Niners in Auckland – Merv Wallace,

Geoff Rabone, Bert Sutcliffe and Johnny Hayes – felt so strongly about the issue that they asked to meet a representative of the committee so they could put their case for change. Iain Galloway met with them at length and eventually nearly all the changes that group recommended were implemented. I was in England at the time, refereeing the series against the West Indies, and filled in my questionnaire there. My comments and those of many other former players were similar. We had all watched with increasing concern what was happening. I was never told in detail the results of those questionnaires, but there must have been an overwhelming consensus of opinion as to what was wrong.

"The outcome, in 1995, was the excellent Hood Report, which emphasised good business practice and organisation and led to the resignation of the entire old New Zealand Cricket board and to a tighter new board of seven members being appointed. This new board was a better balance of sport, business and professional personnel and has proved to be a more successful combination."

The public face of New Zealand Cricket in recent years has been Chief Executive Officer Christopher Doig, a rather innovative early appointment of the board. Doig gained headlines initially not just because of his opera singing ability – not on the C.V. of most aspiring sports chief executives – but because he locked horns with then New Zealand coach Glenn Turner, who retained his job for just one year. There was widespread sympathy for Turner, whom the public felt was beginning to instil some much-needed discipline into the New Zealand side, and Doig struggled for a while in the public relations stakes. However, says Reid, the public was ignorant of Turner's short-comings in the man-management area.

Reid believes Doig has more than shown his worth to New Zealand cricket. "Chris has excellent marketing credentials and showed he knew how to put them to good practical use by running a very successful Wellington festival and also by running the arts centre in Christchurch. He has great communication skills, has gathered a good team around him at cricket headquarters in Christchurch, and has become a respected figure in world cricket administration.

"The very healthy New Zealand Cricket balance sheet is an indication of how good Chris is in negotiations with potential sponsors. He asks people with the appropriate credentials for their input, then makes his decision – unlike the New Zealand Cricket Council regime of the past. Chris is on various I.C.C. committees and has been particularly involved with the planning of tours and with trying to get some order to test cricket, including putting some sort of sensible ranking system in place.

"I feel that through the implementation of the Hood Report, New Zealand cricket administration in the mid-1990s moved into the 20th century, just a few years before the dawn of the 21st century! Cricket in New Zealand is a multi-million-dollar business, involving dozens of men and women. While nothing will ever be perfect, at least it is now run professionally and there is logic and reason for the major decisions that are made."

~

JOHN REID'S VIEW
NEW ZEALAND - THE PLAYERS

Verdun Scott: He was a great chap and, during the 1949 tour, though I was the youngest and he was one of the oldest, he was one of my best mates. As a player, he was much under-rated. People used to remark on his slow scoring, but he scored at a livelier clip than it looked. It's just that he didn't have extravagant strokes. He was a good on-side player, and used to turn and glance the ball effectively. One weakness was that he played away from his front foot. Verdun and Bert Sutcliffe were a world class opening pair. Scotty was also a good fieldsman, showing the athleticism which made him a New Zealand rugby league rep. As an opening batsman, Verdun would rate about on a par with Bruce Edgar of a later generation.

Bert Sutcliffe: I was fortunate to witness the blossoming of one of the best players New Zealand has ever produced. Bert struggled somewhat early on that 1949 tour, but once he found his feet, he played wonderfully well. He was a classic left-handed batsman. He had an air of authority about him and was almost impossible to keep quiet. His hooking was superb. I always felt he had more class than Neil Harvey, the famous Australian left-hander of the same period. Bert was very light on his feet. He was equally as effective as Martin Donnelly, but their methods were entirely different. Bert was a more graceful player. His figures on the 1949 tour were marvellous – his aggregate was second only to Bradman for a tour of England, and he really looked as if he belonged in that company. Bert was one of the younger members of Wal Hadlee's team and we got on well. Whatever his success, Bert never developed a big head. His feet never left the ground. He could concentrate for long periods, as two scores of more than 350 indicate, but he also scored very quickly and proved to be a match-winner on many occasions.

However, I also witnessed some of the problems that he encountered later. He took a terrible hammering in the Ellis Park test in South Africa in 1953 and I believe the blow to the head from Adcock that he suffered affected his confidence for the rest of his career. Whereas previously he'd always looked calm and composed, and been a devastating hooker, the quicker bowlers were always a concern for him after that. He still scored packets of runs and always made them attractively, but he was never as assured against genuine pace. It is one of the great injustices of New Zealand cricket that Bert was never in a test-winning team. He was too sick to play against the West Indies in 1956 and was unavailable for the 1961-62 tour of South Africa. Yet no one did more in the years after the war to give New Zealand cricket some pride at international level. He retained his form so well that in 1965, after an absence from the international arena of five years, he agreed to a request from the national selectors and returned to the New Zealand team to help combat the spin bowling we would encounter in India. It was a job he did very well.

When I look through my photo albums, I note how frequently Sutty's picture pops up. We have been touring companions and close friends for more than half a century. These days Norli and I see Bert and his lovely wife, Norma, regularly.

Merv Wallace: People who judge Merv purely from the record book do him a great disservice. Merv had a test career that lasted more than 15 years, yet played just 13 tests. His test average of 20.90 with five half-centuries indicates a fairly mediocre player. In this case, the stats are misleading. Merv was one of the best New Zealand batsmen I've seen. In 1949, he got the team off to a great start by scoring more than 900 runs in May. He was a middle-order batsman and I had some big partnerships with him. Merv was a complete batsman, with all the usual shots, plus a few of his own. His specialty was the drop kick. He'd pick up the ball from the stumps and drop kick it over mid-wicket or square leg. That shot brought him a lot of runs and frustrated bowlers. Merv didn't hook a lot, preferring to hit the ball in front of the wicket. He had a very good cut. Like many small men, he was light on his feet, though not as quick as Bert Sutcliffe.

Merv, or Flip as we called him, was also the best cricket coach I've come across. He would talk technique with anyone at any time, and he had a lovely way about him. We spent hours in Merv's room in 1949, talking about the day's play, the team we were to play tomorrow, how to play a leg-spinner, what to do on a wet wicket and so on. He really took on the role of senior pro in that team. As team coach, he was a very important part of New Zealand's first test win, in 1956, and it was a tragedy for New Zealand cricket that for one reason or another, he was not retained in that position for years. Merv was great at detecting the cause of a problem and could explain how and why. Lots of players can bat naturally, but few can talk about how it is done. Incidentally, the nickname of Flip was born during his tour of England in 1937 when he constantly used to say, "flippin' heck" in place of the current swear word.

Walter Hadlee: I don't think we saw the best of Wally as a batsman in 1949, though he still had a good tour, with nearly 1500 runs at an average of 35. Wal put a lot of time into his captaincy. He'd be up all hours preparing speeches and planning, and certainly didn't spend as much time on his batting as he would have otherwise. He received a bad knock on the shin at one stage, and that slowed him down for several matches. Even so, he was a classic front foot player, an impressive driver of the ball who was a joy to watch when in full stride.

As a captain, Wal was organised and liked to plan things well ahead. This suited his personality as an accountant. He'd work out who'd be bowling first, who'd take over, and how many overs each bowler might get in a day. His captaincy was a little too stereotyped to my mind. I think you have to try to remain flexible and intuitive. Having said that, he led a team which made the most of their resources in 1949. Wal didn't have a lot of depth in bowling, and we did have to bowl against Hutton, Washbrook, Edrich, Compton and co in the tests, so it can't have been easy. In the county games, Wal was always eager for us to bat last and to chase runs on the last afternoon. He had faith in our batting and figures show his faith was amply repaid.

Martin Donnelly: I feel very fortunate to have toured with Martin, or Squib, as we called him. He is just a name in the record books to most New Zealand cricket followers, because all his great batting feats took place in England. All most can go on is the record book and the accounts of his team-mates. I felt Martin was about on a par with Bert Sutcliffe as a batsman, and you can't get much higher praise than that. But he was a different style of player. He was not a classical stylist; rather he was a clobberer who was lethal hitting through mid-on and mid-wicket, and on the cut. I used to be amazed at the way he batted. He always seemed to play with his feet together. He didn't seem to place his feet near the ball. He must have had a wonderful eye and excellent timing. He used to shuffle across his stumps and belt the ball through mid-wicket. I saw him do it four times in succession to as fine a bowler as Alec Bedser at Scarborough.

Martin was a wonderful travelling companion. He wouldn't say "boo" to anyone, but he was always the best of company. He became known for his shaggy dog stories, and had a tendency to start off by telling one story and for it to drift into another, until he forgot the original story. He was a modest, under-stated person who, though he'd been away from New Zealand since he went to the war, immediately fitted right in with our team.

I was very sorry to learn of his death on October 22, 1999, while preparing the draft of this book. We – the remaining Forty-Niners – sent a combined team message to his wife, Elizabeth, and New Zealand Cricket sent its president, Iain Galloway, and Martin's last captain, Wal Hadlee, to his funeral in Sydney to pay a tribute to a great cricketer and a fine team-mate.

Geoff Rabone: Geoff was a good utility player. He was a very good slip fieldsman, a useful batsman, and an adequate off-spin bowler who also developed into a leg-spinner. He was always a good team man, and a bit of a joker. He led the New Zealand team in South Africa in 1953-54 and did a good job in the circumstances. I don't think he was given the right players and we were outgunned in the test series, but no one could have quibbled with the commitment and leadership Geoff showed. It was a team which unfortunately needed some discipline instilled in it, and Geoff did the best he could in that regard, often without all the support he might have expected. He broke a bone in his foot midway through that tour, which was unfortunate, but which did go to give some credence to his long-standing nickname of "Bonesy" and also triggered the words for a song to the tune of "Dem bones, dem bones, dem dry bones", possibly because of his tall, gaunt stature.

Brun Smith: I liked Brun, and though we were really vying for one batting spot in the test team in 1949, we got on well. He didn't have an entirely happy tour because he suffered from homesickness. He'd often say how much he was missing his wife Jo. As a batsman, he tended to flash, somewhat like Craig McMillan of today's New Zealand team. He was a busy cricketer and things were always happening when Brun was involved. I replaced him in the test side, even though he was averaging 86.5 for the series, so that must have been galling, though he never said anything to me. On a tour of England, it is every batsman's ambition to score 1000 runs. In 1949 Brun walked out to play his final innings of the tour, against H. D. G. Leveson-Gower's XI, having totalled 996. There was no such thing as biding his time. He slashed three boundaries through the gully, to take his tour tally to 1008, and was then bowled by Cliff Gladwin.

Frank Mooney: Having played with Frank in Wellington for many years, I know he was a much better batsman than generally given credit for. He used his feet well to spin bowling and was entrusted with the job of opening the test innings against Adcock in South Africa in 1953-54. He played some valuable innings in 1949, most notably his 102 against the M.C.C., which rescued us from a grim position. Frank wasn't the most athletic of wicketkeepers, but he was a good technician and carried a heavy workload in 1949. His 66 dismissals was a record for any wicketkeeper on tour in England.

Jack Cowie: "The Bull" was the perfect nickname for Jack. I remember him playing cards on our many train journeys. He and Ces Burke were close mates. He was 37 and past his best in 1949, but still a great bowler who could put it on the right spot at a good pace. He had a long run-up and was accurate. He was tall and gained good lift. Even in 1949, he was quicker than Alec Bedser, so I can understand why cricket followers rated him so highly in England in 1937. Jack seemed a rather dour person, but once you got to know him, you appreciated his qualities. He had a good sports career – he became a test cricket umpire, was a rep soccer player and later became the top soccer administrator in New Zealand.

Tom Burtt: In 1949, Tom was easily the best spinner in England. He was a jolly, round person, a joker. He was a good sportsman, having played hockey for New Zealand. Though he was getting on in years and wasn't the most nimble of fieldsmen, Tom should have been retained in the test team for longer than he was. I'd like to have seen him lumbering up to bowl for several more years, and I'm sure Geoff Rabone would have appreciated his services in South Africa in 1953-54. In England, he was our best defensive bowler, and also a most effective attacker, as a tour total of 128 wickets testifies. He had a good change of pace and nice loop. I still regard him our best left-arm spinner, ahead even of Hedley Howarth and today's young champion Daniel Vettori.

Fen Cresswell: Fen was nicknamed "The Ferret" because he used to go in after the rabbits in the batting order. He really knew very little about cricket when we went away in 1949. I honestly don't think he knew which was the leg side. He was a real country boy. But he had a talent for bowling late inswingers. He wasn't as fast as Gavin Larsen, and some days he was hammered. But on those occasions when he got it right, he would run through even good batting lineups. He opened the bowling 30 times during the tour, which is an indication of our limited pace bowling resources, but was a credit to Fen. Against England in the final test, he took 6-168, including Hutton, Simpson, Edrich and Compton, which is not to be sneezed at. And against an Australia B team the following year he took 8-100, so he did have some golden days. It's just that it was hard to get used to hearing the off and leg described as the left and right!

Ces Burke: I have extremely warm memories of "The Burglar". His card sessions with Jack Cowie and Tom Burtt were always a feature of our many train journeys through England. The Bull's loud comments about the injustices of life whenever things weren't going well could be heard throughout the carriage. Tom Burtt had a wonderful season with his left-arm spinners, and his success tended to exclude Ces from displaying his skills as a leg-spinner to best advantage. Nevertheless Ces took a full part in the tour. He captured 54 wickets, and had one golden day against Derbyshire, when he took 6-23. His dry, humorous comments were much appreciated at our sometimes serious meetings.

Harry Cave: I rated Harry Cave very highly. He never stopped trying, whether it was in England, or on the lifeless pitches in India and Pakistan. He was still learning his craft in 1949 and a few years later was a much superior bowler. He was tall and bowled at a lively pace, mainly out-swingers, though he could dip the ball in, too. Harry showed his class as a person and a player with his bowling in the fourth test against the West Indies in 1956. I'd replaced him as the New Zealand captain, yet he offered me total support, and then bowled superbly to take eight wickets in the match to set us on the path to victory. I doubt I have toured with a more popular player. Harry bowled at about the pace of Ewen Chatfield, but did more with the ball.

Johnny Hayes: Johnny was taken away as the quick bowler in the 1949 team. He started well, but pulled a groin muscle and it never really came right. It was a pity because he was the fastest bowler in England – only Tom Pritchard, a New Zealander bowling for Warwickshire – approached his pace. Johnny went some way towards making up for his disappointments in 1949 by bowling well on the next trip to England, in 1958, when he took 62 wickets at 20.20. Overall, I'd say he had enough pace to be an international bowler, but didn't do enough with the ball, though nobody could say he didn't try.

Tony MacGibbon: We called him "Long Hop". He was one of the hardest triers and most reliable team men I toured with. Tony was a great character who gave it everything. He was an effective fast-medium bowler who moved the ball and used his height to get bounce. He got the best batsmen out, which is the test of a pace bowler. In England in 1958, he numbered Richardson (2), Mike Smith (3), Cowdrey, May (4), Graveney, Milton, Watson and Bailey among his 20 test wickets and was easily our best bowler. Early in his career, he was inclined to be a bit wayward – he once hit me on the shins when I was fielding at second slip! – but he got the most out of himself. He wasn't a bad batsman, either, using his height to get well over the ball. I batted him No 3 in 1956 against the West Indies and he did a respectable job. I remember Mac very kindly and always liked having him as part of my teams.

Murray Chapple: I had a lot of respect for Murray as a captain. When I was leading Wellington, we had a strong rivalry with Murray's Canterbury teams. I picked Murray as my vice-captain for South Africa in 1961-62. I rang him late one night and got him out of bed to ask him if he wanted the vice-captain's job. I wouldn't have done that if I didn't have respect for him and confidence in him. I say that because a story did the rounds that we had no time for each other. I didn't think Murray was especially talented as a player, but he forced his way into the test team in 1961-62 and performed quite well. He made two tours of South Africa. On the first occasion, in 1953-54, he could have performed better, but when he returned as vice-captain, he did the job.

Gordon Leggat: He had a tremendous influence on New Zealand cricket. He was unlucky not to tour South Africa in 1953-54. Only his weight prevented his selection. He was not a good fieldsmen, but in those days you could hide one or two players in the field, and I felt he should have gone. He was a solid opening batsman and his wise counsel would have helped on that tour. In 1961-62, he went over as manager and was one of the stars of the tour. His man management skills were unsurpassed, and he was very influential in all aspects of the tour. He could be tough when he had to be. Like all of us, Gordon suffered in India and Pakistan in 1955-56. There are famous photos of him squashed into a tiny basin which doubled as the team bath. I remember him putting his foot on the first step of the team bus one day and then turning and heading for the toilet. We didn't see him for three days! Gordon was one of the giants of New Zealand cricket.

Alex Moir: Alex took a lot of wickets in New Zealand with his mixture of leg-spin and googlies, but wasn't as successful in the international arena. One reason was that generally we didn't have enough runs to be able to bowl him properly. He was not especially accurate, and though he could spin the ball both ways, he was too loose to keep good batsmen under pressure. There is no one in New Zealand cricket today who spins the ball like Alex did.

Jack Alabaster: Alex Moir's Otago team-mate and leg-spin partner, Jack was a much tighter bowler and therefore more effective. He was the best leg-spinner New Zealand has produced since the war. He had the right temperament and was a good team man. Jack was a good thinker and in South Africa he was one of my four wise men, along with Gordon Leggat, Murray Chapple and me. We made a bad mistake when we didn't pick him for the 1965 tour.

Bob Blair: As with Johnny Hayes, so with Blair. At Plunket Shield level, he was a terror, a bully of a bowler. On a Basin Reserve wicket which often offered him plenty of assistance, he had some sensational figures. But Bob never really took the step up to test level. I saw international batsmen like May, Graveney and Les Favell, who could handle his pace, hammer him mercilessly because he did not do enough with the ball. It wasn't until late in his career, when his pace had declined, that Bob started to concentrate on line and length, and became a more respected bowler.

Bob and I had the odd little confrontation. Once, when I wanted half-volleys bowled to me in the nets, he mistook my request and bowled bouncers, until I walked up to his end and had a chat with the bat still in my hand! And again, after I had transferred to Otago, I was playing against Wellington at the Basin and managed to deposit a couple of his bouncers into the adjoining playground during an innings of 72.

Having said all that, "Rabbit", as he was nicknamed, was a giant on the domestic scene. He took 446 first class wickets in New Zealand at an average of just 17.4. Many a batsman had a sleepless night as they contemplated facing Blair on a green Basin Reserve wicket the next day. Bob has had a long career in cricket, coaching in Australia, South Africa, Zimbabwe, Northern Ireland and England, and is still involved with the game today.

Noel McGregor: Noel was reinstated for the South African tour in 1961-62 after missing the 1958 tour of England, when he should have been selected. He got us off to a good start surprisingly often. We used to call him "Snicker", because he did flirt with the slips a bit. People used to complain that Noel never went on to many big innings, but he made a lot of 30s. We knew that and sometimes 30 was more than most of the others were getting! He also made a contribution as an excellent fieldsman and a great companion. And let's not forget: he caught Everton Weekes at Eden Park, one of the most important catches in New Zealand history.

Zin Harris: Parke Gerald Zinzan Harris, Zin to his mates. He played some gutsy innings, especially in South Africa. His century at Cape Town contributed hugely to our win. But one of the innings I most appreciated was in the fifth test at Port Elizabeth when he and Graham Dowling had to withstand 40 minutes of the most ferocious fast bowling barrage imaginable before stumps. Adcock and Pollock really went after them. I'd seen Zin have his face split open by Bob Blair and that must have been in the back of his mind, but he never flinched. He was a good companion and a good tourist. We called him "Broken Bum" on account of his walk, which was the same as we see now from his son Chris. They are very similar, both with a big smile and very little hair.

Dick Motz: I made two big tours with Dick, and he bowled with tremendous courage both times. He was a good workhorse. As an opening bowler, he was about Danny Morrison's pace, though a better bowler. During the 1960s, Dick was one of the best bowlers in the world. He wasn't as good as Hadlee or Cowie, but there haven't been many other New Zealanders of his calibre. He had plenty of fire and aggression. He didn't do a lot with the ball, but moved it away just enough. At Plunket Shield level, he bowled extremely well for Canterbury for years. Dick wrote his name in New Zealand cricket history when he became our first bowler to take 100 test wickets. Dick's batting fell away badly, which was a pity as he has some ability with the bat. However he was a good guy to have on your side.

Gary Bartlett: An enigma. He first made an impression on me when I was playing for Wellington. He was just a teenager playing for Central Districts and he gave me a sample of his pace. I won't forget one ball whizzing past my nose. Gary was really quick, faster than Adcock and at least as fast as Trueman, though nowhere near as complete a bowler. He wasn't far off Tyson's pace, and that's as quick as it gets. He had the ability to bowl the odd really good ball. On the other hand, silly mid-on was in danger sometimes! His pace was so disconcerting that some visiting batsmen accused him of throwing. Ian Craig and Bobby Simpson and the rest of them would pass comments, but I couldn't hear them! Gary toured South Africa in 1961-62 and played all five tests. He didn't take a lot of wickets, but did win the test at Cape Town for us, dismissing McGlew and McLean on a batsman's wicket through sheer pace.

Gary was good to have in the team. Not only did you have a weapon up your sleeve to keep the opposition off balance, but he was a good team man, a useful batsman and a good fieldsman. When I think back, I was probably too tough on him. He had shin splints and wanted to withdraw from a match now and then, but we'd tell him to play. It was a time when shin splints was an unknown term, as was the expression stress fracture. Times change. Fast bowlers put a lot into their work physically and it's easy to overlook their injuries.

Frank Cameron: Our relationship has stood the test of time in our many different roles in New Zealand cricket. Early on, "F.C." was there as a trusted, solid, uncomplaining medium-paced away swing bowler with our team in South Africa in 1961-62. During the tour, his role changed from being a stock bowler to a main strike bowler because of the heat and injuries taking their toll on our other pace bowlers, Dick Motz and Gary Bartlett. Frank was a pleasure to have in a side. He was a real trier and a great team man.

I remember a match early in the tour. We were playing against Rhodesia (the team is now known as Zimbabwe, and I suppose the match would be a test) at Salisbury (now Harare). On the last afternoon, the match seemed headed for a draw. I didn't want the Rhodesians to make a feast of our attack, so I asked Frank to bowl out the remaining overs from one end. He just nodded and got on with it. At the end of the game, I was changing next to him and saw that his boots were running with blood. He had had an operation for piles that morning and had said nothing about it. He just got on with his role of tying up one end as requested by his captain. Frank was of a brisk pace, similar to Martin Snedden, and possibly a shade quicker than Ewen Chatfield. He was very accurate and tended to swing the ball away late, a type of bowler who is essential when conditions are suitable, either overcast, as in England, or well-grassed pitches, as in South Africa.

Our association continued when we were both New Zealand selectors through the 1970s, with Frank the convener and Ian Colquhoun the other member of the panel. We had a fairly successful stint as selectors, settling the number of selections to a more reasonable, acceptable level. We gave some young players – including Geoff Howarth, Jeremy Coney, John Wright, Richard Hadlee and Ewen Chatfield – a start and they formed the basis for the strong New Zealand side of the 1980s. However, it wasn't all plain sailing in the selection room. Eventually each selection was unanimous, but sometimes Ian had gone to bed and Frank and I had kept at it until the wee small hours!

Graham Dowling: We never got the full benefit of his potential. He became a rather dour batsman and he had more ability than that. He played well on occasions – against India in 1968, for instance, when he scored a test double-century – but not so well in England. In South Africa in 1961-62, he popped up when we needed him and played very bravely in the fifth test, standing up to the best that was fired at him. One of his problems was that he used to hit beautiful drives straight to the fieldsman. I remember speaking to him in Timaru after the South African tour and suggesting he should be looking to hit it straight past the bowler and into the gaps. He was almost too correct. When they were going, Donnelly and Sutcliffe would seldom hit to a fieldsman, but Graham didn't have their ability to play into the gaps. He needed to use a bit more right hand.

Artie Dick: Artie was a good fieldsman who kept wicket, and eventually developed into a competent keeper. I've always thought a keeper has to be able to bat – it gives a team such an advantage. Parore, Wadsworth and Mooney were the best we've had in this area. They were better batsmen than Ian Smith. Overseas you think of Les Ames, John Waite, Rod Marsh, Alan Knott, Ian Healy, Alec Stewart... all extremely useful batsmen. Ames not only kept wickets, but found time to score a century of centuries! Artie was a reasonable batsman who used his height to drive well off the front foot, and I used him as an opener in 1965 when Terry Jarvis was unavailable through ill-health. Artie always backed up his captain. He was an outstanding team man.

John Ward: An unlucky player. He was easily the best wicketkeeper in New Zealand in his time, but was plagued by injury. He was ruled out of all five tests in England in 1958 and again in South Africa in 1961-62. In 1965 he played all four against India, but then hurt his finger. He missed all three tests against Pakistan and by the time his finger healed he was able to play only the last test in England. He was a good tourist and he had to be, because in those days when you got injured, there was no easy way home.

Barry Sinclair: I suppose Barry's career turned out to be slightly disappointing. I thought he would take over from me and go on longer than he did. He was a very dedicated cricketer and had a good season in England in 1965. He was a solid, consistent batsman and an excellent fieldsman, a good team man who supported his captain. I really wanted to take him to South Africa in 1961-62, but he just made no runs that season and couldn't be selected. We ended up picking batsmen who weren't as good, but you have to be fair and others were scoring heavily. Barry was one of the shortest men in test cricket – of similar height to Aravinda de Silva today – but he was a fairly aggressive player. He had pleasant strokes all around the wicket, trained hard and used his feet well. Bruce Edgar, another Kilbirnie and Wellington cricketer of a later generation, reminded me of Barry in attitude.

Bevan Congdon: "Congo" was nothing special on tour in 1965, but he was a late blossomer. He watched and learned and improved greatly later on. He incorporated the back movement to get behind the ball and developed into a good attacking batsman who hit the loose ball and played sensibly. He was always a good fieldsman. We will always remember Congo for his consecutive test innings of 176 and 175 against England in 1973. The English joked they'd found out he was weak in the 170s! They must have been two great knocks. If he was playing today, he would be the best batsman in the New Zealand side.

Bruce Taylor: A cricketer who rode his luck. He made his Canterbury debut · as a replacement for the injured Dick Motz, was selected for the 1965 touring team after Gary Bartlett was ruled out through injury, and played his first test, at Calcutta, when Barry Sinclair pulled out with illness. Then "Tails" went out and scored a century and took five wickets! Talk about taking your chances. When I think about his cricket, I feel there was a certain lack of responsibility. He played silly shots when he was set. He was a steady enough attacking bowler, but never a reliable all-rounder. He got a lot of bounce and moved the ball around, but didn't get the most out of himself, especially as a batsman. He was never completely dedicated and too easy-going to reach the top. The pity was he had a ton of ability. That's what makes me mad. When they don't have the talent, you can't do much about it. But when they do and don't use it, that's frustrating.

Richard Collinge: I recall Richard very warmly as a good left-arm bowler. He moved the ball around a bit and brought the odd one back. He was one of our better attacking bowlers, and worried class players. He dismissed Hanif five times in succession in 1965 and later on he bowled Geoff Boycott at the Basin with a peach of a delivery that set up an historic test win. Though he was tall and came bounding in ferociously, he wasn't as aggressive as he looked and off the field was a rather quiet guy.

Vic Pollard: In 1965, he was the up-and-coming star and for a while he really did shine. He won both the Winsor and Redpath Cups and seemed to have the cricket world at his feet. He was an attractive batsman who sparkled in England as a youngster in 1965, and again in 1973, when he scored two successive centuries. I tried to get him to bowl off-cutters like I did because I thought that would be useful, but that didn't really work. Vic was a good team man, but his career closed sooner than it might have because he did not play cricket on Sundays because of his religious views, and by the 1970s, Sunday cricket had become a major part of the game. He was on the quiet side, but was always a gutsy player, and his team-mates respected his religious views.

Glenn Turner: My association with Turner was as a selector, though I played a few matches against him in 1965. He used to just poke the ball around in those days and didn't impress anyone with his stroke-making. Later on he blossomed for New Zealand and Worcestershire. But for me, there was always a question mark over Turner. I had cause to doubt his dedication to the New Zealand team above himself. I certainly don't put him up on the same level as Sutcliffe, Donnelly and Crowe. Turner could bat, without doubt. He made back-to-back centuries against Australia in 1974 in stressful situations, and they were two bloody good innings. It wasn't his batting, but his dedication to the silver fern that was in question. I never did see Turner sacrifice his wicket in his team's cause. More often than not an opening batsman can play a selfish innings and it will still be to his team's benefit. However there are occasions when the team must come first.

I did appreciate aspects of his coaching of the New Zealand team. During his first tenure as coach he oversaw series wins over Australia and England. The second time around, in the mid-1990s, he got some discipline back in the team when it was most needed, but his man-management left a lot to be desired. In spite of his experience, Worcester didn't want him as their captain for long. Turner became a world class one-day batsman, and he was inventive and exciting to watch. But it's interesting that in this brand of cricket, fast bowlers are largely muted because they cannot bowl short.

Hedley Howarth: The senior of the two test-playing brothers, Hedley Howarth always had a difficult job winning me over. It was nothing to do with his ability as a bowler or his attitude. No one fought harder for New Zealand. But rather that I retained memories of Thomas Browning Burtt, our left-arm spinner in England in 1949. I regard Burtt as New Zealand's best left-armer, but I can pay Hedley the compliment of saying he ran him a very close second. Hedley had more flight and variety, but Burtt spun the ball more and was more accurate. Howarth carried the New Zealand spin attack for nearly a decade from 1969 and sometimes – especially in the West Indies in 1972 – I felt he suffered from being asked to bowl too defensively. He was at his best in 1969 when he really won over the critics in England, India and Pakistan.

Ken Wadsworth: What an exciting addition Ken would have made to any team. Again, I was a national selector during part of his test career, and had a close-up view of this excellent cricketer. Ken died tragically young – he was just 29 when he died of cancer. Who can say what cricket feats lay ahead of him? I feel he was in the middle of what would have been a memorable career. As it was, I regarded him as a genuine all-rounder, a classy batsman and a superb wicketkeeper. Allied to that, he had a magnificent, fighting temperament. He feared no one. Players of such talent are rare.

Geoff Howarth: With the best overall winning record of any New Zealand captain (in test and one-day matches) and some very good individual performances under his belt, Geoff is a significant player in our cricket history. When South Africa was on the outer in world cricket in the early 1980s, various rebel teams were touring the Republic. As there had been teams from England, Australia, the West Indies and Sri Lanka, I picked a "wish list" New Zealand team for a rebel tour. Geoff was the obvious captain in such a side, which was also to include players like Lance Cairns, Jeremy Coney and Ewen Chatfield. All this was fine and the tour might have gone ahead if Richard Hadlee had been available. At this time, Geoff was still a world-respected batsman. But soon after, when he was appointed captain of the Surrey county side, he had trouble making the first team. He struck a serious problem which got worse after he had been appointed then reappointed New Zealand coach in the early 1990s. Eventually this problem caused his retirement as team coach. The situation was not helped shortly afterwards by the publication of his biography, which was entitled *Shaken Not Stirred*. I can only surmise that Geoff received some poor advice.

John Wright: John makes my best-ever New Zealand XI, and not only because of his expertise as an opening batsman for New Zealand and in county cricket for Derbyshire for so many years. He is also picked for his attitude towards the traditional spirit in which this game of cricket is played. He seldom has a harsh word to say about anyone and I often wonder how he has managed to retain his laid-back composure during his spell as coach of Kent. John is a part-time coach at the New Zealand Cricket Academy in Christchurch. So far I haven't seen much evidence of players taking notice of his wise words. An old saying is relevant here: you can lead a horse to water, but you can't make it drink. As a left-handed opening batsman, I put him in the same class as the Australian Mark Taylor.

Sir Richard Hadlee: I was a selector when he was first picked, which was ironic in a way because his father had first picked me for New Zealand! It was obvious early on that Richard was going to be a good player, and he had the ability to run through test batting lineups. I missed his best years because I was living in South Africa, though he bowled with Clive Rice for

Notts, so I knew him through that. He was a model bowler who made a wise decision to cut his run-up, though he was initially heavily criticised. I thought that for some years he was the best bowler of his type in the world, and as a New Zealander was very proud when he set the world record for most test wickets, eventually getting to 431. He was a unique bowler because even off his short run-up, you could not call him a medium-pacer of the Alec Bedser mould. Richard still had the ability to bowl a genuinely quick delivery, and he had a superb change of pace. I was interested to hear Sir Donald Bradman single out Richard for special praise when discussing the great bowlers he had seen. The other thing I really liked about Hadlee was his attitude. He just got on and bowled. No histrionics.

Jeremy Coney: These days Jeremy Coney is regarded as a brilliant public speaker and a world-respected cricket broadcaster. He became a fine batsman and led New Zealand to a test series win in England. Yet when I was a New Zealand selector, there were question marks over Jeremy. He was a rather hesitant schoolteacher and it took him several years to book a permanent place in the New Zealand team. But his ability as a performer must have already been deep within, and when he got onto the international stage, with a big crowd watching, he rose to the occasion. By the 1980s, Jeremy had become a top-flight middle-order batsman with a special ability to pace a run chase in a one-dayer, a dispenser of useful dribbly in-swingers, and one of the best slip catchers New Zealand has fielded.

Ian Smith: I know how long Ian Smith's international career lasted – it mirrored almost exactly the time I lived in South Africa. However I did see enough of Ian to appreciate what a huge contribution he made to the successful era in the 1980s. He was an athletic, energetic keeper who was at his best standing back to quicker bowlers. This suited New Zealand's purposes well, as their attack was build around Richard Hadlee and a supporting cast including Lance Cairns, Martin Snedden, Ewen Chatfield and Danny Morrison. Smithy always looked to have a bounce in his step and this is an important attribute for a wicketkeeper who can really lift a team during a long day in the field. He now holds all the major New Zealand wicketkeeping records, a fair indication of the contribution he made.

I didn't rate Smithy so highly as a batsman – he was nowhere near the class of Ken Wadsworth, for instance. However, he did have his days. He hit two test centuries, including that never-to-be-forgotten 173 (off only 136 balls!) against India at Eden Park in 1990. These days I enjoy Ian's work on television. He is one player who has made the step across to broadcasting so successfully that he now covers rugby as well as cricket.

Martin Crowe: Though I missed a lot of his best innings, it was obvious he had all the trappings of a great batsman. He scored fast, had a very solid technique and was a good all-round batsman, up there with Sutcliffe and Donnelly. He always looked to have time to play his shots, even against the extreme pace of the West Indians, and that's an indicator of a class player. For someone who obviously thought deeply about the game, I was a bit disappointed with his captaincy and his overall attitude.

John Bracewell: I toured England in 1996 with "Braces". He was coach and I was manager of the New Zealand under-19 team. I had not had a lot to do with John, but knew about his reputation as a player – he is one of the very few New Zealand cricketers to have taken 100 wickets and scored 1000 runs in test cricket. I understood that he was a good off-spin bowler with an abrasive attitude and he knew about me as a strict "old" New Zealand captain and a current I.C.C. referee who was inflexible and probably would want to interfere with his role as coach. We were both wrong. I found Braces to be a very good coach, up with all the modern coaching techniques. He ran innovative fielding sessions (which I was more than pleased not to have to take part in!).

His abrasive attitude, if he had one, had disappeared and his man management skills were excellent. I imagine that one day he will make an excellent coach of the New Zealand team. I had to be convinced that his insistence on a review of each session by the captain (plus coach's comments) before the team went to lunch or tea was a good idea, but Craig McMillan, the captain, handled it well and the team was certainly a very happy, positive, winning unit, which is all anyone can ask. Braccs has had a couple of seasons as Gloucester county coach and by all accounts has done a very good job, which will give him a solid grounding for any future appointments.

Chris Cairns: I've watched Cairns play test cricket for more than a decade, and until 1999, he didn't rate particularly high in my book. He is prone to injury and though he had ability, there seemed to be something lacking. His attitude, initially very bad, has improved over the last couple of years. This is fortunate as he wasn't the right role model for young New Zealanders. I regard him as a better bowler than batsman, but, despite some good performances in England in 1999, he must be rated an under-achiever by a long way when his career as a whole is viewed.

Having said that, his play in the test series against England in 1999 was outstanding, and if he is able to build on that he could become a genuine world class player. The day after New Zealand had clinched the series against England 2-1, I ran into Chris in the Kensington High Street underground shopping mall. I congratulated him on the series win and said I was sorry to have missed his whirlwind 80 in the final test. This must rank as one of the great test innings, especially as New Zealand was 39-6 at the time. I was interested to hear him discuss his change of attitude. He insisted that the Oval win was a team effort, which indeed it was, with Stephen Fleming making a fighting 66 not out in the first innings, a half-century from Daniel Vettori, plus Shayne O'Connor, Dion Nash and Cairns chipping in with vital wickets and some brilliant fielding. We gave England a lesson in every department and I feel won every session except one in the four-match series.

Cairns' maturity was all the more remarkable to me because I was present at a camp for the test players in 1994 and heard him rubbish the value of team spirit at an evening talk session given by Gilbert Enoka, the current team's psychologist. Cairns said then that he sometimes appreciated the performances of team-mates, but often hated some of them. He was supported on this theme by Dion Nash, and only one player, Chris Harris, got up and publicly said they were on the wrong track. The next morning when I addressed the team I made my thoughts on the subject plain. I said there was a very real need for team spirit and that they were not good enough individually to get by without each others' support.

When I mentioned this to Cairns during our discussion in London, he attributed his attitude back in 1994 to the lack of senior figures around to look up to and learn from. When I thought about this, perhaps Geoff Howarth, the coach, Ken Rutherford, Martin Crowe and Danny Morrison didn't stack up too well when I compared them to the senior players in my formative years – Merv Wallace, Martin Donnelly, Wal Hadlee, Tom Burtt and Jack Cowie.

Now that Chris Cairns is one of those senior players that the youngsters in the test team look to for encouragement and confidence, he has a new-found sense of responsibility. Perhaps it has awakened an urge to give cricket fans around the world a consistent look at his undoubted ability. What has also helped is that Cairns seems to now regard himself as a bowling all-rounder and not as a batsman first who bowls a bit.

Stephen Fleming: I found it difficult to captain New Zealand at the age of 27, so it must be said that Fleming was given one of the hardest tasks in cricket – the captaincy of New Zealand at the age of 23. He was really the only suitable person for consideration, but I don't think it was in the best interests of his batting, which requires quite a bit more development. He should be allowed to get on with his batting, which is the area he can be of most use to New Zealand. He needs to learn how to build on a good start and score centuries. Too often he has given away his wicket after reaching 20 or 30. After leading New Zealand to the series win over England in 1999, he can only go from strength to strength as a captain.

Chris Harris: My assessment of Zin Harris' son has to be based on two years of occasional coaching at the New Zealand Cricket Academy, on following his fortunes from the V.I.P. boxes at various New Zealand venues and, of course, on television. I have been sorry to see Chris pigeon-holed as a one-day specialist. Only on vary rare occasions is a talented player unable to expand to the five-day test arena – perhaps Gavin Larsen may be one. There is no better example of the right cricket attitude than Chris, who is a great fieldsman, a bowler of unusual technique and a batsman who can be very effective. Why somebody has not got hold of him and eliminated the areas where he has trouble with the bat is beyond me. There are plenty of former test left-hand batsmen to call upon. Surely a plan should have been drawn up to improve his play against spin and to teach him how to play back properly. It is still worth the trouble, for Chris has the talent to be a very solid test player.

Dion Nash: Dion must now be considered a genuine all-rounder and some of his more recent performances have elevated him to the point where he can sometimes be regarded as New Zealand's main strike bowler. I was disappointed when I heard that "our" promising new bowler had signed to play county cricket for Middlesex in 1995 because I knew that he would have to do the hard yards as a county work horse, and so it proved. He developed a back injury and some bad "falling away" bowling habits. It is all right for a promising batsman to play in county cricket as the more times he bats, the better, but not for a young bowler. I have been impressed with the way Dion has regained his place in the New Zealand team and admire his ability to produce a big performance when it is most required in the international arena.

I can accept Dion's macho aggressive attitude, but only in small doses at the right time and when kept within the rules of the I.C.C. Code of Conduct. If you are good enough, there is little need to talk about it – the performance will speak for itself. His deliberate bumping of Sachin Tendulkar during the second test at Kanpur in 1999 was silly. That sort of action can bring only negative vibes for himself and New Zealand cricket. Unfortunately, it wasn't Dion's first transgression.

Nathan Astle: He has played some spectacular innings in both the test and one-day arenas and clearly has a lot of talent, but like many modern batsmen, he keeps reinventing the wheel. Astle, like several of the current New Zealand team, keeps pushing forward and it gets him into trouble, as we saw during the 1999 World Cup. They want to hit hard, but haven't developed their attacking back foot strokes. The other area of concern is that they decide to rush down the track for no good reason, get nowhere near the pitch of the ball and find themselves stumped or get an edge. Like several of our batsmen, Astle needs to get himself better organised at the crease and take more notice of the technique of other players – some of them his opposition. Most top players look to get across to the line of the ball, usually by moving the back foot to the off stump.

Adam Parore: To me, Parore fits in the pre-1999 Chris Cairns mould. He has been a player with considerable talent, but seems to have a poor cricket attitude. When I was a youngster in the 1949 team, I would sit around and listen in the hope of picking up advice and information that would help me improve. I'm not sure a lot of that goes on these days. Besides often under-performing as a player, Parore's behaviour on the field sometimes leaves a lot to be desired and falls short of what is required for role model status. Hopefully the message is being received that for such a valuable all-rounder, questionable on-field behaviour is not only unnecessary, but can only be detrimental to the team and to New Zealand cricket.

Craig McMillan: Craig is another product of the New Zealand under-19 touring schedule. He toured Pakistan in 1994 and captained the team to England in 1996. I was the manager on both occasions and it has been my great pleasure to again observe at close quarters a special cricket talent beginning to blossom. Already Craig has commentators talking about his belligerent, aggressive attitude... and this is before he even gets to the crease! As a batsman, he reminds me of Brun Smith in full flight, and can be a match-winner on his day.

I am a little disappointed that after an unbelievably good start in international one-day and test cricket (his first series was against an Australian team including Glenn McGrath and Shane Warne), Craig has struck a bit of a lean patch, due mainly, I feel, to the fact that he hasn't progressed by watching, listening and learning to copy the back foot techniques of some of his opponents. I understand that you can't put an old head on young shoulders, but cricket experience these days is not about how old you are, but about how many times you have visited the crease. Craig has made that journey fairly often now. Having said that, I have a lot of faith in Craig and am sure he will ride out the storm. I can see a potential New Zealand captain waiting in the wings in a few years' time.

Just a quick word of warning/advice about his attitude: as a youngster he has been on the receiving end of some aggressive comments on the field. I hope Craig is able to keep his composure and let his bat do the talking for him. That is always the best answer.

Daniel Vettori: I rate Dan the most exciting player to have appeared on the New Zealand scene since the arrival of Martin Crowe in the early 1980s. I was fortunate to observe Dan closely when I managed the New Zealand under-19 team to England in 1996. The long hair didn't appeal to me greatly, but his bowling and positive attitude most certainly did. His bowling has improved and kept up with the standard of his opponents until these days he is probably the best left-arm slow bowler around. He turns the ball, has a great loop and is very accurate. Even at this early stage of his career, I feel strongly that Daniel can be compared very favourably with Hedley Howarth and our best left-arm bowler, Thomas B. Burtt.

I can't believe the improvement in his batting – lofted straight drives, square cuts, defence as needed – he has the lot. What I also like about his attitude is the fact that he does not get carried away with his success. He gets on with his role, bowling or batting, despite some intimidation on occasions, and has put his studies on hold.

∿

It is very distressing to me to feel it necessary to talk about the behaviour and attitude of some of the present New Zealand team members. In 1955-56, our New Zealand team came a poor second on our tour of Pakistan and India. Primitive accommodation, poor general playing conditions, sub-standard umpires and excessive amounts of sickness all combined to make the tour an uncomfortable and rather unenjoyable experience. But we still played the game in the spirit which is traditionally expected and New Zealand Cricket still proudly displays a model of "Kim's Gun", containing the following inscription:

For when the great scorer comes to write against your name,
He makes not that you won or lost,
But how you played the game.

Presented by the Pakistan Eaglets Society in appreciation of the sportmanship displayed by the New Zealand cricket team during the test match played at Lahore in October, 1955.

∿

Having provided such a full summary of New Zealand's leading players of his time, I asked Reid to select a New Zealand XI since the Second World War. Sometimes, through a sense of modesty, authors picking such teams omit themselves, but this would be farcical in Reid's case. He was judged good enough to captain a genuine Rest of the World XI and is obviously a must inclusion in any New Zealand team. I have therefore placed him at No 5 in the batting order and asked him to fill in the other 10 names.

Reid's comments: "Some players pick themselves, but overall, it wasn't an easy side to select. Bert Sutcliffe is an obvious choice for one of the opening batsmen. He is well clear of any other New Zealand opener of my time. But his partner had me scratching my head. Initially I wrote down Glenn Turner's name. It's difficult to ignore his run-scoring – 103 first class centuries and nearly 35,000 runs. But I have problems with Turner. He made packets of runs in county cricket, and I don't rate county cricket particularly highly. In the test arena, he wasn't as convincing against good attacks, and, of course, he withdrew from the test team for basically the last six or seven years of his career. In the end, my rationale was that this is my team, and I didn't want him in there as I couldn't guarantee he would put New Zealand first.

"So, if not Turner, then who? Verdun Scott was a very good opener, and there is the added advantage of him having batted so much with Bert. I liked Verdun. He was a great team man and difficult to dismiss. But I've finally gone for John Wright. Like Turner, he had a distinguished county career, and I liked the way he fronted up to the world's best pace bowlers for New Zealand year after year. Wright had the sort of courage and temperament I admire. So he opens with Bert, which gives us two left-handers – not such a bad thing.

"At No 3, Martin Crowe walks into this side. He is on the top rung of New Zealand batsmen. He could score quickly or defend, according to the circumstances. I wasn't overly enamoured with his attitude towards the end of his career, but in a team of this calibre, I think he'd be proud to be included and more than happy to fit in.

"Merv Wallace is my No 4. His batting in England in 1949 was superb. He scored so heavily, especially over the first month, that we seldom found ourselves 40-3 and under pressure. This was 12 years after his first England tour, when he led the averages. Merv had a terribly disjointed career because of the war, but I haven't seen any other batsmen since who would displace him. We've had several other good middle-order batsmen. Wal Hadlee could fill the role when required. Barry Sinclair and Bevan Congdon were world class players. Geoff Howarth had a golden run for three or four years. Andrew Jones was a gritty player who was never overwhelmed by the opposition. But none of them scored more heavily than Merv, and none had his elegance and style.

"I see I've been placed at No 5, which, given the batsmen preceding me, is a pleasant thought. Just in case our batsmen have an off day, or we're caught on a tricky wicket, we've got Martin Donnelly at No 6. If we're in trouble and need to fight our way out, Martin is the man. If we're on top and want quick runs, Martin is still the man. They don't come better than him.

"The wicketkeeper caused me deep thought. The two obvious contenders are Ken Wadsworth and Ian Smith, and I've gone for Wadsworth. He was the better batsman and did nothing wrong as a keeper. I had tremendous respect for Wadsworth. He was combative and loved a fight. His wicketkeeping improved every year, and by the mid-1970s he was batting as well as many of the specialist batsmen. But for his tragic early death, he might have been New Zealand's wicketkeeper well into the 1980s. Smith, too, had some glorious days with the bat, especially his famous 173 against India at Auckland. But he wasn't the pure batsman Wadsworth was.

"Richard Hadlee is at No 7, which not only gives us one of the world's best bowlers, but a batsman who scored two test centuries and 15 half-centuries.

"Who is to be his fellow opening bowler, and who will take the containing role? Jack Cowie, Bruce Taylor, Dick Motz, Harry Cave, Lance Cairns, Ewen Chatfield, Danny Morrison, Chris Cairns and Richard Collinge all come into the reckoning. Cowie was a marvellous bowler, but he was undoubtedly a better bowler before the war. My selection span stretches back only to the end of the war. By the time Jack went to England in 1949, he was aged 37 and well past his best, though he could still be menacing. Instead, I've chosen Motz and Taylor. Motz was tremendously gutsy and is a clear choice. He could open the bowling or bowl into the wind, and he never stopped trying.

"Taylor shades Cave, Frank Cameron and Chatfield for the third pace bowling selection. At his best, Taylor was a match-winning bowler, capable of running through good lineups, as he did in the West Indies in 1972. His inclusion gives the attack more penetration. The trick with Bruce was to ensure he was really applying himself, which was not always the case. His selection also gives me a valuable lower-order batsman. I greatly admired Cave for his bowling at home against the West Indies in 1956. He was a much better bowler than his test bowling average indicates. Cameron was a magnificent team man who, though usually selected as a third pace bowler, was capable of opening the attack. Chatfield was accurate and persistent, but Cave did more to worry a batsman. Of the others, I feel none would give me the potency of Taylor at his best, though all of them had their great days.

"That leaves me with one place left, for a spinner. The spinners who come to mind are Tom Burtt and Hedley Howarth, the left-armers, Jack Alabaster, the leg-spinner, and John Bracewell with his off-spin. Bracewell was an aggressive off-spinner and won several tests, but given the choice, I like to have a bowler who can make the ball spin away from the batsman. What's more, I'm there to bowl some off-cutters, so I'm looking for someone to balance the attack.

"It could be Burtt, who was a notch above Howarth, and who was superb in England in 1949. But I've gone for Alabaster. His wrist spin was more difficult to read, and therefore more penetrating, and he was equally as accurate, which is unusual for a bowler of his type. Alabaster, bowling as he did in South Africa in 1961-62, was our best spinner since the war."

Here is Reid's New Zealand XI, with their test statistics:

			Batting						Bowling			
	M	I	NO	HS	R	Avg	100	C/S	R	W	Avg	5I
Bert Sutcliffe	42	76	8	230no	2727	40.10	5	20	344	4	86.00	0
John Wright	82	148	7	185	5334	37.82	12	38	5	0	-	-
Martin Crowe	77	131	11	299	5444	45.36	17	70	676	14	48.28	0
Merv Wallace	13	21	0	66	439	20.90	0	5	5	-	-	-
John R Reid	58	108	5	142	3428	33.28	6	43/1	2835	85	33.35	1
Martin Donnelly	7	12	1	206	582	52.91	1	7	20	-	-	-
Ken Wadsworth	33	51	4	80	1010	21.49	0	92/4	-	-	-	-
Richard Hadlee	86	134	19	151no	3124	27.16	2	39	9611	431	22.29	36
Bruce Taylor	30	50	6	124	898	20.41	2	10	2953	111	26.60	4
Dick Motz	32	56	3	60	612	11.55	0	9	3148	100	31.48	5
Jack Alabaster	21	34	6	34	272	9.71	0	7	1863	49	38.02	0

18 | STEERING THE SHIP

The expression "a thousand words" is well-known by players captained by John Reid. If a player, or the team collectively, had performed below standards, the skipper often delivered what he termed "a thousand words" at the end of play, or at the next team meeting. It was not an experience to be relished, for it was a case of Reid, with his seniority, his considerable stature as a player, and his forceful personality, putting the acid on under-achievers.

Artie Dick, who made two overseas tours under Reid, recalls those "thousand word" sessions well. "I think John was quite proud of them," says Dick. "He believed in confronting the problem, discussing it, then leaving it behind. You would never classify it as bullying, but it was certainly a case of the captain letting his team know that better was expected."

Reid seemed quite young when he took over the test captaincy in 1956. In fact, he was 27, and was in his eighth year as a test player. When he led New Zealand to their first test victory, over the West Indies in 1956, the image that sticks is of a virile young man leading from the front, rather than a wily old campaigner.

He had had considerable captaincy experience, having led his Hutt Valley High School First XI, and taken over from Trevor Barber as Wellington Plunket Shield captain at the end of 1951. In addition, he had played under a variety of captains – Walter Hadlee, Bert Sutcliffe, Merv Wallace, Geoff Rabone, Harry Cave for New Zealand, and Stewie Dempster and Joe Ongley for Wellington.

"I quickly discovered that a successful cricket captain must have a high degree of skill in man-management. This was an area in which I was lacking in my early days as captain. If a bowler wasn't putting the ball where it needed to be put to test the batsman's weak points, I tended to grab the ball and try to do it myself. Sometimes I might well succeed. But while this is all very well, and might come under the heading of 'leading by example', it is not the way to encourage the development of team spirit. It was the same with batting. I might have been able to play certain opposition bowlers without undue difficulty, but I had to learn that other batsmen in the team might have more trouble.

"It soon dawned on me, particularly when I was leading New Zealand, that the most important thing I could do as captain was build a really strong team spirit. We needed that as we were generally not over-endowed with naturally talented players in my time as captain. The real art of captaincy is to be able to get the best out of your players.

"But a captain can't do it alone. He needs help. On the tour of South Africa in 1961-62, I gathered around me a first class manager in Gordon Leggat [a former test cricketer], a loyal, supportive vice-captain in Murray Chapple, and a 'senior pro', Jack Alabaster. I'm sure Wal Hadlee felt the same when he captained the team to England in 1949. He had Jack Phillipps, who was a magnificent manager, Merv Wallace as an extremely knowledgeable, astute and reliable vice-captain, and two senior pros in Martin Donnelly and Jack Cowie. Of course, the captain makes the final decision, but generally has that back-up and support from what might be termed his 'executive'."

Dick says that, while Reid was a strong-willed captain who liked to back his hunches, he was always ready to take on board the opinions of others. "He had his own ideas, but I always found he was happy to listen to advice. That was good because, as well as giving John something else to consider, it helped others feel they were contributing."

It's often said that captains are born, not made. While agreeing with the proposition in general terms, Reid says cricket is the exception which proves the rule. "I believe there is such a thing as a natural leader of men, as has been proven many times over on the battlefields of the world, but in cricket there are so many aspects to consider that it takes time and experience to improve. A good natural leader does not necessarily make a good cricket captain. Ian Botham was a commanding figure on the field, and a dominating influence in any situation. Yet his tenure as England captain was far from successful.

"I'm sure I improved as a captain over the years. I was a bit dogmatic early on and expected a higher standard of performance than some of my players could produce. At team talks I would generate tremendous expectations of beating our opponents, no matter who they were, and probably believed my own rantings. Then I'd be disappointed the next day when it didn't happen quite as I'd envisaged. I feel my captaincy came of age on the 1961-62 tour of South Africa. I had learned the skills of man-management, helped immeasurably by my employment as a representative for the B.P. oil company. I'd been thrown into the deep end and been let loose on the territory of Central Otago. During my four years – 1955-58 – based in Oamaru, I was successful in my job, and developed the skills of dealing with people. I learned when to be forceful, when to pull back, when to be insistent and when to give way. The same skills were easily transferable to captaining a sports team.

"I'm afraid I upset some of the Otago supporters of long-time provincial captain Langford Smith when I was transferred to Oamaru at about the same time as I was appointed captain of the New Zealand team. I had previously captained the Wellington team. I insisted I also captain the Otago team because I knew I needed the practice of captaining a first class team. Like most things in life, the more you do, the better you get. As golfer Gary Player once said, 'The more I practise, the luckier I get.'

"The weather, the state of the pitch, the strengths and weaknesses of eleven opposing players, the balance of runs and time, the fact that a match can stretch over five days... these are all important factors, yet I can think of no other sport which incorporates all of them. For instance, we say field placing is an integral part of captaincy. This is a constant challenge and even slight alterations can be crucial. A captain has to have a very deep knowledge of cricket to be able to look at a batsman's stance, grip and propensity for favouring certain strokes to know how to work out his faults and find his weak points. Then he has to know which of his bowlers can best exploit those weaknesses, and give his bowler suitable advice, while setting the correct field after consultation with his bowler."

Reid feels a key aspect of being a good captain is being an automatic choice as a player. "There must be no doubt about his ability as a player, otherwise his authority is immediately undermined. No cricket captain is worth his place just for his captaincy. When we think of some of the successful captains, such as Bradman, Benaud, Ian Chappell, Border, May, Lloyd, Cronje and Imran Khan, it can be seen they were all outstanding cricketers who would have walked into their sides purely as players. The problems arise when captains are not producing the goods as players. There was a constant swirl of discussion about Mike Brearley, who, though he was a fine skipper, did not score enough runs to justify his test place. Geoff Howarth and Mark Taylor are two others who at various times of their careers, faced this unpleasant fact. There can be no question that once a captain is not earning his keep as a player, the murmurings will start, and that can be very counter-productive for a team."

In 1991, Reid and Clive Lloyd ran a coaching seminar in South Africa and produced this outline of the requirements of a good captain:

1. Must have the trust, respect and confidence of the players.
2. Must be a leader.
3. Must know his players.
4. Must have discipline on and off the field.
5. Must know the laws of the game.
6. Must know the strengths and weaknesses of the opposition.
7. Must sort out field placings beforehand.
8. Must be able to motivate team-mates.
9. Must anticipate what will happen during the game and be aware of the game situation.

10. Must communicate with bowlers all the time.
11. Must lead by example.
12. Must be a strong character.
13. Must be able to read wickets.
14. Must take a leadership role in training.
15. Must be calm in tight situations.
16. Must have a good relationship with the manager and/or coach.
17. Must always know how much time (or overs) is left in the match.
18. Must sometimes be firm and take the initiative, even when making a decision against the views of the team.
19. Must not be afraid to try different tactics in order to get a wicket.
20. Must play fair and not let the team get involved in intimidation.

Reid had one of the longest unbroken reigns in cricket history as a test captain (see table, page 232). He became the New Zealand captain in early 1956 and by the time he retired, in 1965, he was into his 10th year in the job. During that time he led New Zealand in 34 successive test matches. Even today, when test cricket has become an all-year merry-go-round, Reid still holds the record for having led New Zealand in the most tests.

Overseas, others since have captained test teams on many more occasions, but that is primarily because of the explosion in the number of test matches played these days. For instance, Allan Border was Australia's captain for nearly as long as Reid and during that time led his country in 93 tests.

So where does Reid rate in terms of captaincy? Former New Zealand wicketkeeper and double All Black Eric Tindill, who played with Reid in the late 1940s, and then umpired in many first class and test matches involving Reid, is not a man given to over-statement. But, says Tindill, Reid must be ranked near the top of any list of New Zealand captains.

"The quality I liked most about John Reid's leadership was his optimism and how positive he was. No situation was too daunting for him. He was always trying to make something happen, believed in persistent attack. If something wasn't working, he'd change it. Sometimes he was a bit unorthodox, but he was a thinker. He'd shake up his team, hurry them on. He was a great example to his players."

Reid's record of three wins in 34 tests as captain does not seem very impressive on paper. But it must be put in the context of its times. When Reid was captain, New Zealand generally had just two genuinely world class batsmen, himself and Bert Sutcliffe. His teams had some good pace bowlers, but no match-winner of the class of a Richard Hadlee, Dennis Lillee or Fred Trueman. And for most of Reid's career, New Zealand lacked penetrative spin bowlers of the calibre of Ramadhin, Laker, Lock and Benaud. Only Jack Alabaster in 1961-62 provided him with a spinner approaching world quality.

By comparison, Geoff Howarth fashioned a fine record in the early 1980s as a test and one-day skipper. But he did have players like John Wright, Bruce Edgar, Martin Crowe, John F. Reid, Jeremy Coney, Ian Smith, Richard Hadlee, Lance Cairns, John Bracewell and Ewen Chatfield in his side. What difference would even three or four of those players made to Reid's teams of the 1950s and '60s?

Some of the longest-serving captains since the Second World War have been:

	Years as captain		Tests as captain
Bobby Simpson (Aust)	16	(1963-78)	39
Javed Miandad (Pak)	15	(1979-93)	34
Nawab of Pataudi (Ind)	13	(1962-74)	40
Clive Lloyd (WI)	12	(1974 -85)	74
Arjuna Ranatunga (SL)	11	(1989-99)	56
John Reid (NZ)	10*	(1956-65)	34
Colin Cowdrey (Eng)	10	(1959-68)	27
Sunil Gavaskar (Ind)	10	(1976-85)	47
Imran Khan (Pak)	10	(1982-91)	48
Allan Border (Aust)	10*	(1985-94)	93
Mohammad Azharuddin (Ind)	10	(1990-99)	47
Greg Chappell (Aust)	9	(1975-83)	48
Jackie McGlew (SA)	8	(1955-62)	14
Gary Sobers (WI)	8*	(1965-72)	39
Viv Richards (WI)	8	(1984-91)	50
Peter May (Eng)	7	(1955-61)	41
David Gower (Eng)	7	(1983-89)	32
Wasim Akram (Pak)	7	(1993-99)	22
Abdul Kardar (Pak)	6*	(1952-57)	23
Richie Benaud (Aust)	6	(1958-63)	28
Geoff Howarth (NZ)	6	(1980-85)	30
Graham Gooch (Eng)	6	(1988-93)	34
Mark Taylor (Aust)	6*	(1994-99)	50
Hanse Cronje (SA)	6*	(1994-99)	44
Ray Illingworth (Eng)	5	(1969-73)	31
Ian Chappell (Aust)	5*	(1971-75)	30
Mike Brearley (Eng)	5	(1977-81)	31
Kapil Dev (Ind)	5	(1983-87)	34
Mike Atherton (Eng)	5*	(1993-97)	52
Ted Dexter (Eng)	4	(1961-64)	30

* Unbroken sequence
Figures correct to October 1999.

19 | TECHNICALLY SPEAKING

John Reid says the Ellis Park test at Johannesburg at the end of December 1953 was the critical match of his career. New Zealanders recall the match for the extraordinarily dramatic day's play on Boxing Day. Naturally Reid does, too. But it was also the match which led to him altering his batting technique. He became, he says, a much better test batsman after the 1953-54 tour of South Africa, and figures back him up.

Here's a comparison between his test batting until the end of that Johannesburg test, and for the rest of his career.

	M	I	NO	Runs	Average
1949-53	10	17	0	281	16.52
1954-65	48	91	5	3147	36.59

The statistics don't surprise Reid. "When I look back, I don't think I really knew how to bat before that South African tour. I had a poor technique. My batting was somewhat hit and miss, relying very much on natural ability. I went through a bad patch in test cricket in the early 1950s and it was obvious I needed to sort out my technique.

"It was the Ellis Park match that did it. Our batsmen were given a terrible time by Neil Adcock. Ironside was fairly vicious, too. We were pummelled. We were badly battered and bruised. The wicket was a green snake pit. We simply couldn't play Adcock. Granted he was fast, but we had a pretty quick bowler, too, in Bob Blair, while Tony MacGibbon and I were sharp. Yet the South Africans didn't seem to have any trouble playing us. They had time to spare. Endean, McGlew, McLean, Waite, Funston and the rest of them could handle quick bowling. They looked comfortable. I wondered why that was."

The answer was supplied by Eric Rowan, a fine South African test batsman who was not long retired. "He was very wise in the ways of cricket and we got on with him well. He looked after us socially, and we talked a lot of cricket. I used to keep a register of how I got out, and how I batted. I could see I was getting caught behind far too often. One day I got talking to him, and he said we New Zealanders were getting into trouble because we were basically front foot players. He said that, especially against pace bowling, it was important to get onto the back foot as much as possible. He then suggested the technique of moving slightly back and across to the off stump – a movement of about 15cm – marginally before the bowler delivered the ball, with the weight slightly forward, but no big commitment either way, forward or back."

Reid pondered this advice, felt it was sensible and subsequently adopted it, not only against the quick bowlers, but all the time. "You go back and across with the intention of going forward, and you move early," is how he describes it. "Against really quick bowlers, you are already back and can play your strokes. Against off-spin bowlers you have taken away their target. It is the best advice on batting I can give anyone.

"In the innings after Eric spoke to me, I scored 135. I hit a 6 that day and broke a little girl's arm. I remember later on I signed her cast. It was obvious to me that what Eric said was right, but I still had to learn the technique. I didn't always do it correctly for a start. I found I was playing half-volleys off the back foot!"

There was a suggestion, especially early in Reid's career, that he was susceptible to good spin bowling, especially off-spin. He tended to play forward with his front leg too straight and had a gap between bat and pad. But his batting figures indicate that once he adopted the back-and-across technique, spin bowling held few terrors for him. He scored a magnificent Plunket Shield century against Jim Laker, hammered Sonny Ramadhin in English league cricket, and prospered against Hugh Tayfield, Ian Johnson, Fred Titmus, and other world-renowned spinners. In South Africa in 1961-62, Jackie McGlew seemed reluctant to bowl his spinners at Reid. "There might have been a weakness there early on, but once I adopted the technique suggested by Eric Rowan, I always felt confident that in normal circumstances, I could handle any bowling. I'd still get myself out, but I could trust my technique."

Merv Wallace supports that view. "In John's early days, he wasn't that great against off-spinners. His pick-up meant he had no coverage of the wickets. He had a high backlift and a short arc of the bat. But he overcame that problem later on by moving across his stumps and created a longer arc for himself. He developed the ability to let the ball come on to him, and then he would hit the ball like a rocket."

Wallace says Reid was very good against quick bowling. "He used his feet well, getting across and in line. Against spin, he wasn't the sort of batsman who tried to get down the wicket. He developed his own technique and it worked very well for him. He found that there are many more scoring shots off the back foot."

Throughout the rest of his career, and on to this day, Reid has been at pains to promote the importance of playing off the back foot and of using the back-and-across technique against quick bowling. Sometimes he addresses the subject with an almost religious fervour. Looking through various clippings files on Reid, it is incredible to see how many times in interviews all around the world he has expounded the benefits of the technique.

The key point to stress, he says, is that most of the great batsmen of history were back foot players. "You'll get the odd few who were front foot players. Tom Graveney was a beautiful driver and murdered our bowling. He always looked to have time to play the ball. But he was 6ft 2in. He could get well forward and over the ball. If you read the history books you'll sometimes find examples of other very tall men, like Frank Woolley, who were terrific front foot players. But the great majority of the best players got onto the back foot whenever they could.

"I once asked Don Bradman about it. He said to me, 'I only went forward to drive.' People used to remark on the time Bradman had to play the ball. I believe that was partly because he got onto the back foot. In addition, his great scoring strokes, the hook, pull and cut, were back foot strokes.

"The West Indians have generally been back foot players. Gary Sobers used to take the step back and across. So did Clyde Walcott, a magnificent player off the back foot. Walcott once said that the place to hit really fast bowling was to and through mid-on. To do that, a batsman has to be back and right across. Brian Lara, today, is another of the top players who gets onto the back foot whenever he can. The best recent West Indian exponent of the back foot technique has been Carl Hooper, a technically brilliant batsman. Steve Waugh, Greg Chappell, Ian Chappell were back foot players. Barry Richards always looked at ease at the crease. People used to remark on the amount of time he had to play his strokes. It's because he employed this back-and-across technique and had played half his shot before the ball had been delivered. You don't commit yourself forward or back, but you make sure you are already in line with the ball. If you think about the great names, you'll see many of them followed the same policy. As a variation, the top English batsmen, such as Colin Cowdrey, Peter May and Len Hutton, mainly got into a half-cock position, the front foot advancing three or four inches across to the off stump, but ready to push back if required.

"Some players used to get back and across as I did, when the ball was being delivered. Others remained still, but preferred to play as much as possible off the back foot. It's really one technique, which you can take to whatever lengths you want. I took it further than most and moved across to off-spinners as well. It left them with nothing to bowl to as you covered up the gap between bat and pad."

Gren Alabaster, one of New Zealand's better off-spinners through the 1960s, is in no doubt Reid is correct with his back foot theory. "He played off-spin very well. He was the only leading New Zealand batsman of that period whom I didn't get out. I've listened to the Bradman audio tapes. On the second tape, Bradman stresses the importance of back foot play. He said that playing a bowler of Larwood's pace he tried to be back and across at the point of delivery. Bradman emphasises the point again in an article of his that I have. His attitude was that you played forward if the ball was pitched up and you wanted to attack it, but that most of the time, you were better off playing back and getting behind the ball."

Reid tried to convince his Wellington and New Zealand team-mates of the wisdom of the technique, but not always with success. "Some of our players were true front foot batsmen and couldn't change. They paid the price when they got on wickets where the ball was doing a bit. Lawrie Miller was a case in point. Lawrie, a left-hander, used to put his right foot well down the wicket and play everything from that position. The technique served him well in New Zealand, where the bowling was not always of the highest class, and he scored very heavily for several seasons. But when he got to England in 1958, he had all sorts of problems. Fred Trueman, Peter Loader and Brian Statham sorted him out so that in his four tests he scored just 92 runs at an average of 11.5.

"I suppose my suggestion didn't suit some players, and to them I might have sounded like a broken record, but I was convinced, and still am, that if our batsmen wanted to play long test innings, that was the way to go."

One who elected not to follow Reid's suggestion was tall Wellington opening batsman Bruce Murray, "Bags" to cricketers everywhere. "I was just a young fellow, probably a bit brash, and still at university," says Murray, "when Bogo tried to introduce me to his back foot technique. But I wasn't the sort of person who would do something on trust. I wanted to be able to see the logic myself. On the one hand, there was Bogo himself, and he was a brilliant batsman. He had some good people on his side, starting with Bradman. But when I looked at it, I felt it didn't suit me.

"I was a tall front foot player who didn't have great power, and liked to drive. Players like Bogo, Everton Weekes and other well-known back-foot players seemed to me to be shorter and very strong. In New Zealand Barry Sinclair and Graham Dowling, two of our best batsmen in the 1960s, were both back foot players. They liked to hit the ball hard to the on. I was an off-side player. I looked about and thought I'd take some advice. We happened to be playing Canterbury, and so I asked Walter Hadlee, who was managing their team, what he thought. I'm a lot older and hopefully wiser now, but at the time it was an innocent inquiry. Walter advised me that he favoured the batsman keeping perfectly still until the ball was delivered, his logic being that that minimised the amount of head movement, and should therefore assist with timing.

"What I didn't know was that Bogo and Walter didn't always see eye to eye, and had locked horns on various issues. Walter himself had been a tall, front foot player with a particularly strong drive. I duly reported back to Bogo what Walter had said and received a fairly heated reaction! [Reid's response: 'To my knowledge, I have discussed only wicketkeeping technique with Wal. He was insisting that Godfrey Evans waited until the ball pitched, even from Bedser, before he moved to outside the leg stump to take the big in-swingers. I didn't agree. I never discussed back foot play because I knew that on that subject he would be as dogmatic as me!']

"As I look back, I can see the merit in both concepts. So many great batsmen have been back foot players, and so many have used the short initial back-and-across movement that it obviously works for many people. But like all things, you can't be hard and fast about it. It's a horses for courses type of thing. I'd say if you were under six feet tall, then the half-step back and across is very worthwhile. I happened to have developed a technique where I looked to go forward, and because of my height – nearly 6ft 3in – I found I could get over the ball most of the time. I was very rarely in trouble with bouncers.

"It reminds me of the time I asked Bogo about the best way to play off-spin and he mentioned 'hitting them over the top'. I soon discovered this method probably suited him, with his immense strength, more than me, because I found myself getting caught in the deep!"

These days, Reid agrees with Murray that there will always be exceptions. "I have watched Sachin Tendulkar," he says, "who I think is a wonderful player, and I can't say he favours one foot or the other. He does not move before the ball is bowled, and is a very balanced batsman. He has rare talent.

"But when I look at New Zealand's batsmen in recent years, I've no doubt that the likes of Nathan Astle, Roger Twose and Craig McMillan would have done better if they'd paid more attention to learning how to play back properly and had made a point of getting across behind the line of the ball. Astle and McMillan have had some memorable days in one-day and test cricket. They have good timing and attack the bowling. But I'm convinced they'd have more consistency, be a lot more secure and not lose any of their scoring strokes if they adopted the back and across policy."

20 | COACHING AND SELECTING

Back in the 1980s, the term "coach" was generally deemed to be insulting to top cricketers. When Glenn Turner first worked with the New Zealand team in 1986, he was not called the coach, though that's what he was. "It bruises egos and some of the players feel it is demeaning," he explained at the time. So Turner and other coaches of the time were termed "assistant managers", "technical advisers" and the like.

Now, of course, the term coach is not only widely accepted, but actively embraced. The New Zealand team don't have just a coach, but a "technical coach" as well, plus a psychologist/motivator/mental skills expert. England's team has an even larger number of assistants with each facet of cricket – batting, bowling and fielding, as well as the usual doctor, physio, psychologist – assigned to an expert in that area. It would be difficult to imagine a test team turning up for a game these days without a coach.

But how important is the coach's role? Is his position over-rated? Walter Hadlee wonders where the coach and other advisers would have fitted into the 1949 team to England. "There wouldn't have been room," he says. "We had all aspects covered." A biased view from a proud captain? "No, Wal's right," says John Reid. "That team had a core of very experienced players who were brilliant at passing on knowledge. Merv Wallace was absolutely outstanding in this regard. A coach would have been entirely superfluous."

Similarly, would a coach have assisted Don Bradman's famous Invincibles team of 1948? Did Bradman, Hassett, Brown, Barnes, Morris, Tallon, Miller, Lindwall, Harvey, Johnston, Johnson and the rest of them suffer through lack of advice?

Reid has mixed views on the role of the coach: "I would not say categorically that a test team do not require a coach, but I would say the position is vastly over-rated. I've watched test cricket closely throughout the 1990s, and each year I see players turn up and make exactly the same mistakes as the previous time I saw them. That does make me wonder what effect the coach is having.

"For example, take the case of Graeme Hick. Quick bowlers all over the world know that he is susceptible to the short-pitched ball. When he comes into bat, the opposing captain will bring on his fast bowlers. That's the standard way to attack Hick. I wonder what work has been done by Hick and the various England coaches to overcome this weakness. Very few batsmen enjoy being on the receiving end of short-pitched bowling, but if you handle it right, maybe hook a couple to the boundary or duck comfortably under some bouncers, you'll stop being the target of special treatment. But if you don't get behind the ball, and instead hang out the bat, you encourage the bowler to give you a few more.

"I've yet to see a coach make a difference to a player with a technical problem. The trouble is, a lot of the coaches are not very good. It's one thing to put on a baseball glove and go down in front of the pavilion and start hitting high catches to the players; it's quite another to really provide them with the knowledge they need.

"However, having said that, a genuinely good coach can be a treasure. Australian cricket was turned around when Bobby Simpson came on board in the mid-1980s. The New Zealand team had Merv Wallace as coach in 1956 and '57 and he was of huge assistance to me as captain, and to the players. We were a rather young side, not exactly brimming with naturally-talented players, and had a very poor test record. It was extremely helpful having Merv with us."

Reid has considerable experience as a coach. For several seasons in the early 1950s, he was employed as a coach by the Wellington association. This entailed him doing the rounds of local schools and junior clubs to offer advice and encouragement, and also working with the association's various rep sides. At the same time – 1952-54 – while playing for Heywood in the Central Lancashire League, Reid was expected to coach the club's A and B teams during evening net practices. While he was New Zealand captain, Reid took part in the release of two records – 45s as they were – called *John Reid on Cricket*, which preceded the modern coaching video.

During the 1980s, Reid had a successful spell as manager-coach of Northern Transvaal, instilling cricket habits and discipline into a team where these attributes had been noticeably absent. He offered some, but not overwhelming, technical advice, and worked hard on making the Northern Transvaal players believe that if they put in the practice, they had the ability to take on the best players in South Africa.

When he looks back on his time in South Africa, Reid says he was generally rather more mellow and not too demanding of his players. It's an interesting thought. Certainly the South African players did not see it that way. Even now the Reid years at Northern Transvaal are spoken of the way New Zealand youngsters talk about having completed the course at Outward Bound. They're proud to have been part of it, to have got through it, and acknowledge it altered their outlook considerably.

While he feels that at lower tiers of cricket, up to domestic first-class level, it is important to have someone to give players technical assistance, Reid says it is reasonable to expect test players to have their techniques fairly much worked out. "A coach can do very little technically during a test or one-day series. In fact, if he starts making radical alterations to a player's technique at that time, he will almost always do more harm than good. The time to put in the hard work on technique is between tours or series, back home.

"Therefore my feeling is that at international level, the coach's major contribution must be in the mental area. He must be able to instil self-belief in his team, and also help them overcome difficulties they will face at that level – how to deal with hostile crowds, comments out in the middle from the opposition, the need to concentrate for long spells, play session by session and so on. There must also be some continuity in the role. Some countries seem to have a new coach every year."

Reid feels the coach, providing he is not a one-series wonder, must be a selector as well. "When I was captaining New Zealand, I soon realised I had to have a say in the selection of the teams I was being asked to lead. Otherwise what happens is you are given teams you're not comfortable with, then when you lose, you get the blame. It's the same now with the coach. It's his job to prepare the team; he must have plenty of input into the selection. The captain, too, must be asked his views. I don't say the selectors must automatically go along with every wish of the captain, but his opinions must carry some weight.

"Some people say that having the coach also on the selection panel makes things more awkward for him when dealing with players. The theory goes that they will be less willing to confide in the coach if he has the power to drop them. If they tell him they are having trouble facing pace bowlers, or can't bowl to left-handers or whatever, then the coach will be more inclined not to select them. I don't follow that reasoning. If the coach is worth his salt, he'll already know his players' weaknesses and be working to overcome them. If the player needs a shoulder to cry on, the manager should be his first port of call."

One of the prerequisites of being a good coach at international level, says Reid, is to have played plenty of big cricket. "I would say it's almost imperative. Occasionally you might find a good coach who was not a test player, but not very often. I'm certainly not saying all good players will be good coaches, but when you do find one like Merv Wallace who can transfer his knowledge to players, then he is at a massive advantage.

"For a start, he will have increased stature in the eyes of the team. That cannot be overlooked. I noticed when I coached the Northern Transvaal team that their attitude towards me was considerably more accepting when they'd looked me up in *Wisden* and realised that this old bugger who was telling them this and asking them to do that had actually played a lot of test cricket himself and scored a few runs. You can say it shouldn't matter, but it's an undeniable fact that it does. Players are going to be far more receptive to a famous former test star than to someone they've never heard of. It's human nature.

"The other reason I much prefer former test players as coaches is that they have experienced so many different situations in the middle. It must be very difficult to offer advice on how a player should handle himself during a heated one-dayer or a long, drawn-out test match if the coach has not experienced those situations himself. If you've batted in India and taken guard to a fast bowler, and know what it's like to have a capacity crowd chanting and screeching as he runs in to bowl, you will have some idea of what advice to offer. If you've never been in the situation, I imagine it must be much more difficult."

A danger of the modern trend towards over-coaching, says Reid, is that players are less inclined to work things out for themselves. "We all need help, of course, but the person primarily responsible for a player's technique and form is the player himself. I used to keep a record of my innings – how I'd done against various bowlers, how I'd got out, things I'd noticed while batting. It's important to be self-analytical, and, after all, every player is a little bit different.

"Furthermore the players on a team must help each other. If a team-mate feels you aren't doing something right, he should mention it. Perhaps if it is a fault it can be ironed out at the nets. There is a lot of knowledge within an international team, and it's important that that knowledge be pooled. The 1949 team was the best example. We didn't get much help at all from the English pros, but spent hours in the evenings discussing cricket, dancing about the bedroom moving inside bouncers or playing imaginary off-breaks. These days most international cricketers are full-time pros. It amazes me how many basic mistakes they make, and I question how much they are observing, talking to other players and really trying to improve.

"Ideally, instead of a coach, I would prefer a team to have a player-coach, though I know there aren't too many of those sorts of people around. I wanted Merv Wallace to fill that role for us in England in 1958. I'm sure Bobby Simpson adopted the same role with the young Australian team in 1977-78 when he was brought out of retirement to help the test team during the years the Australian board was in dispute with Kerry Packer."

Whereas the modern coach is as visible as his players, selectors are very much shadowy figures in the background. Yet they're equally important.

Reid had two spells as a national selector, totalling 10 years. He says selecting is an interesting balancing act. "You have to be guided to some extent by statistics. Cricket is a game of statistics – runs, wickets, catches. They are important. But a selector must also use his knowledge of cricket to make intuitive decisions. You can't simply look up the latest averages and choose from that list.

"What I wanted more than anything from selectors was consistency. If you see a player chosen for one match, then dropped for the next, it is not the player's fault, but that of the selectors. They don't know what they're about. I remember Noel McMahon, a big-hitting batsman from Waikato, being chosen to play against the Australians at Carisbrook in 1950. He scored 0 and 12 and was never selected for New Zealand again. But have a look at the background: he'd made his first class debut in 1936-37, as a spin bowler. Over the next 13 years he played just three first class matches, scoring 12 runs at 3.25 each and taking three wickets at 32 runs each. He was chosen for New Zealand purely on the basis of a hurricane century he scored in a two-day against the Australians.

"Noel was nearly 34 when he was chosen, and was out of his depth. I spoke to the Australians later and was left in no doubt that they were amazed by the selection as they had not taken the Waikato fixture very seriously at all. My point is: McMahon was criticised in some quarters for failing in the 'test', but he wasn't the culprit. The finger should have been pointed at the selectors. The experienced selection panel of the time – Walter Hadlee, Merv Wallace and Jack Kerr – should have known better.

"When I became a selector my priority was to get consistency into the selections. For years we'd picked players for one match, or one tour. It's interesting that when we toured South Africa in 1961-62 (and drew the series 2-2), we took with us Murray Chapple, Zin Harris, Noel McGregor and John Guy, all of whom had toured with New Zealand teams previously but had missed the last major tour, to England in 1958. For that South African tour, we took only one youngster who was basically untried. That was left-arm spinner Bryan Yuile, who did not force his way into the test team in South Africa, but did end up playing 57 matches for New Zealand over the next decade.

"Selectors don't get it right all the time. I still shake my head and wonder how Gordon Leggat, Merv Wallace and I could have omitted Jack Alabaster from our touring side in 1965 and taken an untried teenager like Graham Vivian instead. Over the years, Vivian became a punishing batsman and a brilliant fieldsman, but his spin bowling was never more than a part-time activity. Even in 1965, when he was picked for his bowling promise, he bowled just 113 overs on the full tour and took just eight wickets. By comparison, Bevan Congdon bowled 164 overs and the regular bowlers, such as Motz, Cameron, Taylor and Collinge, all got through more than 500 overs.

"Picking Vivian was a poor decision, especially as it went against the policy of consistent selection that we had established over the previous few years. What made it worse was that we left Alabaster at home. He had missed selection for Otago in some games that season, but he should have been included in the touring side. I was captain and knew his ability. He'd been superb in South Africa a few years earlier. We all make mistakes and his omission in 1965 was one of them. Jack would have made a big difference. It would only have been a matter of bowling him into form.

"And I still regret that we were unable to take Barry Sinclair to South Africa in 1961-62. But you have to pay some heed of figures. In the season before, Sinclair had an appalling run, whereas some of his rivals for a touring spot, such as John Guy, scored very heavily. I knew how good Sinclair was because I'd played with him for some years in the Wellington side. But you have to be fair and Guy deserved to be chosen. His run-scoring demanded it."

Reid says the panel he was on in the 1970s (Frank Cameron, Ian Colquhoun and Reid) worked very well. "We – especially Frank and me – debated for hours into the night, but in the end all selections must be unanimous. Once you have made your decision, that must be the end of it."

One player Reid always pushed for was an all-rounder, either a wicketkeeper good enough to play as a batsman, or a genuine batting-bowling all-rounder. "In my time, players like Keith Miller and Gary Sobers gave their sides a tremendous advantage by covering two positions. More recently, Ian Botham, Richard Hadlee, Kapil Dev and Imran Khan have all been good enough to represent their countries as batsmen or bowlers. Heading into the 21st century, South Africa is very well stocked in this area, with players like Jacques Kallis and Lance Klusener lethal with either bat or ball, and Shaun Pollock not far off genuine all-rounder status, either. An all-rounder greatly alters the balance of a team. It means you can field six batsmen, and still have five genuine bowlers. If none of the top six bowl and one of them isn't the wicketkeeper, your attack will generally be thin. My advice to young players today would definitely be to try to develop as both batsman and bowler.

"With so much one-day cricket played now, any player who can fill two roles will have a big advantage in catching the eyes of the selectors.

"We did have a couple of notable successes. New Zealand won the third test against India in 1976, at the Basin Reserve, by an innings and 33 runs, and Richard Hadlee cleaned up the Indians on the fourth morning, taking 7-23. His match figures were 11-58. It was his first great test performance. Yet before the game there was some anxious discussion before Hadlee was chosen. The three leading pace bowlers were clearly Richard Collinge, Lance Cairns and Dayle Hadlee. Richard Hadlee had been omitted from the first test team, and had taken 1-139 in the second test. The Basin wicket looked as if it would suit seam, though the Indians went into the match with just two pace bowlers and their three world class spinners – Bedi, Chandrasekhar and Prasanna. We decided to omit our one spinner, Hedley Howarth, and chose Richard Hadlee as a fourth pace bowler. It was a gamble, and it paid off massively.

"A couple of years later, the selectors again faced a tricky problem choosing the New Zealand 12th man for the third test – it's the selectors, not the captain who choose the 12th man in home matches. Geoff Howarth had been playing test cricket for more than four years and had generally not produced anything like the runs a player of his class should have. In the 1978 test series against England, he had scored 13, 21, 5 and 1. For the third test we called in a very promising young Wellingtonian, Bruce Edgar. Most predicted Edgar would play and Howarth would carry the drinks. But after some careful consideration, we opted to go with Howarth, a fateful decision. He scored 127 and 102 and his career blossomed. For the next three years he was New Zealand's best batsman and developed into a world class test and one-day captain.

"I mention these two examples to give weight to what I say. Selectors should pick the best players and then, within reason, stick with them."

Besides their role in picking teams, selectors fulfil other functions behind the scenes. Reid, never one to shirk a confrontation, become something of a trouble-shooter in the 1970s. He recalls meeting Glenn Turner at Wellington airport one summer's day in the mid-1970s and driving him to Lyall Bay for a chat. "We both had a few words to say. Glenn at that time was having a running battle with the New Zealand Cricket Council over his professional demands for himself and other players. I had no objection to that. In fact, he was some years ahead of his time. My problem was what the selectors perceived to be his selfish actions and attitude. I reminded Glenn of the high regard in which he was held in world cricket, but said he would get my endorsement only when I saw him willing to sacrifice his wicket in the course of chasing a New Zealand win. He countered by saying I was too dogmatic.

"Later our selection panel recommended to the council that Glenn be appointed to captain the New Zealand team that was to tour India in 1976. I can't say his attitude had done an about-turn, but because of his obvious Indian connections – he was married to an Indian – we felt it would be a good appointment. But Glenn was not really a success as captain and was not retained long. He withdrew from playing test cricket for New Zealand in 1977 and returned for just a couple of matches against Sri Lanka many years later.

"Another chat I recall well was with Geoff Howarth. He, too, was a budding New Zealand captain in the mid-1970s, but again there were problems. I spoke to him about his attitude and demeanour around the dressing room. Howarth was very much a loner in those days and used to have his after-match 'toot' by himself. We selectors did not feel this was the best way to help generate a good team environment. Hence my talk with Geoff."

21 | UNSPEAKABLE ACTIONS

For a reason that is not easy to fathom, being labelled a "chucker" seems to be the most heinous fate that can befall a cricketer. A chucker, of course, is a bowler who throws. These unfortunate individuals are sometimes also called dart-throwers or spear-throwers.

I am unsure that delivering a cricket ball with a bent elbow instead of bowling it is a more shameful activity than dropping an easy catch or making a pair of ducks. Yet bowlers who have been called for throwing in major cricket matches have had their careers, and even their lives, ruined. Ian Meckiff, the Australian paceman who was called in a test against England in 1963, never played again, or got over the shame of it all. He wrote a bitter book and called it *Thrown Out*.

The fuss in recent years has revolved around Sri Lankan off-spinner Muttiah Muralitharan, who was called for throwing during the second test against Australia at Melbourne in 1995, and then seven times the following week in a one-day international between Sri Lanka and the West Indies at Brisbane. The Sri Lankan has run into "throwing" trouble since in Australia. Not surprisingly, the Sri Lankans defend their spinner vigorously. They claim that the Australian umpires who have called him, Darrell Hair, Ross Emerson and Ern McQuillan, had made their decisions in advance.

They could be correct. Almost always, it is the square leg umpire who no balls a bowler for throwing. After all, how can the umpire at the bowler's end watch the position of the bowler's arm and feet at the same time and still make considered decisions on such matters as lbw appeals?

Yet Hair was at the bowler's end when he no-balled Muralitharan on the opening day of the Melbourne test. Hair's umpiring partner, Steve Dunne, did not call the Sri Lankan, and neither did Hair after his opening burst. Perhaps he felt he had made his point. In the one-dayer, Emerson called Muralitharan seven times and McQuillan once (concurrently).

Muralitharan has caused great divisions since. Umpire Emerson, when demoted by the Australian cricket authorities in 1999, claimed that he had been told by leading test cricketers that if the world's leading batsmen were asked about Muralitharan's delivery and could answer without fear of reprisal, 100 per cent of them would say he threw.

Throwing has been a source of controversy since before bowling progressed from roundarm to overarm in 1864. John Willes was the first person no-balled for throwing, when he bowled roundarm for Kent against the M.C.C. in 1822. He was also so incensed that he vowed never to play again. There was a rash of throwing in England in the 1880s. Every county, it seemed, had a fast chucker, and on the rough pitches of the day, they could be almost literally lethal.

At Lord Harris' instigation, the "absolutely fair" clause was added at this time to the bowling law. The worse offender was a Lancastrian named Crossland, and several counties refused to play against Lancashire until Crossland was removed from the team.

The first bowler to be no-balled for throwing in a test was the Australian speedster Ernest Jones (the man who at Melbourne in 1898 bowled a ball through W.G. Grace's beard and then called down the wicket, "Sorry Doc, she slipped." Jim Phillips, one of the most respected umpires of his time, was the man who called him and so earned himself a share of cricket immortality. Jones continued to play for Australia until 1903, making 19 appearances in all.

Left arm spinner Tony Lock was the first English bowler to be no-balled in a test, against the West Indies in 1954. Lock ran into trouble when he delivered his quick one. He was called by umpire Perry Burke when he bowled his faster one to Gerry Gomez, just after bowling George Headley with a similar ball. Lock had been no-balled previously for Surrey, and was to be no-balled several more times over the next few years, before he remodelled his bowling – switching to a slower pace.

At the end of the 1950s, throwing was rife in top cricket. Besides Meckiff, Australia had Jim Burke and Gordon Rorke, South Africa had Geoff Griffin (who was called 11 times in a test against England in 1960) and the West Indies had Charlie Griffith.

Griffith was a hostile opening bowler. There is always the suspicion that opposition batsmen are pleased to see such bowlers labelled chuckers in the hope that it will force them to slow down. Photographic evidence indicates that Griffith delivered the ball with a bent arm, but that is not the same thing as saying he threw.

Because of the trouble at the time, the International Cricket Conference focused on the problem at its meeting in 1960. Sir Donald Bradman led the charge to eradicate what he called "the biggest curse in the game today".

A new definition of throwing was devised: "A ball shall be deemed to have been thrown if, in the opinion of either umpire, the bowling arm having been bent at the elbow, whether the wrist is backward of the elbow or not, is suddenly straightened immediately prior to the instant of delivery."

Since then, there hasn't been a really bad outbreak of throwing, but the subject bubbles along never far from the surface.

Although things get very heated at the time, some throwing incidents are

A CRICKETING LIFE

humorous in hindsight. For the rare Aboriginal cricketer, throwing has been a recurring problem. In a match at Sydney, in November 1900, between New South Wales and the Next XV, the Aboriginal fast bowler J. J. Marsh was no-balled by umpire Curran, who was standing at square leg. After an argument, and a refusal by Marsh to accede to his demand, Curran left the field in a huff.

In 1904, the M.C.C. played New South Wales and found another Aborigine, named Henry, mustering incredible pace. Herbert Strudwick, in *Twenty-Five Years Behind the Stumps*, wrote: "Henry bowled one at Braund which hit the sightscreen on the second bounce and came halfway back to the wicket. The Aborigine, following up his run, stood a couple of yards from Braund when Len looked around. There is not the least doubt it put the wind up Braund. After the next ball, he backed away as far as the square leg umpire would allow and, pushing his bat at the ball, poked it to point with the bottom of the bat.

"Did you ever see anything so fast in your life?" Len said when we asked him about his retreating tactics. "There was no way I was going to stop there to be shot at by that black devil."

Don Bradman had an equally frightening encounter with yet another Aboriginal fast bowler, Eddie Gilbert, while playing for New South Wales against Queensland in 1931. "Gilbert took 3-12 and sent me down the fastest period of 'bowling' I can remember," recounted Bradman in *Farewell to Cricket*. "All players thought his action was decidedly suspect, but certainly on the green top wicket, the ball came through at bewildering speed, which seemed accentuated because Gilbert shuffled only about four quick steps before delivering the ball. One delivery knocked the bat out of my hands. He was faster than Larwood or anyone else I faced."

There was an amusing sequel to Bradman's brief innings. When he returned to the pavilion, a team-mate commiserated with him for failing to score. "Luckiest duck I ever made," said Bradman. Marsh was not the only bowler to resort to wearing splints to prove the correctness of his action. C. B. Fry, a legendary England batsman of the golden age of cricket, before the First World War, was so furious when called for throwing that he turned up with splints, but found he could not bowl the ball effectively.

New Zealand has had its share of throwing wrangles. Our first genuinely fast bowler, George Dickinson, was often said to be a "chucker". Later came the Bartlett furore. When he was just a teenager, Bartlett mustered fearsome pace and certainly rattled the visiting English and Australian teams. England, backed by their tabloid press, naturally labelled him a chucker, a tag that haunted Bartlett over the next decade. In 1968, when Bartlett was recalled from the cricket wilderness to play against India, he clearly frightened the Indians, taking 6-38 in Christchurch. In response, Abid Ali deliberately threw one ball of that test and was duly called by umpire Fred Goodall.

There was a fuss in the early 1990s when England left-arm spinner Phil Tufnell was described as a thrower when touring New Zealand. Then

Muralitharan toured and the New Zealand media and some players pointed the finger at him.

It is customary when a player is accused of throwing for his team-mates to support him by accusing a player on the opposing team of the same crime (a sort of cricket version of nuclear deterrence). Certainly when the Aussies were accusing Bartlett of throwing, they had several bowlers with suspicious actions. When Muralitharan had the finger pointed at him in New Zealand, his Sri Lankan team-mates nominated Kerry Warmsley as a thrower. In India, when the New Zealanders suggested an Indian bowler threw, they replied by stating that Dion Nash's action was questionable.

Considering it is such a touchy subject, it is perhaps surprising that only nine bowlers have been called for throwing in the history of test cricket, and two of them, Ali and David Gower, did so on purpose. The other offenders have been Ernest Jones, Tony Lock, Geoff Griffen, Haseeb Ahsan, Ian Meckiff, Henry Olonga and Muralitharan.

Despite the apparent scarcity of throwers, the I.C.C. takes the issue very seriously these days and Reid is on an advisory panel chaired by Sir Clyde Walcott. Other panel members have included Brian Basson (South Africa), Javed Burki (Pakistan), Kapil Dev (India), Doug Insole (England), Michael Holding (West Indies), Ranjan Madugalle (Sri Lanka), Nigel Plews (England), Andy Pycroft (Zimbabwe) and Bobby Simpson (Australia). "A report can be received only from the umpires or the referee. Umpires can report what they suspect is an illegal delivery to the referee. The referee will then arrange with the producer of a television company to confidentially film the bowler from three or four angles. That film is sent to the I.C.C. with the referee's report and as soon as possible the I.C.C. will send copies of the video and the letters to the members of the advisory panel.

"A conference call will be arranged. During the call each panel member comments on what he has seen. The call is chaired by Sir Clyde Walcott. After all panel members have spoken, the chairman will sum up the feeling and then decide what action is required. Either the bowler will be deemed not to be a thrower, or it will be decided he has a doubtful delivery, or it will be decided that we need more film. A copy of that report is then sent to the board of the country involved. In recent years Muralitharan has certainly had the most publicity over his unusual action, but he has been far from the only bowler to have been scrutinised.

"If the advisory panel feels there is a problem with a bowler's action, the bowler will be sent to London and given remedial work by Fred Titmus, the former England off-spin bowler, or another qualified person, and the panel will have another look at his action after that has been done."

Reid says cricket followers would be surprised at how much work has been done involving illegal deliveries. "A lot of the work isn't reported on. Cricket authorities acknowledge that with a problem delivery, action needs to be taken early."

22 | WE ARE FAMILY

It must be difficult growing up in the shadow of a famous parent. One celebrated case concerns Don Bradman's son John, who eventually changed his surname to Bradsen. He meant no disrespect to his father, but had found years of living in a fishbowl environment because of his surname got just too stifling. Imagine if Michael Jordan's son wanted to be a basketballer in the United States, or if one of John McEnroe's children was inclined towards tennis. Would not their fathers' fame make things very much more difficult?

In New Zealand terms, it cannot have been easy growing up in the 1960s and '70s in the shadow of John Reid. Though Reid largely predated the television age, he was a national celebrity. He held centre stage for so long that he became a household name.

John and Norli had three children: Alison, Richard and Ann. All had their own strengths and, in fact, they each displayed prowess at a different sport. But because the central theme of this book is cricket, and for no other reason, there will be more words in this segment on the Reid family devoted to Richard than his two sisters.

The saying goes that behind every successful man there is a woman. In John Reid's case, that woman has been Norli Le Fevre. They were married in Wellington in 1951, after an unusual start to their relationship. Norli was the admitting nurse at Hutt Hospital in 1946 when John was bundled in with his second bout of rheumatic fever. Romance blossomed from that point and was not dented even by the fact that John spent more than half of 1949 overseas with the New Zealand cricket team. Theirs has been a partnership in the fullest sense of the word.

"Norli has been a tower of strength," says John. "She has been the assistant manager, and sometimes the manager, of our various business ventures, and my best friend for more than 50 years. It's amazing how quickly those years have flown by.

"We travelled to England by ship in 1952 for the first of seven consecutive summers. I played league cricket in Lancashire in the northern summer, and would then return to coach in Wellington. Travelling on the big liners in those days was a wonderful experience, though very time-consuming, as it took a month or more to get from England to New Zealand."

It would be incorrect and somewhat demeaning to describe Norli as a sports widow, even in the 1950s and '60s, for she was always a personality in her own right. However, it must have been difficult for her to be alone so often while raising their young children. Alison was born in 1955 and was just three months old when her father set off on a long tour of Pakistan and India. Richard was born in 1958, soon after his father had returned from a tour of England. Ann was just three months old when her father headed to South Africa for the 1961-62 tour.

Norli was always keen on sport. She played tennis at school and after the children had grown up a little, became a B grade squash player. The support and encouragement she gave her husband should not be underestimated. I noticed it while preparing this book. Draft chapters would be read by both John and Norli, and often Norli's handwritten notes in the margin signalled a sentence or a phrase that was either incorrect or unclear.

"I can't image how I would have survived if Norli hadn't been around to supervise my various business interests over the years," says John. "There is really no way of saying thank you enough to a wife who has made such a huge contribution to our unique lifestyle and who is still involved in our current business, running a homestay enterprise – dinner, bed and breakfast – in Taupo. One benefit of the work I do now for the I.C.C. is that Norli can sometimes accompany me on overseas trips.

"New Zealanders generally, myself included, are not very demonstrative regarding their family affection, unlike the French or perhaps the Italians. But I have been very fortunate as I have received a tremendous amount of support from my family. The girls give me a very hard time with their selections for birthday and Christmas cards, so there is never any possibility of me getting a swollen head!"

Alison, the oldest of the three children, studied as a microbiologist, and became an A grade squash player who toured New Zealand with a national colts team. This was an interesting time. "When Alison was selected for the squash team, I was president of the Commercial Squash Centres Association and was battling to have the commercial centres represented at New Zealand association level, and was negotiating to stop legislation being passed which would class all who worked at a commercial centre – including the receptionists – as professionals. Back then, professionalism in squash was still a dirty word and professionals were barred from entering New Zealand association events. It was a farcical situation. Norli had taken up squash only to face being classed as a professional in her first B grade tournament because she worked at our squash centre!

"Anyway, Alison didn't seem to meet any resistance during her time as a competitive player, and I was pleased about that. She later travelled to Britain, Europe and North America, where she married Dick Orgias, which delighted us as he had been a long-time friend of the family. From America they joined us in South Africa, where their daughter Christina was born. They are now settled in Auckland."

John and Norli see their younger daughter, Ann, frequently as she and her husband, Gordon, also live in Taupo. "Ann's passion at school was athletics, and she was a good sprinter. She was naturally gifted at sport, and at school shaped up as a good tennis player. But she has now changed tack and has taken up squash. She completed her education in Taupo, where we moved in 1978, and married Gordon Fraser in 1981, just before we moved to South Africa. Gordon and Ann lived in Wanganui for some years, but since moving to Taupo, Gordon has established a thriving painting/decorating business. They have one daughter, Megan."

Unlike Alison and Ann, having a famous cricket father was definitely a factor in Richard's career. He was a naturally gifted young sportsman, one of the best squash players in the country for his age, and a talented cricketer. John Reid gauges that by the time Richard was captaining the Scots College First XI, Richard was a better player than he had been as a schoolboy. Richard had an interesting, if disjointed, cricket career.

He represented Wellington for two seasons in the early 1980s, and his play from that time is best remembered for the game against Central Districts in Palmerston North when he broke his arm in two places while trying to take an awkward catch in the outfield. "At this time," says John, "I was a radio comments man and was covering another match. I nearly had a fit the next day when I heard that Richard had batted for 40 minutes for three runs, with his right arm in plaster and in a sling to save Wellington from defeat."

Shortly after, Richard went to South Africa, where he coached in Johannesburg and had several seasons playing club and minor rep cricket. He returned to New Zealand keen to re-establish his first class career. What happened defied belief. He played first class cricket for Auckland and then Wellington, and did reasonably well. But his career really took off when he began opening the innings. He turned out to be an exciting and punishing batsman, especially at one-day level. In 1990-91, when he and Martin Crowe were opening the batting for Wellington, they drew huge crowds to the Basin Reserve. Spectators would ensure they were there at the start of play and were seldom disappointed. It reminded older cricket fans of the impact John Reid had had on cricket lovers in the capital three decades earlier. Crowe and Reid scored so fast that often by the time their partnership was broken, they had won the game for Wellington. Reid's scores in the Shell Cup competition that season were: 89 (from 90 deliveries), 95 (73 deliveries), 12, 91 (68 deliveries), 14 and 47 (44 deliveries).

Richard was an uncompromising attacker, and really smashed the bowling with big hooks, drives and cuts. As he piled up the runs, he attracted the attention of the national selectors, who had dabbled with him for a couple of games back in 1988, then discarded him. Richard was called into the New Zealand team that went to Australia in early 1991 and even at that level proved successful. He was a disconcerting player because he always looked so laid-back. He was not in the best physical condition and some cricket followers wondered about his application. In his case, appearances were deceiving. He cherished his national team selection, and for a time thrilled New Zealand crowds.

"I heard all this from afar," says John. "I was still in South Africa then, but of course I was pleased and proud that Richard had got into the New Zealand team. I hoped he would play in the 1992 World Cup, and was back in New Zealand by then. But Richard had secured a good job at Nike and by 1992 that was taking priority."

You could say it turned out all right for Richard. He played 43 first class matches between 1979 and 1992 and nine one-day internationals from 1988 to 1991. In those nine one-dayers he made 248 runs at 27.55, hinting at the ability he had.

Richard was never the most competitive or ambitious of cricketers. He says: "Dad and I have had some interesting discussions, not just about our attitude to cricket, but to life. He strongly believes if you are going to do something, you must do it as well as you can. I agree with that in some areas, but only if it matters a lot to you. I never felt like that about my cricket. I'm not a lazy person; it's just that cricket was never the priority for me that it was for dad. You could say we've agreed to differ on that one."

Without wishing to become an amateur psychologist, I have a feeling that Richard was discouraged from being too ambitious at cricket because of some early experiences when he seemed to suffer through being the son of a famous former New Zealand captain. Certainly when I knew him at primary school, he was as competitive a young sportsman as could be found.

John says he felt frustrated watching from the sideline as his son received harsh treatment from some age rep selectors of the time. In the Reids' garage in Taupo is a scrapbook of Richard's early newspaper write-ups, caringly collected and stuck into the book by a proud father. But Richard faced more problems than most boys his age hoping to progress with their cricket. "Richard was forever playing in my shadow," says John. "His performances had to be twice as good as the next player, not just better, for him to be selected for various teams. He was a very good schoolboy batsman, who scored a double century in the open 2C grade competition and produced other big scores. I always felt sorry that I couldn't help him more – I could have confronted the small men of this world, but that would have meant he would never be selected for anything."

Richard, who has two boys, Oliver and Angus, was the New Zealand managing director of Nike until 1999 and then took up a two-year contract for a firm based in Nigeria.

23 | FINAL THOUGHTS

THE INFLUENCES OF ONE-DAY CRICKET

The benefits and pitfalls of one-day cricket are well-documented – much better fielding, less technically correct batting, the emphasis on tight bowling. For John Reid, another noticeable change has been the virtual extinction of the tail-ender.

"In the 1950s and '60s, captains used to write down the names of their tail-enders and hand the list to the opposition. There was an unwritten rule that fast bowlers would not bowl short to these players. But that's long gone. Now, even the worst wielder of a bat, the chap who comes in just before the roller, is kitted out with all the usual gear – bat, pads, box, gloves – and also a chest guard, inside thigh pad, helmet and arm guard. He is expected to cope with a bouncer or two in the first over, if he survives that long. Perhaps the game was changing anyway, but I'm sure one-day cricket has hastened the new attitude.

"There are no tail-enders now. Every player is expected to be able to bat at least usefully, and wicketkeepers who can't bat well are rare. And whereas when I played you might be able to hide a couple of your fieldsmen at fine leg and third man, every player is now expected to be able to field to a high standard. I watch big pace bowlers like Allan Donald or Glenn McGrath finish an over and wander down to fine leg. Within a moment, they'll be sprinting around the boundary, diving to save an extra run, and firing in a return.

"The fielding these days is a joy to watch. Some, such as Jonty Rhodes, Ricky Ponting and Chris Harris, are supremely good, and the overall standard is vastly better than in my playing days. Back then, the standard fell away quickly after the best few fieldsmen in a team. Now everyone is competent and in some teams nearly everyone is outstanding."

Reid says the attitude towards spin bowlers has also changed since his playing days. "Spin bowlers were an integral part of cricket and teams' bowling attacks were generally made up of two spinners, three quicker bowlers and an all-rounder. There were exceptions, such as the Bodyline series in 1932-33. But even the attack Len Hutton took to Australia in 1953-54, which boasted Tyson, Statham and Bailey, also included spinners Bob Appleyard and Johnny Wardle.

"These days it is not unheard of to find five pace bowlers in a team, and four is relatively common. There is often much discussion about whether a spin bowler will be included. In my time, spin was almost always a key factor of any test attack. Richie Benaud, Hugh Tayfield, Jim Laker and Tony Lock, Jack Alabaster and myself, Lance Gibbs... we were critical to our attacks. And that's discounting the Pakistanis and, in particular, the Indians, who had a succession of brilliant spin bowlers.

"A few years back, I feared for the future of spinners. In one-day cricket they were virtually extinct, and they were being phased out of test play. But Shane Warne's arrival has altered people's thinking. Warne is not only a potent attacking weapon, but he is as economical as many quicker bowlers. Since Warne's successes, other spinners such as Kumble, Vettori and Strang have begun to make an impression, though the standard of spin bowling around the world is still nowhere near what it was 40 years ago."

John Reid would have been a natural one-day cricketer. Without altering one jot his attitude to the game, he would have been the sort of player who scored at a run a ball (a strike rate of 100 as modern terminology has it), would have been able to bowl whatever was required and would have been one of those outstanding fieldsmen who secures the match-altering catch or run out. The one-day game is about dominating the opposition, so it's not surprising Reid is a fan.

"It has changed the face of cricket, with the 'flannelled fools' looking more like court jesters bedecked in colourful pyjamas. I like the buzz around the ground during a big one-day international. The abbreviated brand of cricket has attracted a new breed of younger fans who are possibly just as interested in the social occasion as the mechanics of cricket. They enjoy having a few drinks at the game, and get caught up in the excitement of the occasion. This is marvellous. These converts to cricket are most welcome, for in the end it's bums on seats that counts. Cricket must retain its viewing audience to prosper."

But while Reid is all for the pace and drama of one-day cricket, he is far from convinced by some of the batting he now sees. "From a former player's point of view, I find it difficult to accept that it is necessary to pick a test team and then a separate side of one-day specialists, and even a different captain. My thinking is that surely if a batsman is good enough to play test cricket, he is good enough to bat the ball around with less restrictive field placings and very few fieldsmen in short catching positions. Greg Chappell, Martin Crowe, Viv Richards, Sachin Tendulkar, Brian Lara, Mark Waugh – they are or were all wonderful test players who also shone at one-day cricket without having to dramatically alter their techniques."

ABOUT FAST BOWLERS

The question of pace bowling is an interesting one. Throughout cricket history, observers have maintained their era produced the fastest bowlers – whether they were Lockwood and Ernest Jones at the turn of the century, McDonald and Larwood in the 1920s, Lindwall, Miller, Tyson and Adcock in the decade after the Second World War, Hall, Griffith and Bartlett in the 1960s, Lillee, Thomson, Roberts and Holding of the 1970s or Marshall, Ambrose, McGrath, Donald, Wasim, Waqar and Shoaib Akhtar of more recent years.

Logically, bowlers might have got a shade quicker. In athletics, field events competitors are throwing further and sprinters are running faster. Fast bowlers are a bigger breed these days. Ambrose and Walsh are taller than any of the famous genuinely fast bowlers who preceded them.

But Reid doubts there is much difference in pace between the quickest of his era, Frank Tyson, and today's speedsters. "Tyson was hurling them down at about 93mph (148km/h), which is about the speed they're reaching today. In fact, the bowling today might even be a fraction slower when the new front foot no-ball rule is taken into account. Now the ball is delivered from behind the popping crease. That means that bowlers like Lindwall and David Larter, who had a drag of at least a metre, would have had to deliver the ball from much further back. The ball, travelling at the same speed as it does now, had a shorter distance to travel."

UNDER-19 TEAM EXPERIENCES

In 1994 and 1996 Reid took a break from his refereeing duties to manage the New Zealand Under-19 team on tours of Pakistan and England respectively. The 1996 team, captained by Craig McMillan, included players like Matthew Bell and Daniel Vettori, and performed very well, winning the "test" series.

During the England tour, the young cricketers received lessons not always linked with cricket tours. "I spelled out what I expected in terms of late nights, shaving, dress code, table manners, how to share the photos taken on tour... all sorts of things. I spent a lot of time teaching the boys about etiquette at meal times. They were the sort of lessons I learned on my first tour, in 1949.

"Because I had a refereeing appointment in Sri Lanka, I had to miss the last match of the 1996 tour, and therefore the farewell dinner, so planned a practice dinner instead. We issued invitations, decided on the No 2 dress for a formal dinner, and organised the use of the hotel restaurant. I explained what the term "7pm for 7.30pm" meant. Then we went through the meal. I showed them how to eat soup, which utensils to use for each course – things some people might take for granted, but which still have to be learned. Craig McMillan, the captain, made a presentation to the coach and to me, and there were some short speeches.

"As I was leaving, I asked them to keep in touch. They sent me a message after their final match, saying the farewell dinner had gone well and they hadn't let me down."

Reid recalls that under-19 tour of England for another, less happy, incident as well. "I was appalled by the behaviour of the boys in the England team. At the time I was an I.C.C. match referee and if I'd been acting in that capacity, I'd have taken some severe action. Instead, I had to deal with it as the New

Zealand team manager. Things reached a head during the 'test' at Manchester, after which I wrote this letter to Micky Stewart, the Director of Coaching and Excellence at Lord's:

"Even after sleeping on it, I still feel so incensed at witnessing such an act of unsportsmanlike behaviour by members of your England under-19 team during the match at Old Hill that I don't fancy a telephone call.

"Relations between the two teams during the first test at Old Trafford were hardly cordial due to the amount of sledging that was being thrown back and forth. Both teams were at fault, but when one of your team three times called 'yes', imitating the batsman's call for an indecisive run during the last innings, I thought it was time to talk to Graham Saville and see what could be done to stop it.

"We agreed that before the next test, we would get the captains, umpires and ourselves together and endeavour to halt this I.C.C. Code of Conduct breach. Then yesterday, with one run required for a New Zealand win with Matthew Bell not out on 99 and on strike, there was a conference of several England players, who then contrived to get the bowler to bowl a wide down the leg-side. The situation was saved only by the umpire, who refused to call the ball wide, thereby saving a very nasty media-based incident and striking a blow for sanity by restoring some of the spirit of the game of cricket back into proceedings.

"I am appalled by this deliberate act, which strikes at the heart of the renowned English sense of sportsmanship and fair play. I would appreciate you taking some action regarding the players involved, as this must certainly come under the umbrella of striving for excellence in the game that has its roots in England where the term 'It's not cricket' originated.

Code one, Code two and Code five of the I.C.C. Code of Conduct are worth reading and unless we start insisting that the Code is acted upon at this level, there is certainly going to be a lot of work for the I.C.C. in the future."

Reid says it would be nice to report that his letter drew a positive response, but he received no such feedback.

LIKE FATHER, LIKE SON

As with many fathers, John Reid was very proud of his son Richard's cricket ability. But unlike most fathers, Reid was able to get a close-up look at his son's batting and be on the spot to offer tips when needed.

"When Richard was captaining the Scots College First XI," says Reid, "the team coach was my former Wellington and New Zealand team-mate Trevor McMahon. Scots, who played in the Wellington association senior grades, was not over-burdened with outstanding young cricketers. So I sought and received permission from the Wellington association to be regraded to third grade, on the condition that I would not score more than 50. I then played the season with Richard. One particular thrill was having a long partnership with him while he scored 150. I made a quiet 50 at the other end."

GONE FISHING

John Reid has had a lifelong love of fishing. His first recollection of fishing is of using a very small hook on a light line to try to catch herrings from the Seatoun Wharf in Wellington. He recalls, at the age of eight, accepting a ride in a motorboat out into Cook Strait in pursuit of blue cod. "I don't remember how successful we were fishing for cod, but I do know my mother was most unimpressed with the Cook Strait excursion."

When the Reid family moved to Lower Hutt, the teenaged Reid and his friend Ming Nightingale struck fishing riches at "the groin", a pipe from a sausage factory that was discharging offal into the Hutt River. The offal proved a big attraction for herring, kahawai and the odd trout, and provided the youngsters with some happy fishing days, even if it was illegal to catch trout, meaning the fish had to be smuggled home.

Reid's fishing career took another turn after his marriage when for a Christmas present his wife, Norli, bought him a fly-fishing outfit to fish in the Wainuiomata River, near where they built their first home.

"I furthered my fishing experience while working for B.P. in Central Otago in the 1950s. I had a huge area to cover, and it was virtually compulsory to spin and fly fish in the Waitaki River and in Lakes Wanaka and Wakatipu."

After Reid retired from cricket, he applied himself more seriously to learning how to fly fish at Hatepe. There was plenty of trout fishing when the Reids later bought a bach near the Waitahanui River.

These days the Reids live at Five Mile Bay, near Taupo. Their home is just two kilometres from the famous Waitahanui River Bridge Pools and the "Picket Fence" at the river mouth. When he's not in a fly-fishing mood, Reid will sometimes drag a dinghy across to the Five Mile Bay beach and head onto Lake Taupo where he estimates he catches an average of one super rainbow trout for every hour spent fishing.

"Once I took up fishing relatively seriously, I found it an ideal way to relax and get away from the pressures of work, where I was with people continuously and assailed by the noise of a squash centre that ran from 7am until after midnight. I have heard it said that every hour spent fishing adds an extra day to one's life, and I can believe it."

PAYING YOUR WAY

As New Zealand's test cricketers these days are professionals, they are well paid when they tour overseas. All are on substantial contracts with New Zealand Cricket and there are various incentives, such as win bonuses. It was a vastly different scene when John Reid was playing test cricket.

When he embarked on his first overseas tour, to England in 1949, he was a clicker in a slipper factory. There was no pay for him while on tour, but he was fortunate that the Hutt Cricket Club did some vigorous fund raising and was able to present him with a cheque for £1014, a substantial sum in those days.

Reid's next tour was to South Africa in 1953-54. As by then he was playing league cricket in England during the New Zealand winters, he received no income except for a minimal daily expense allowance.

By 1955-56, when New Zealand toured Pakistan and India, Reid was employed by B.P., who kept him on full pay while he was overseas, but withdrew his company car. In 1958, when he led a New Zealand team to England, he was again paid by B.P., and this time the car was left for his wife to use in his absence.

In 1961-62, Reid captained the New Zealand team to South Africa and was again paid by B.P. In return, he did a large amount of public relations work while on tour, opening service stations and making appearances when required.

Reid's last tour was to India, Pakistan and England in 1965. By then he was self-employed, running John Reid's Squash Centre, so he received no financial compensation for touring.

JOHN REID II

When he retired, New Zealand cricket followers sighed and said there would never be another John Reid. They were wrong. Within 15 years another John Reid was playing for New Zealand, and proving to be one of the mainstays of the middle-order batting.

John Fulton Reid was an Auckland wicketkeeper and left-hand batsman who made his debut for New Zealand in 1979. He went on to play 19 tests for New Zealand, scoring 1926 runs at 46.28 an innings, with an impressive six test centuries.

Not surprisingly, the name John Reid became a matter of some confusion. Cricket fans took to calling them "Reid the elder" and "Reid the younger". The second initial became crucial. Was it John R. Reid or John F. Reid who was being referred to? These days John R. calls himself "the original"!

"My surname has been a constant source of confusion through my time in cricket," says John F. Reid. "I've had mail delivered to me by mistake, and have long ago lost count of the times I've been asked if I was related to J.R. Many people assume I'm his son. I still get mail from overseas for him. Sometimes there are requests for autographs and it's not always clear which one they want."

John F. Reid has stayed involved in cricket, as an official and a coach. These days he is the Operations Manager for New Zealand Cricket, and has more to do with John R. Reid than ever. "It's caused a chuckle between us," says John F. Reid. "We refer to each other as J.F. and J.R."

The I.C.C. took some time to unravel the mystery of the two Reids. John F. Reid is on the I.C.C.'s Cricket Committee and John R. Reid is not only a test referee, but is on the I.C.C.'s illegal deliveries advisory panel. As John R. Reid says, "For quite a while I was getting Cricket Committee material sent to me in Taupo while all the material on illegal deliveries was going to J.F. at New Zealand Cricket in Christchurch. Thankfully, I think we've now sorted out the I.C.C."

A CENTURY IN CHRISTCHURCH

Most of John Reid's famous innings were punishing, hard-hitting affairs, but there was one century he is particularly proud of that was totally out of character. It came in the third test against England at Christchurch in 1963 when Reid twice fought virtually a lone hand as he defied Ted Dexter's Englishmen. The match was played just weeks after his fabulous innings of 296 at the Basin Reserve, when he hit his world record 15 6s.

The England attack was decidedly useful. It was spearheaded by Fred Trueman and lanky David Larter. Barry Knight was the third seamer and the spin was handled by Fred Titmus with Dexter himself to provide a few overs.

In the first innings Graham Dowling and Barry Sinclair reached 40, but wickets fell too frequently and only Reid, with an aggressive 74, was able to shore up the innings. Lancaster Park had not been a happy hunting ground for him and this was his best effort there in 14 years. New Zealand totalled 266 and then bowled out an England batting line-up which included David Sheppard, Ken Barrington, Dexter and Colin Cowdrey for 253.

Desperate to build a score in their second innings as they chased their first test win over England, New Zealand's batsmen could not counter the skill of Trueman, Larter and especially Titmus. However Reid, in what some rate as his finest innings, scored precisely 100. It included 13 boundaries, but took him more than four hours and was full of watchfulness and concentration. There were no extravagant 6s this day. As the New Zealand batsmen came and went with alarming frequency, Reid desperately farmed the strike. When he reached his century (of 142 scored in that time), the England players applauded generously. Off the next ball, Reid became the ninth batsman dismissed. He was given a standing ovation by the Lancaster Park crowd.

While Reid scored 100, the other 10 New Zealand batsmen totalled just 50, with extras contributing nine. The innings folded for 159 and England cruised to a seven-wicket victory. The innings is easily lost in the mists of time, but Jack Alabaster considered it as fine an innings as he saw Reid play, comparable in its way to anything he produced in South Africa.

Dexter was full of praise for Reid, saying at the time: "I could never play an innings like that." These days he recalls Reid as a "sturdy opponent of international stature" and says: "At that time, John was very much carrying the New Zealand line-up and was the chap we always wanted to get out. He held us up in Christchurch with a magnificent fighting innings."

That day in Christchurch, Reid scored 62.89 per cent of his team's total. At the time only Australian Charles Bannerman, who scored 165 not out of his team's 245 in 1877, had a higher percentage for a completed test innings. Even now, Reid is still fifth on the list.

APPENDIX

JOHN RICHARD REID
Born: Auckland, June 3, 1928

PLAYING CAREER

			BATTING						BOWLING			
	M	I	NO	HS	Runs	Avg	100	C/St	Runs	Wkts	Avg	5I
First class (1947-65)	246	418	28	296	16,128	41.35	39	240/7	10,535	466	22.60	14
New Zealand (1949-65)	163	274	18	203	10,287	40.18	24	146/7	6495	244	26.61	4
Tests (1949-65)	58	108	5	142	3428	33.28	6	43/1	2835	85	33.35	1

- Was dismissed three times in the 90s in test cricket and eight times in all first class cricket.
- Made four double-centuries.
- Twice totalled 200 runs in a test match.
- Three times scored a century and a half-century in the same test match, the most by any New Zealander.
- Is one of nine New Zealanders to score centuries in two successive test innings.

WORLD RECORDS (AT TIME OF RETIREMENT)
Most 6s in one innings: 15 (Wellington v Northern Districts, 1963)
Most consecutive test appearances: 58

NEW ZEALAND TEST RECORDS (AT TIME OF RETIREMENT)
Most test runs: 3428
Most test wickets: 85
Most test catches: 43
Most test appearances: 58
Most times captained New Zealand: 34

RECORDS IN ALL MATCHES FOR NEW ZEALAND (AT TIME OF RETIREMENT)
Most wickets: 243 (Bill Merritt next with 221)
Most runs: 10, 287 (Bert Sutcliffe next with 8245)
Most centuries: 24 (Bert Sutcliffe next with 21)
Most appearances: 163 (Bert Sutcliffe next with 125)

- Won the Redpath Cup (Best Batsman): 1955, 1956, 1960, 1962, 1963
- Won the Winsor Cup (Best Bowler): 1955
Note: Only two players, Reid and Vic Pollard, have won both the Redpath and Winsor Cups. Reid won them in the same season.
- Scored a century before lunch three times.

ON TOUR
England

1949	1488 runs at 41.33	13 wickets at 30.00
1958	1429 runs at 39.69	39 wickets at 22.74
1965	799 runs at 31.96	4 wickets at 41.25

South Africa

1953-54	1012 runs at 37.48	51 wickets at 19.54
1961-62	1915 runs at 63.39	27 wickets at 29.00

Note: In 1953-54 Reid became the first cricketer to score 1000 runs and take 50 wickets on a tour of South Africa. In 1961-62 Reid set a record for runs on a tour of South Africa that has not been beaten.

In India and Pakistan

1955-56	1024 runs at 53.89	39 wickets at 23.87
1965	494 runs at 41.18	8 wickets at 38.75

ADMINISTRATION
New Zealand selector: 1958-65, 1975-78
Manager/coach Northern Transvaal team: 1983-1989.
Managed South African team; 1985-86
Managed Transvaal team: 1990
Managed New Zealand under-19 team to Pakistan: 1994
Managed New Zealand under-19 team to England: 1996

REFEREEING
John Reid's appointments as an I.C.C. referee

Date	Tour	Teams
1993	Sri Lanka	Sri Lanka v South Africa
1994	West Indies	West Indies v England
1994	Pakistan	Pakistan/South Africa/Australia
1995	Australia	Australia v England
1995	England	England v West Indies
1996	India/Pakistan	World Cup
1996	Sri Lanka	Sri Lanka v Australia
1996	India	India v South Africa
1997	Malaysia	I.C.C. Trophy
1997	Sri Lanka	Sri Lanka v India
1997	Sri Lanka	Asia Cup
1998	South Africa	South Africa/Pakistan/Sri Lanka
1998	Australia	Australia v England
1999	England	World Cup
1999	Australia	Australia v Pakistan

HONOURS
New Zealand Sportsman of the Year, 1955
Wisden Cricketer of the Year, 1959
South African Sportswriters' Cricketer of the Year, 1962
Awarded O.B.E., 1963
Captained Rest of World XV, 1965
Inducted into New Zealand Sports Hall of Fame, 1990
Is an Honorary Cricket Member of New Zealand Cricket
Is an Honorary Life Member of the M.C.C.
Is an Honorary Life Member of Lord's Taverners

BIBLIOGRAPHY

Barclays World of Cricket, E.W. Swanton (editor), Willow Books, 1986
Bat and Pad, Ron Palenski (editor), Benton Ross, 1987
Between Overs, Bert Sutcliffe, Whitcombe and Tombs, 1963
Big Names in New Zealand Cricket, Dick Brittenden,
    Moa Publications, 1983
Cavalcade of International Cricketers, A, Brian Crowley, MacMillan, 1989
Century of Great New Zealand Cricketers, A, Joseph Romanos,
    David Bateman, 1993
Conflicts in Cricket, Jack Bailey, Kingswood Press, 1989
Cricket Almanack of New Zealand, 1948-64, Arthur Carman and
    Noel MacDonald, Sporting Publications
Cricket Companions, Alan Mitchell, T Werner Laurie, 1950
Encyclopedia of New Zealand Rugby, The, Rod Chester,
    Neville McMillan and Ron Palenski, Hodder Moa Beckett, 1998
England Test Cricketers, Bill Frindall, Collins Willow, 1989
Farewell to Cricket, Don Bradman, Hodder and Stoughton, 1950
Finest Years, The, Dick Brittenden, A.H. and A.W. Reed, 1977
Great Days in New Zealand Cricket, Dick Brittenden,
    A.H. and A.W. Reed, 1958
Great New Zealand Cricket Families, Joseph Romanos,
    Random House, 1992
Guinness Book of Cricket Facts and Feats, Bill Frindall,
    Guinness Publishing, 1996
Guinness International Who's Who of Sport, Peter Matthews,
    Guinness Publishing, 1993
Innings of a Lifetime, The, Walter Hadlee, David Bateman Ltd, 1993
John Arlott's 100 Greatest Batsmen, John Arlott,
    Macdonald Queen Anne Press, 1989
John Reid's Kiwis, R.S. Whitington, Whitcombe and Tombs, 1962
Jubilee Book of Cricket, The, K.S. Ranjitsinhji,
    Thomas Nelson and Sons, 1897
Kiwis Declare, Nigel Smith, Random House, 1995

Leading from the Front, Mike Gatting, Macdonald Queen Anne Press, 1988

Memorable Moments in New Zealand Sport, Don Cameron (editor),
Moa, 1979

Men in White, Don Neely, Richard King and Francis Payne, Moa, 1986

Million Miles of Cricket, A, John Reid, A.H. and A.W. Reed, 1966

New Zealand Cricketers, Dick Brittenden, A.H. and A.W. Reed, 1961

One-Day International Cricket Lists, Stephen Samuelson,
Ray Mason and David Clark, Five Mile Press, 1998

One Hundred Greatest Cricketers, John Woodcock, MacMillan, 1998

On Reflection, Richie Benaud, Willow Books, 1984

Oxford Companion to Australian Cricket, The, Richard Cashman,
Warwick Franks, Jim Maxwell, Brian Stoddart, Amanda Weaver,
Ray Webster, Oxford University Press, 1996

Oxford Companion to Australian Sport, The, Wray Vamplew,
Katharine Moore, John O'Hara, Richard Cashman, Ian Jobling,
Oxford University Press, 1992

Phil Edmonds' 100 Greatest Bowlers, Phil Edmonds,
Macdonald Queen Anne Press, 1989

Shell Cricket Almanack of New Zealand, 1965-99, Arthur Carman and
Noel MacDonald/Ian Smith and Francis Payne,
Sporting Publications/ Moa/Hodder Moa/Hodder Moa Beckett

Silver Fern on the Veld, Dick Brittenden, A.H. and A.W. Reed, 1954

Sword of Willow, John Reid, A.H. and A.W. Reed, 1962

Test Cricket Lists, Graham Dawson and Charlie Wat, Five Mile Press, 1998

Tortured Genius, Joseph Romanos, Hodder Moa Beckett, 1995

Twenty-five Years Behind the Stumps, Herbert Strudwick,
Hutchinson, 1926

Wellington's Rugby History, Arthur Swan and Gordon Jackson,
A.H. and A.W. Reed, 1951

Wisden Cricketers' Almanack, 1864-1998, John Wisden and
Co/Macdonald and Jane's

100 Summers, Don Neely, Moa, 1975

ABOUT THE AUTHOR

Joseph Romanos is a Wellington-based sports journalist and author who has written books on tennis, athletics, cricket, rugby, basketball, softball and netball. He collaborated with Walter Hadlee in *The Innings of a Lifetime* and has also written *Tortured Genius*, a biography of Martin Crowe, plus *Great New Zealand Cricket Families* and *A Century of New Zealand Cricket Greats*.

Romanos, a passionate cricket follower with a deep interest in the history of the game, has long wanted to write a book on Reid, whom he considers New Zealand's finest all-round cricketer.

In addition to his book-writing, Romanos has been the *Listener*'s weekly sports columnist since 1989. Previously he worked on newspapers in New Zealand, Australia and England and was a professional squash coach in Germany. Romanos and his wife, Gael, also a journalist, have four children, Dominic, Amelia, Alexander and Eliza.